Then the Whisper
Put on Flesh

Then the Whisper Put on Flesh

New Testament Ethics in an African American Context

Brian K. Blount

Abingdon Press / Nashville

Then the Whisper Put on Flesh:
New Testament Ethics in an African American Context

Library of Congress Cataloging-in-Publication Data

Blount, Brian K., 1955-
    Then the whisper put on flesh : New Testament ethics in an African American context /
Brian K. Blount.
        p. cm.
    Includes bibliographical references and index.
    ISBN 0-687-08589-6 (alk. paper)
    1. Ethics in the Bible. 2. Bible. N.T.—Criticism, interpretation, etc. 3. Afro-Americans—
Religion. I. Title.

BS2545.E8 B56 2001
241—dc21

                                                                                    2001053528

04 05 06 07 08 09 10—10 9 8 7 6 5 4 3 2

MANUFACTURED IN THE UNITED STATES OF AMERICA

For Hendrik Boers

Contents

Preface

My excitement for this project arises from the opportunity it has afforded me. For the first time in my academic career I have been able to combine the three research interests that intrigue me most: cultural interpretation of the New Testament, biblical ethics, and African American Christianity. Having already explored the influence of context on New Testament interpretation in my dissertation and first book, I forged ahead in my second work by analyzing a biblical text from the perspective of the African American church. That work on Mark's kingdom message and its meaning for the contemporary black church became a kind of inspirational foundation for this broader New Testament study that covers the Synoptic Gospels, John, Paul, and Revelation.

My work as pastor of the Carver Memorial Presbyterian Church in Newport News, Virginia, whetted my appetite for the study of biblical ethics. Long fascinated by the writings of the New Testament, I found during that time of church leadership that neither the church nor the people who wrote in support and nourishment of it could ignore the ethical quandaries surrounding the many social and political issues that demanded its attention. Given the dire circumstances of many African American communities, African American ministers and teachers must, I believe, evaluate how members of different communities read and interpret the gospel message and, just as important, how their contextualized readings can and do affect the way they ethically construct their lives.

That is what this book tries to do. It is an attempt to help readers who live outside of an oppressed circumstance read the New Testament through the circumstance of oppressed others. It is for this reason that I have consciously chosen to read the writings of the primary New Testament writers from an ethical perspective through the lens of African American slaves. Through that lens, which is the formative one for the African American experience, I hope to show how the New Testament texts are accessed primarily through the thematic window of liberation, and then detail exactly how such a reading influences an understanding of New Testament ethics from an African American perspective. I am, of course, fully aware that there are contemporary voices in New Testament ethical studies who argue that liberation is an improper focal point for doing New Testament ethics. I would maintain that those who make such an argument can do so only because they do not appreciate the impact of culture on biblical interpretation. In an attempt to find an "objective" way of doing New Testament ethics, such researchers are implicitly making the claim that context does not matter, that there is one interpretative strategy for accessing the ethical thought of the New Testament that must work no matter where or how one lives. My work in this book demonstrates how very much I disagree. Our context shapes the kinds of questions we bring to the biblical material. Those questions shape the window through which we investigate the text. What I hope to demonstrate here is that the questions that have been the most formative and frequent in the recent history of African American Christians have operated from the theme of liberation. It is for this reason that, for this community, when the New Testament is brought into contact with ethical consideration, the operative, analytical lens must also be that of liberation.

Because I am so excited about the work of this book, I am deeply grateful for the many persons who have played a role in helping to materialize it into print. I am most appreciative of the editors at Abingdon Press who have helped me shepherd it from theory to reality. Rex Matthews, now a senior editor for the Society of Biblical Literature, helped me initially to shape the idea into a publishable form. He then demonstrated valuable support across the years when my efforts to establish my teaching career put the writing phase of the project on hold. Ulrike Guthrie followed up with guidance and support until Michael Russell helped me to bring the work to its final form.

I am also thankful for the support and dialogue from my students at Princeton Theological Seminary. Their questions, classroom discussions, and engagement with critical issues over the span of three courses on New Testament ethics have been invaluable. One student I must single out for particular gratitude: Brent Driggers, my research and teaching assistant. Brent has provided immense help in gathering resource material, looking up minute research details, and reading and responding to the manuscript. And then there is my family, my wife, Sharon, and my two children, Joshua and Kaylin. I am particularly blessed to have their support and encouragement through all the many different ups and downs that occur as one goes through the long research, writing, and publication process. Finally, I want to acknowledge two of my Emory professors and colleagues. I am deeply grateful to Professor Theodore Weber, whose seminars in Christian ethics and Christian political thought continue to be an inspiration to me and provide fodder for new ways of approaching the biblical materials. Most especially, I acknowledge yet again my gratitude to my friend and adviser, Professor Hendrik Boers. I am deeply grateful that through his guidance, direction, teaching, patience, and friendship, I have been introduced to a methodology that enables me to do the kinds of things I was able to do in this book. Without his foundational help, my interest in cultural interpretation, New Testament studies, and biblical ethics would remain just that—an interest. He helped me find the method to bring them into what I believe is fruitful and provocative dialogue. For that, I am deeply grateful.

Brian K. Blount
Princeton, NJ

CHAPTER ONE

Liberation as Lens

Loving God is like loving silent movies. There are kaleidoscopes of colorful emotion, juggernauts of reeling action, autographs of written text, and narrative schemes of implied ethical direction. But there is no sound. Yes, there is a voice; every story, every power has a voice, a way of viewing the world and being viewed by it, that signals a message as much by *how* it "speaks" as by *what* it "says." Voice, though, does not require sound. It needs only an audience and a channel to reach it. The physical ear need not be involved.

The human spirit must be involved. The spirit is a kind of inner ear. It is the instrument upon which the reverberations of God's voice make an impact. It is the human spirit that translates what our eyes see, our fingers touch, our noses smell, our bodies experience, and our ears do not hear into the voice of God. That is why even though God does not talk, humans are capable of listening to God's voice.

The role of the spirit is a constant. Laced into the fabric of all of our human being is that part of us that reaches beyond the boundaries of our flesh and blood and touches the essential voice of God's own Holy Spirit. In every time, in every place, in every moment of history, the spirit plays this interlocutory role. It is how we "hear" God, and through this hearing, when we are fortunate, it is how we hear each other. The spirit is a constant.

The "human" is not. Humanness signals contingency, limitation, and context. Because we are human, our spirits always encounter God through the context in which God finds us and we find ourselves. This means that although God is always the same, and we always perceive God through the interactive channel that links our spirits with God's Holy Spirit, we always perceive God and what it is that God wants from us differently.

God's voice, then, is like an inaudible whisper whose breathings, gentle and fierce, jangle the nerves of the human spirit until, tensed and alert, it attends to what it is that God wants to "say." And what God says will be different according to the variable conditions in which the human spirit who encounters it finds itself. When that spiritual whisper becomes an incarnate word, gripping *human* spirits where they live, it takes up the causes of the people who encounter it in the situations of that encounter. It is in this way that God's eternal voice for all becomes a living word exclusively *for them.* The whisper takes on flesh.

The African American slaves of the antebellum United States understood this instinctively. Whether or not they always thought of the Christian Deity, and whether or not their stories always chronicled the exploits of biblical heroes and heroines, their spirits were in contact with the power of a Holy Spirit who attuned them to the voice of God. In their narrative accounts of cunning animals capable of outwitting creatures of greater strength, ferocity, and appetite; in their sorrow songs, whose melodies envisioned joy in heaven and freedom on earth; in their tales of conjurers brewing the dissolution of a master's being and the enhancement of a slave's soul and body; of testimonies, prayers, songs, and sermons that called on Moses and Jesus to lock forces with African ancestors in a battle for spiritual and physical salvation; or stories of mythological figures who stood by the side of a beaten-down slave and sounded the voice of a coming jubilee—these human possessions themselves possessed the ability to *listen* for God's direction in and for their lives. What they sensed was the drumbeat of freedom. "African Americans under white slavery glued themselves to a theology filled with the 'let my people go' witness of Yahweh in the Old Testament and with Jesus the Liberator of the poor in the New Testament."[1] This is why Zora Neale Hurston wrote what she did about the mythological figure High John De Conquer, whose spiritual presence gave slaves a reason to hope for a tomorrow infinitely better than their today: "High John de Conquer came to be a man, and a mighty man at that. But he was not a natural man in the beginning. First off, he was a whisper, a will to hope, a wish to find something worthy of laughter and song. Then the whisper put on flesh."[2] The whisper encouraged a faith that fostered an ethics—a liberation kind of ethics.

This is precisely the point that Vincent Wimbush wants to make in the powerful and provocative introduction to his work *African Americans and the Bible.* He argues forcefully that the Bible has always been read through the experience of the people holding it. The meaning they draw and the ethics they build are directly related to the kind of lives they lead. It is no wonder that for a people trapped in slavery and yearning to be free that the Bible would mean and encourage liberation.

Wimbush also realizes, however, that the life experience of some peoples has been historically favored. The meaning and ethics they draw from that experience are also favored. Their reading becomes the standard for all other readings; their experience becomes the lens through which everyone should approach and engage the biblical text.

Neither Wimbush nor I would want the reader to be confused. The African American slave experience is not that standardizing lens. That status of recognition belongs to the conglomeration of Euro-American scholars, ministers, and layfolk who have, over the centuries, used their economic, academic, religious, and political dominance to create the illusion that the Bible, read through their experience, is the Bible read correctly. This is not to say that Euro-American scholarship has historically allowed that Bible reading is a contextual affair. Its proponents have argued forcefully that it is not, or at least that it should not be so. Scientifically objective methods of exegesis must be put in place to ward off the influence of a reader's experience. And so they were. The problem was that the methods themselves came out of the Euro-American experience. The methods did not control the experience; they were *a part of* the experience. And so methodological study of the Bible became, in essence, an exercise in reading the Bible through a Euro-American lens. "In this age people of color have been dominated by a pejorative Eurocentrism which tends to take a one-sided approach to theological scholarship, and particularly to hermeneutics and ethics."[3] The whisper took on a white flesh.

Wimbush and the scholars who write with him have cobbled together a response. They posit an alternative reading that would challenge the very foundations of Euro-Americanized New Testament inquiry. Why not, he asks provocatively, read the New Testament "through African American experience"?[4] Why not, indeed? Because "centering the study of the Bible upon African Americans would be a defiant intellectual and political act."[5] It would not only threaten the scholarly pretension that only the Euro-American exegetical perspective can convey an appropriate "reading" of the New Testament, but it would also yield a very different kind of "reading." It would initiate a "more consistent and intense and critical focus on the *Bible as script/manifesto that defines and embraces darkness*."[6] In other words, it would prompt an interpretative reading in which the Spirit's whisper becomes a human cry of and for liberation. The "biblical exegete who is faithful to the sociological particularity of Black suffering will always 'cut the cheese' in the direction of historical freedom."[7] This whisper puts on a flesh of color.

I want, then, following Wimbush's challenge, to launch an academically unorthodox experiment. I will use the enslaved African American religious experience as a window into understanding the ethical perspective of the New Testament materials.

New Testament Ethics Today: A General Discussion

Before considering New Testament ethics through an African American lens, there is the necessary matter of analyzing New Testament ethics itself. What is "New Testament ethics," and how do the narratives and letters of the New Testament point us to it? Actually, there is an even more fundamental question prior to this one: Does the category exist? In his presidential address to the Society of Biblical Literature, Leander E. Keck records the opinion of many who argue that "it is not evident that the New Testament has any ethics to be studied."[8] I, along with Keck, want to make the case that it does.

Halvor Moxnes would disagree. In a 1993 article he argues that, as far as the New Testament is concerned, it would be more appropriate for researchers to use the terminology of morals—"that is, norms and rules of behaviour accepted within a certain group or culture." He goes on to say: "Instead of 'ethics' in a modern sense, it is more appropriate to speak of a 'moral understanding,' i.e., a reflection over actions that gives an answer to the question of 'why' this particular norm is valid."[9] Eduard Lohse essentially agrees. Pointing out that the New Testament does not know the term *ethics*, he reasons that it instead reflects "on the nature of the moral life, and sometimes indicates what corresponding action should be."[10]

Even as they argue the point, Moxnes and Lohse raise an important matter that they themselves do not fully address. Before one can really ascertain whether the New Testament is limited to "moral" reflection or also includes "ethical" reflection, the key terms must be defined. Here Keck's article is of immense help. He acknowledges that too often the terms *moral* and *ethical* are used interchangeably, even though they do not carry the same meaning. Morals exhort particular kinds of behaviors; ethics reflects upon those morals and categorizes them into systems. "In other words, if morality describes and prescribes proper behavior as well as proscribes what is unacceptable, ethics is a critical reflection on the prescribed and proscribed, the allowed and the forbidden, the urged and the discouraged."[11] Ethics, then, is the rationale, the philosophical structure of reasoning behind the moral exhortation.

Although this clarification is helpful, the critical question remains: Does the New Testament have such a structure of reasoning undergirding its hodgepodge of moral exhortations? Keck answers yes. New Testament ethics may not look like what we have come to expect from a "critical reflection on morality" because it is its own brand of ethics. It is not ethics formed around a philosophical construct. It is, instead, "event ethics." It is ethics oriented toward and structured around the event of Jesus' life, death, and resurrection.[12]

This Jesus event is, of course, captured in the narratives and correspondence that make up the New Testament. New Testament ethics, then, is the ethics of the New Testament texts. Dan O. Via recognized that this statement is not as self-evident as it may on the surface appear. Researchers, he stresses, must declare whether they are doing Christian ethics, which makes use of the New Testament and other materials, or New Testament ethics, which derives exclusively from the narratives and correspondences that make it up.[13] Keck is more blunt: " 'New Testament ethics' is the ethics of the New Testament texts, period."[14] Frank Matera agrees:

"Since the New Testament is a collection of writings, in my view the primary subject of *New Testament* ethics is the ethical teaching of these writings."[15]

Via goes on to demonstrate how narrative works like those that comprise the New Testament have a positive relationship with ethics. Narratives, and even correspondences, tell a story. The story models and prescribes, particularly in the case of the letters, certain kinds of behavior. Even more important, stories reflect on the structures that categorize those behaviors as preferred or non-preferred. It is at this level of reflection that the story contains and projects an ethics. "It is through metaphors organized into a story that we receive our vision of the world and of our condition. This vision sheds light on what we are to do but also on what is for Christian ethics the more important problem of how to do it."[16]

In the New Testament, then, ethics exists at the literary level of narrative and correspondence. It is the rationale, the reasoning, as Keck puts it, that lies behind the exhortations and moral directives and gives them structure and coherence.

> Given the diverse grounds for moral exhortation in the New Testament, a major task is twofold: first, to analyze the material formally in order to identify the reasons given for or against behavior—the warrants and sanctions—and then to develop a taxonomy of adduced reasons. That would yield a useful overview of the "moral reasoning" of the New Testament.[17]

This "taxonomy of adduced reasons" is the stuff and reality of New Testament ethics. It is not so much a matter of finding a unity of ethical thought, which would be impossible given the eclectic nature of the materials that comprise the New Testament, but rather a sense of coherence or, as Keck calls it, constancy. Daniel Patte calls it a "broader conceptualization."

> The very diversity of ethical teachings in the NT requires that any scholar who undertakes to write a study of "the Ethics of the NT" posit a conceptualization of ethics broader than those of any of the NT texts. This broader conceptualization of ethics provides categories and criteria in terms of which the specific conceptualization of ethics by a given text—the S[ermon on the] M[ount], for example—is determined.[18]

This "constancy" or "broader conceptualization" is a lens that gives the New Testament its sense of ethical coherence, while simultaneously beckoning the human spirit that engages it to see and listen through it for the reverberations of God's voice.

That lens is *the* event of Jesus' life, death, and resurrection as they are chronicled in the various New Testament materials. The Jesus event is the element of constancy that gives coherence to the New Testament's various forms of moral exhortation. That event, then, is the foundation of New Testament ethics. But it is precisely here where space—the cultural context of the individual interpreter and his or her community—begins to play a critical interpretative role. According to the sociological methodology of Enrique Dussel, an interpreter's "spatial, worldly setting" is a primary and reliable indicator of the perspective that structures and gives focus to that interpreter's work. "I am trying, then, to take space, geopolitical space, seriously. To be born at the North Pole or in Chiapas is not the same thing as to be born in New York City."[19] Whether we are considering something as significant as a community's evaluation of a momentous event in world history or something as isolated as a private individual's reading of a newspaper editorial, Dussel would propose that one's spatial and political location in life determines what one sees, or at least how one sees.[20] Thus our space, like the space of the first readers in the first century C.E., influences how we read that Jesus event. That is to say, our space becomes a communal and/or personal lens that influences how we read through the event lens that provides a sense of constancy for the New Testament's moral reasoning. Our looking glass has at least these two layers.

Obviously, I operate against the grain that there is some objective ethics that we can uncover absent the influence of the space we inhabit. Because we operate from in front of the text, the Jesus event we engage, the moral reasoning we adduce through it and the taxonomy we build from it will necessarily be in large part directly attributable to variables like "who we are" and "where we live." It is in the interchange between that space, the Jesus event, and the text that New Testament ethics will *develop*. It is not found; it evolves as a result of an active, dialogical interaction. Our (communal and/or personal) reading lens interacts with the text's shaping (Jesus event) lens in such a way that the text becomes

19

meaningful *for us*. What occurs as a result is an ethics that is a word-on target for our time.

In this same way, the ancient New Testament narratives and letters became an ethical word-on target for antebellum African American slaves. For them, as we will soon see, the event of Jesus Christ, engaged as it was through the oppressive reality of their horrific space, encouraged a particular kind of interpretative constancy. For them, Jesus means freedom.

And it begins and ends with a social emphasis. Of course, a prominent criticism against individuals and communities who read from "in front of the text"—that is, who allow their cultural and methodological space to influence their interpretative process, is that they read into (*eisegesis*) rather than out of (*exegesis*) the text. One could very easily, then, dismiss a slave's unlettered, untrained ethical appropriation of the New Testament as a negatively biased reading that has no merit beyond that particular slave's individual or communal existence. If, however, one could show that the New Testament has a vast meaning potential that includes emphases toward social and political concerns, then the case could be made that, because of their unique social and political circumstance, African American slaves were uniquely outfitted to interact with that part of the meaning picture that other communities overlooked or dismissed. That is to say, they could see into and interact with a part of the New Testament that other communities, because of their space implications (limitations), could not. The space we come from encourages the questions we ask. The questions we ask help to prefigure the answers we get; those questions direct us toward particular areas of a text's meaning potential. This does not mean that because we see the text differently from others that we are right and they are wrong or, heaven forbid, that they are right and we are wrong. It could well be, and very often is, that one community has seen something that has eluded another.

Stephen Charles Mott demonstrates quite nicely that there is a social-ethical emphasis in the New Testament that a slave or a slave community could have "exegetically" engaged. He points out three key elements that provide a framework for a *social* New Testament ethics. We will soon see that in their own way the African American slaves recognized and worked with each one of them.

First, Mott notes, the framework for a social New Testament ethics arises from the integral connection between the New and the Old Testaments. "Jesus has inherited and is passing on to the new messianic community the social role and *raison d'être* of Old Testament Israel."[21] The emphasis on justice for the most oppressed persons in society passes on through the prophets to Jesus. Jesus does what the prophets did, only this time as *the* representative of God's desires *and* as God's person on earth.

Second, Mott argues that the concept of status plays a key role in New Testament ethics. Jesus' ministry was a transformative one. People and entire communities of demeaned and ostracized social status, like sinners, tax collectors, women, and even Gentiles, could find themselves, through following Jesus and doing the will of God as Jesus proclaimed and modeled it, included as integral parts of God's kingdom vision. In other words, Jesus means *social* and *political* redemption. "The purpose of justice in biblical terms is to restore the community. Jesus' way of dealing with the inequalities of status and his activity in bringing people back into community would constitute a ministry of justice."[22] A ministry of *social* justice.

Finally, Mott notes that there are the principalities and powers, and, though spiritual in origin, they influence and destroy human social and political relationships. "My argument," says Walter Wink, "is that what people in the world of the Bible experienced and called 'principalities and powers' was in fact real. They were discerning the actual spirituality at the center of the political, economic, and cultural institutions of their day."[23] God is at war with these principalities and powers; we are enlisted in the battle on God's side. This is the language of social and political liberation. Not only does it describe the state of the world and God's *event*ful actions through Jesus Christ to redeem it, but it also offers an ethics, a *social* ethics, that helps humans determine how they are to conduct themselves as a result.

A Final Opening Thought

There is, of course, a thread of tension running throughout the argument I wish to make. This tension is inherent to my very process of research. In utilizing the enslaved African American

21

religious experience as my window onto the world of New Testament ethics, I have decided that a specific communal space will consciously orient the kinds of questions I bring to my investigative task. Since, as I have already noted, the questions help to prefigure the answers, my perspective on New Testament ethics will be shaped in very large part by that space. I say "in large part" intentionally. Here is where the tension surfaces, for it is also clear that I am a part of the wider interpretative community that is the guild of North American New Testament scholarship. My training, teaching, research, and writing experiences within this guild remain a critical part of my space and thereby also shape my interpretative questions. Both of these spaces, then, are always operative. Sometimes they complement each other; at other times, they stand in vociferous opposition. The result of this uneasy pairing is an interesting dialogue between spaces that enriches my process of meaning discovery. While some conclusions will be visible only through the perspective of the slave tradition, they can also be quite usefully mined in the guild. Others will be initially visible only through the methodological procedures and perspectives developed and nurtured in the guild. I hope to show, however, that they can be usefully mined by inhabitants of oppressed spaces like those of the African American slave or the contemporary African American Christian. By placing the spaces in constructive dialogue rather than isolating them according to competing, exclusive claims, I hope to show that the enterprise of New Testament ethics can take on a new life and thereby give even very diverse communities operating from the New Testament some common direction for ethically shaping that life.

CHAPTER TWO

Reconfigured Ethics

Where should a study of New Testament ethics in an African American context begin? I believe it should begin where African American theology and, indeed, the African American church itself began: with the African American slave. The slaves understood how important their space was to the interpretation of biblical stories. Necessity, of course, has often found itself laboring over the birth of some new invention or inventive strategy. The slaves needed something that could enable biblical commentary in spite of the fact that few among them possessed the skills for even the simplest Bible reading. They found their salvation in their own steel-trap memories and vivid imaginations. As Albert J. Raboteau records:

> Illiteracy proved less of an obstacle to knowledge of the Bible than might be thought, for biblical stories became part of the oral tradition of the slaves. Oral instructions and Sunday School lessons were committed to memory. As one missionary to the slaves reported: "To those who are ignorant of letters, *their memory is their book.* . . . In a recent examination of one of the schools I was forcibly struck with their remembrance of *passages of scripture.*"[1]

As far as the Bible was concerned, then, the slaves lived in a contextually sensitive oral culture. "African American slaves, female and male, created an oral text from a written text (the King James Version of the Bible). They composed this oral text by extracting from the Bible or adding to biblical content those phrases, stories, biblical personalities and moral prescriptions relevant to the character of their life situation and pertinent to the aspirations of the slave community."[2] The important point is that theirs was a *compositional* process. Fusing biblical material with their own life situation and concerns, their space, they *composed* a biblical witness that was uniquely their own and spoke to their uniquely tragic circumstances. In other words, they contextually constructed *their* biblical story. The oral quality of their engagement with the text induced a reading that was particularly susceptible to—indeed, inviting of—the influences of their social, cultural, and political circumstances. It is no wonder that the "Bible" they ended up "reading" and the "Christ" whom they ended up worshiping and serving were neither the same Bible nor the same Christ proclaimed to them by white slave owners and missionaries. They were a Bible and a Christ borne out of and uniquely responsive to the context into which the slaves were condemned. And since that enslaved space differed so radically from the enslaving space enjoyed by their captors, it is not surprising that what they might have called New Testament ethics also looked and sounded radically different.

Contemporary African American Space: Slavery's Legacy as an Interpretative Lens

Space *still* matters—at least it should. Given the disparity in quality of life space that exists between contemporary African Americans and European Americans, one wonders how New Testament ethics could mean the same thing in the different communities. The perspective from which most African Americans peruse the New Testament texts, if they peruse them at all, occurs from a brutal, sharply drawn angle of oppression. To be sure, it is not as devastating a context as the one stomached by their slave forebears, but the pallor of suffering clouds it still.

I have already attempted to document the desperate nature of the African American circumstance in an earlier writing. In chapter 14 of *Go Preach! Mark's Kingdom Message and the Black Church Today*, I contend that African Americans exist today under a state of what can only be termed "psychological occupation."[3] A brief and very partial statistical sampling suggests the kind of persuasive evidence that is available. In 1996, 26.4 percent of all African American families were poor. Even more astounding, for black children under the age of six, the poverty rate (1993) was over 50 percent; 46.8 percent of African American households are headed by a female; almost half of those families are poor. Unemployment of African Americans over the age of sixteen is almost twice that of European Americans; African American males are unemployed at three times the rate of European American males. These economic figures are only a frightening indicator of the magnitude of the problem. Even a cursory reading of a daily newspaper brings to light the perpetual problems facing the African American community. In a November 29, 1999, editorial referring to judicial matters, journalist Tom Teepen makes the following references:

> The pattern is consistent: At every step, blacks are more likely than whites to get the short end of the stick in comparable circumstances. Take kids. According to the U.S. Department of Justice, black youths between 10 and 17 account for 26 percent of arrests but 32 percent of juvenile court referrals, 41 percent of kids detained, 46 percent of juveniles sent to correctional facilities and finally 52 percent of youths transferred to adult courts—at the end, nearly double their in-take proportion. Or look at drugs. The U.S. Public Health Service found that 14 percent of drug users are black, but African-Americans account for 35 percent of drug arrests, 55 percent of convictions, 74 percent of prison sentences. Some 65 percent of crack users are white, but a 1992 study found 93 percent of crack convictions were of African-Americans. The list goes on.[4]

Socially and politically, fueled by an intransigent racism that refuses to surrender its hold over much of white America, African Americans continue to experience discrimination in housing and, therefore, school segregation; diminished educational opportunity; high rates of crime and susceptibility to drugs, drug cultures, and gang activity; law enforcement profiling; explosive rates of incarceration for black males; and suicide and homicide rates of epidemic proportions. The effects are dizzying.

In addition, while being destroyed from without, the African American community is also disintegrating from within. Consider, for example, the relations between African American males and females. Orlando Patterson documents the severity of this particular problem with a blizzard of staggering statistics. His conclusion: "Afro-Americans are the most unpartnered and isolated group of people in America and quite possibly the world."[5] Not only are they segregated from the sources of power and wealth vested primarily in Euro-American families and institutions, but they are also separated from each other by layers of mistrust, jealousy, and failures of commitment. Patterson attributes the cause to the conditions and consequences of a slave system whose date of demise is less than three generations old and whose hold on the American psyche has yet to loosen its fanatical grip.

> Something else must be at play. Something that runs deep into the peculiarities of the Afro-Americans' own past. In searching for it, we are inevitably led back to the centuries-long holocaust of slavery and what was its most devastating impact: the ethnocidal assault on gender roles, especially those of father and husband, leaving deep scars in the relations between Afro-American men and women.[6]

This is not a sociological survey of the contemporary African American circumstance, so I will not spend more time attempting to document the severity of the situation by doing the kind of work that is better suited to sociologists like Patterson. What has been presented, however, is enough to support the conclusion that an oppressive wind still cuts through the communal life and existence of African Americans. The space is still very much a haunted one. The reality and effects of that space should play an invited role in the way African Americans seek ethical interpretation and guidance from the New Testament materials, just as a similar, though even more hostile, space once did for their ancestors.

The Slave Narratives: A Liberation Lens

The gruesome reality of the slave space is immediately recognizable in the eclectic literature that is often referred to as the slave narratives. Experiences communicated in those narratives became the lens through which the biblical stories were read, and an informal, intuitive ethics from those stories was developed.

> Scholars who have studied a variety of sources have concluded that "there are questions about the slave system that can be answered only by one who has experienced slavery. How did it "feel" to be owned? What were the pleasures and sufferings of a slave? What

was the slave's attitude toward his owner, toward the white man's assumption of superiority, toward the white man's God? Did the slaves want to be free? Did they feel it was their right to be free?[7]

The African slaves provided their own answers—answers that were not refracted through the bias of white apologetic interest. As one former slave put it:

In all the books that you have studied you never have studied Negro history, have you? You studied about the Indians and white folks, what did they tell you about the Negro? If you want Negro history you will have to get from somebody who wore the shoe, and by and by from one to the other you will get a book.[8]

But the oral and written sources for that "book" were not of a single type. As Joan M. Martin explains, "the slave narrative is a source of enslaved 'witnessing' which can be characterized both as an individual document and as a wide ranging, broad corpus of autobiographical and narrative writing."[9] She goes on to include journals, newspaper articles, magazine interviews, church records, personal letters, folk stories, and dictated autobiographies as the kinds of material included in the genre.

Helpfully, she has also categorized the material. She sees three particular timeframes as important for the creation and classification of the narratives. The period between 1619, the year that saw the introduction of the first slaves onto North American soil, and 1703 comprised an era before the existence of any significant slave narrative material. The first period of production began immediately afterward, from 1703 to 1830. "During this period, slave narratives took on specific purposes which varied in different historical eras."[10] In other words, the narratives were context sensitive.

The unifying goal of the first timeframe, however, seemed to be exposing skin color as the basis of social prejudice. In the second period (1830–65), a new purpose for the narratives emerged. Now they played the role of propaganda and political entreaty as the ex-slaves, having fled to the North, abandoned the discussion of skin color and directly attacked the institution of slavery itself. The narratives took on an abolitionist agenda. In the final period, from Reconstruction to 1944, different aims were achieved. Some narratives reminded readers of the past horror and made them hope that the present struggle for justice would not falter. Others offered strategies for surviving the segregationist confines of the "Jim Crow" South.[11]

Despite acknowledging the variation in material type through and across time, Martin and others seem united in their conclusion that the primary norm for these narratives was an abiding fixation on liberation. Liberation is the lens that slaves and ex-slaves used to bring focus and clarity to their thoughts about their world. As Martin puts it, "thus, the slave narratives provide a 'continuous record of that institution' which reveals a legacy of struggle for self-expression by humans considered to be non-humans. These pages exemplify the thought, language and action of those yearning for legal, political, social, religious and economic rights required for human dignity."[12]

Following extensive research on the same material, Dwight N. Hopkins had already reached an identical conclusion:

> In addition, an investigation of the disparate sources points to a consistent norm in the type of theological thinking held by African Americans in their religious culture. Within each paired guideline, put differently, the majority's liberation and the quest for full humanity became the consistent conviction and major motivation.[13]

Even in non-Christian materials like the secular folk tales (of which the Brer Rabbit collection is a good example), the theme of freedom provided a sense of constancy.[14] Other materials, like the spirituals, maintain the liberation emphasis, even if it is cloaked in the disguise of innuendo and double talk. Ex-slave Frederick Douglass makes the point: "On the lips of some [the symbolic language in the spirituals] meant the expectation of a speedy summons to a world of spirits, but on the lips of our company it simply meant a speedy pilgrimage to a free state, and deliverance from all the evils and dangers of slavery."[15]

Indeed, where such an important matter is at stake, perhaps the authors of the slave narratives should be allowed to testify for themselves. It is, after all, from their words that scholars like Hopkins and Martin come to the conclusion that the driving force behind their narratives is liberation. And so, ex-slave Henry Bibb, writing in a letter to Albert G. Sibley on November 4, 1852, argues that the Christian faith and the institution of slavery are irreconcilable. The very identity and reality of God insist upon human freedom. "I mean that you shall know that there is a just God in heaven, who cannot harmonize slavery with the Christian religion."[16] Ex-slave James Curry is more specific: "Of course, no slave would dare say, in the presence of a white man, that he wished for freedom. But among themselves, it is their constant theme."[17] Lewis Clarke speaks in a way that characterizes much of the slave narrative material and its emphasis on liberation:

> Of course, the slaves don't tell folks what's passing in their minds about freedom; for they know what'll come of it, if they do. . . . The fact is, slavery's the father of lies. The slave knows he ought to have his freedom; and his master knows it, jest as well as he does; but they both *say* they don't; and they tell me some folks this way believe 'em. The master say the slave don't want his freedom, and the slave says he don't want it; but they both of 'em lies, and know it.[18]

This emphasis on liberation is encoded in the slave narratives in many significant ways. In order to illustrate a process that I cannot possibly document fully, I shall mention three that have already been documented by Hopkins.[19] First, the narratives sketch a reciprocity between males and females that is not represented in the surrounding Southern culture. It is not simply the manner in which the narratives suggest a kind of equanimity between men's and women's roles; it is the even more surprising discovery that God is characterized quite approvingly as cherishing female as well as male behaviors and traits. "Whether the slave narratives recount women and men enduring the same types of labor, whether the spirituals sing stories of the male and female nature of Jesus, or whether autobiographies indicate the role of female and male leadership in the secret religious worship services of the slaves, one has to acknowledge gender complementarity."[20] Cheryl Towsend Gilkes sees this development as a reorientation that is as startling as it is radical. "Black people imaged a God of power as both male and female although they were initially presented with a patriarchal God in an androcentric text."[21]

Delores Williams chides Gilkes for overemphasizing the slave's liberation from patriarchy and playing down too greatly the sexism that also abounded in the slave world. But she, too, recognized the presence of a liberating emphasis in the slave narratives that was directly linked to, as it reacted against, their inhuman space.

> Whereas Gilkes concludes that this woman-inclusive strain among the Christian folk is part of the formation of an Afrocentric biblical tradition, I suggest that this egalitarian strain has to do with the interpretative principles (hermeneutics) the folks used in their interpretation of the Bible. And these interpretative principles derived from their life-situation and community aspirations.[22]

Syncretism also developed out of that life situation; it exemplifies a second encoding of liberation. The slaves felt themselves free to merge religious realities from many different West African spiritualities with their understanding of the Christian God. Consider, for example, the circumstances surrounding the indigenous West African belief in a high god who "ruled all creation with justice and compassion for the weak."[23] This god of justice is equally concerned with the spiritual welfare of the individual *and* the political welfare of the community of which that individual is a part. "African traditional religions did not see the possibility of saving the spirit or the soul while the freedom of the body went unattended."[24] This traditional belief obviously would have had dramatic liberation implications for the African slaves. How could a God who cared about their individual welfare approve of their corporate enslavement? How could such a God be preoccupied with the matter of saving individual souls when the physical bodies that housed those souls were so systematically abused? Such a God could not; the God the slaves brought with them and syncretistically introduced to the Christian God of their masters could not. *This* God would have presided over a particular kind of ethics. The "ethical" follower of such a God could not focus exclusively on personal, spiritual salvation. For the follower of such a God, the definition of *ethics* would have been dramatically reconfigured. Suddenly, "to be human was to be ethically communal in outlook and life."[25] And that communal ethics, like the God upon whom it was founded, would, necessarily, have been focused on sociopolitical as well as spiritual liberation.

Third, as the discussion on the second point implies, in this newly fashioned, syncretized belief, faith and politics were always considered together. They were not two separate entities with their own unique fields of concern; to speak of faith was to speak of politics, and to speak of politics was to draw the God of one's faith into the conversation. It was for this reason that a longing for spiritual liberation and heavenly redemption connected so integrally with the hope for social and political salvation from the clutches of historical slavery. The words of ex-slave Fannie Moore prove the point:

> I'se saved. De Lord done tell me I'se saved. Now I know de Lord will show me de way, I ain't gwine to grieve no more. No matter how much you all done beat me and my chillen de Lord will show me de way. And some day we never be slaves.[26]

Where does such liberating vitality come from? It comes from slave religion. This newly configured, heavily syncretized slave Christianity creates the kind of communal and individual, social and spiritual space a liberation lens needs to sprout, to survive, and to succeed. The more we understand the religion, the more we will understand why the image of liberation is so important to it and why its Bible and the ethics that Bible helps to develop cannot occur without it.

A Contextual Engagement with the Bible: Reading, Respecting, and Sometimes Rejecting

It all begins, of course, with the Hebrew Bible. The exodus account anchors an understanding about the Hebrew God that merged in principle and deed with the indigenous West African concept of a deity whose primary concern was for the oppressed and the poor. "In this biblical paradigm American slaves discovered the *nature* of God as the One who sees the afflictions of the oppressed, hears their cries, and delivers them to freedom."[27] But the slaves did more than discover the nature of God; they used that discovery to reconfigure their own reality. Certainly their owners wanted them to perceive reality as they had constructed it; the slave lot in life was not only mandated by law, but was foreordained by God. God backed the bonds that held their lives in check. God made white folk free and gave them stewardship over any and every black person they could afford. In an attempt to draw God's role as an accomplice even more sharply, slave owners and the theologians who supported them offered the Bible as the state's primary piece of evidence for the secondary status of black Africans and, therefore, the divine prerogative of white Americans.

But the slaves took this evidence and reconfigured it in the light of *their* space. The Moses story became critical for them; not just Israel's savior, Moses became *their* liberator, too. They identified so greatly with the Hebrew slaves held hostage in Egypt that the ancient reality became their contemporary one. Israel's myth became their myth. Raboteau points to the recollection of a white Methodist minister pastoring a black congregation of 1,400 in Charleston, South Carolina, in 1862. The minister records the jubilation of his charges whenever he spoke about the "law of liberty" or "freedom from Egyptian bondage." The reason: "What was figurative they interpreted literally."[28] They interpreted it not only as a literal occurrence of exodus for the ancient Hebrews, but as the literal assurance that God's nature was one of deep concern for the ultimate liberation of captives like themselves. Their faith in the reality of Israel's story was also the foundation for their hope that their own story would end similarly. "The sacred history of God's liberation of his people would be or was being reenacted in the American South."[29]

This Old Testament opening to the Christian faith provided the backdrop to the most dramatic reconfiguration of all. Jesus, God's Son, was seen not on his own New Testament terms alone, but through the liberating lens of the exodus. We are not just talking spiritual liberation anymore. When Jesus operates in the same story universe as Moses, then Jesus, like Moses, cannot tolerate the oppression endured by the oppressed. Jesus, all of a sudden, means freedom—social and political freedom. Raboteau records the disapproving thoughts of a white Union Army chaplain in Decatur, Alabama:

> There is no part of the Bible with which they [the slaves] are so familiar as the story of the deliverance of Israel. Moses is their *ideal* of all that is high, noble, and perfect, in man. I think they have been accustomed to regard Christ not so much in the light of a *spiritual* Deliverer, as that of a second Moses who could eventually lead *them* out of their prison-house of bondage.[30]

The chaplain's concern is ill-founded. This Moses-Jesus connection does not mean that Jesus is no longer praised for suffering on human behalf. His suffering and its redemptive value continue to be highly celebrated in the slave world. Indeed, Jesus is an even closer companion to the slave believer because Jesus suffered as the slave suffers; Jesus can understand the pain, the tragedy, the hopelessness, the sorrow, and, most important, the hope. Only one who has suffered as much can hope as steadfastly, and, if given the power that Jesus has been given, drive that hope toward a transformed—that is, liberated—reality. All of a sudden, Jesus' monumental death on the cross and his resurrection from the grave, while continuing to signal human liberation from sin, take on the added significance of breaking the authority of the principalities and powers who preside over the institution of slavery.[31]

Paul, and those who wrote later in his name, do not fare quite as well. It was in this section of the Bible, with the disputed slave statement by Paul in 1 Corinthians 7, and the slave endorsing statements in Ephesians (6:5), Colossians (3:22; 4:1), and Titus (2:9), as well as in 1 Peter 2:18, that the masters found the words that suggested divine endorsement for the slaves' heinous state. As I will show in the section on Pauline ethics, the slaves, ex-slaves, and their descendants looked upon the apostle to the Gentiles with an uneasy sense of skepticism and even outright hostility. Even some of the greatest African American thinkers saw Paul as a threat rather than as an ally to their hopes for liberation. "Partly because of the slavery passage, interpreters like Howard Thurman have little to do with Paul's writings."[32]

Jacquelyn Grant is correct when she notes that "what we see here is perhaps more than a mere rejection of a White preacher's interpretation of the Bible, but an exercise in internal critique of the Bible."[33] Relying upon their oral understanding of God and Jesus, the slaves, using the lens of liberation, decided for themselves which material deserved a cherished place in their canon. Speaking of Linda Brent, the pseudonym ex-slave Harriet Jacobs gave herself in her autobiography, M. Shawn Copeland reflects that "Brent's experience of oppression forced her 'to retain the right, as much as possible, to resist those things within the [dominant] culture and the Bible that [she found] obnoxious or antagonistic to [her] innate sense of identity and to [her] basic instincts for survival.' "[34] Her space meant *that* much.

Oddly enough, this challenge to the Bible comes because of the way slave owners first dictated that blacks learn the biblical stories. Denied access to the written text, the slaves met the Bible on an aural level. There was, therefore, more room for the influence of their own experience in the interpretative process. The slaves did not so much read the story as participate orally with it. "That is, since slave communities were illiterate, they were, therefore, without allegiance to any official text, translation, or interpretation; hence once they heard biblical passages read and interpreted to them, they in turn were free to remember and repeat in accordance with their own interests and tastes."[35] This meant that when the imagery in the story contrasted with experience, a critique was raised.

This does not mean that the New Testament text lost its sense of authority for the slaves. But it does mean that their perception of God in their midst is *more* authoritative. The text must be in line with God's being and agenda of liberation. Where it is not, the text, because of the frailty of the humans who composed it, must be challenged and, if need be, resisted as much as the system of slavery it was purported to support. In this way the slaves were perhaps the first biblical critics in North America to read so aggressively from "in front of the text" that they could recognize the text for what it really was: the *words* first-century human writers employed in their attempt to convey the *Word* of the eternal God.

Slave Hermeneutics: A Reconfigured Reading

Slave masters were not simply afraid of the liberation message inherent in the biblical materials; they dreaded the thought that their "illiterate, ignorant slaves" might possess minds sharp enough to catch hold and make use of it. "The danger beneath the arguments for slave conversion which many masters feared was the egalitarianism implicit in Christianity."[36] Why else would the slave owner be so concerned over the fact that his chattel had become interested in praising the same God whom he himself adored? Ex-slave Isaac Throgmorton, interviewed in 1863, explained just how jittery the Southern power brokers had become:

> I knew a man who would let his slaves carry on a meeting for a while, but when they got a little happy, the overseer would come and whip them. I have known him whip a woman with 400 lashes, because she said she was happy. This was to scare religion out of them, because he thought he wouldn't be able to get anything out of them if they were religious. He said he would rather see them stealing and swearing and whoring than be religious.[37]

It was not so simple a matter as fearing that too much consideration of the spiritual might result in physical laziness; it was a concern about recalcitrance and resistance. Slave owners figured a religious slave was a freedom-thinking and, therefore, work-resisting slave in the making. In the words of one ex-slave, "White folks 'fraid the niggers git to thinkin' they was free, if they had churches 'n things."[38] The comment was right on track: "A continual complaint of masters was that Christianity would ruin their slaves by making them 'saucy,' since they would begin to think themselves equal to white folks."[39] The concern turned out to be an appropriate one. One minister explained that "the 'general indifference' of even churchgoing planters to the [religious] instruction of their slaves was 'the untoward haughty behaviour of those Negroes who have been admitted into the Fellowship of Christ's Religion.' "[40] The Reverend James Blair, who represented the bishop of London in Virginia, wrote in 1729 that he doubted the sincerity of many Negro converts. He was convinced that they had turned to the faith hoping as much for social freedom as for a release from the bondage of sin. Two years later he announced that his fears had proved correct:

> Notwithstanding all the precautions which the ministers took to assure them that baptism did not alter their servitude, the negroes fed themselves with a secret fancy that it did, and that the King designed that all Christians should be made free. And when they saw that baptism did not change their status they grew angry and saucy, and met in the nighttime in great numbers and talked of rising.[41]

What to do? Prior to 1740 and the Great Awakening the problem was not widespread, since before this time the evangelization of the slaves had not met with promising results. But the religious fervor that accompanied the Awakening created a significant shift that would ultimately result in massive conversions of African Americans at the close of the eighteenth and the beginning of the nineteenth centuries. White concern over the impact of the faith on the social and political aspirations of African Americans shifted into higher gear as well. Even though the Great Awakening focused on the conversion and transformation of the inner soul rather than the outer social and political condition, owners continued to evidence their trepidation. New laws, like the 1800 measure in South Carolina that forbade slaves to meet and assemble for worship,[42] were legislated for the express purpose of curtailing the thoughts and actions of liberation that the slaves were developing through their interaction with the biblical stories.

Something strange had happened. The literate, powerful, wealthy slave lords had configured the Christian faith in such a way that every emphasis on freedom and liberation was either spiritualized beyond recognition or directed only at white human beings who had been exclusively created in the image of God. These slave lords are living testimony to the contention that space matters. *Their* space mattered completely. They operated directly from it. As Katie Geneva Cannon explains, "Beneath their rhetoric and logic, the question of using the Bible to justify the subordination of Black people was fraught with their desire to maintain their dominance, to guarantee their continued social control."[43]

But the illiterate, disempowered, and impoverished slaves, while living in their slave owners' space, refused to direct their focus on the biblical texts through it. Instead, they grounded their Bible "reading" in their own space and used the interaction between that space and the biblical witness to reconfigure the faith that had been offered them. They not only saw the liberation motif that existed in the biblical witness, but they also forged an alliance with it and made it their lens through which to view and reshape their world and their response to it. Slave Christianity's common thread became the denominator of deliverance. It was around this hinge that they reconfigured the faith their masters presented to them as a tool of bondage until it became an instrument of freedom. Given the context in which they lived and the power the slave institution held over them, what they did was nothing short of miraculous. Speaking in particular reference to the spirituals, Thurman makes the more universal point: "The existence of these songs is in itself a monument to one of the most striking instances on record in which a people forged a weapon of offense and defense out of a psychological shackle. By some amazing but vastly creative spiritual insight the slave undertook the redemption of a religion that the master had profaned in his midst."[44] Patterson makes the very same point: "Because political resistance would have been suicidal, Afro-Americans rationally, heroically, and successfully resisted the dominant group in its own cultural domain that they had usurped, subverted, and mastered: religion."[45] They did it by being critical, by focusing on their liberating God and God's liberating message in the biblical story. This allowed them to critique not only the slave owners' biblical interpretations, but even, and more important, the "Bible" from which they crafted them. "According to Lewis and Milton Clarke, slaves believed that there existed somewhere a real Bible from God, "but they frequently say the Bible now used is master's Bible," since all that they heard from it was 'servants, obey your masters.' "[46]

They were intelligent enough to notice the incongruity their masters had hoped they would miss. As Mrs. Joseph Smith relays, "The ministers used to preach—'Obey your masters and mistresses and be good servants'; I never heard anything else. I didn't hear anything about obeying our maker."[47] The slave masters and their theological minion were doing much more than trying to control religious thinking. They were trying to manipulate thought, because they knew that for the slaves, as for most of us, religious thought directed ethical thinking and behavior. But, as Mrs. Smith clearly explains, the slaves understood that obeying God is the prime directive. And if God is a God of liberation, then the ethical thinking and behavior that derive from that God must be liberation oriented. That's why slave owners could not present the Christian faith as a matter of obeying God; they knew that in the reconfigured faith of the slaves such a proclamation would have been counterproductive to the institution upon which they so desperately depended. They also knew that the slaves had seen past their propaganda and had created on their own something as dangerous as it was novel. "Therefore the meaning which the missionary wished the slaves to receive and the meaning which the slaves actually found (or, better, made) were not the same. The 'inaccuracy' of the slaves' translation of Christianity would be a cause of concern to missionaries [and the institution of slavery itself] for a long time to come."[48]

Reconfigured Ethics

The "inaccurate," reconfigured slave understanding of the Christian faith along the axis of liberation contributed to a reconfigured ethics that was as evident in the structure of their slave communities as it was in the content of their theological thinking. This reconfigured faith was centered around the clandestine community of believers that has been termed "the invisible institution." South Carolina was by no means the only Southern state to legislate against independent slave worship and prayer services. Every state legislature committed to the perpetuation of slavery recognized the danger. Such activity had to be overseen by "competent" whites. As a result, "Slaves faced severe punishment if caught attending secret prayer meetings."[49]

Despite the danger, the slaves kept meeting, worshiping, and praying. They gathered together in secluded woods, gullies, ravines, and thickets called "hush harbors."[50] Hopkins refers to the time of their gatherings as "sundown to sunup," a time when folk enslaved in the present could talk about a God who was even then mapping out plans for future freedom. In the words of ex-slave Simon Brown, "Yes sir, there was no pretending in those prayer meetings. There was a living faith in a just God Who would one day answer the cries of His poor black children and deliver them from their enemies. But the slaves never said a word to their white folk about this kind of faith."[51]

Just as the seer John understood it would when he wrote the Revelation for his seven churches in Asia Minor, so also this kind of liberating and empowering future vision enabled enduring and resisting present behavior. Indeed, the very existence of this "invisible institution," this underground slave church, symbolized slave defiance. This people who believed in a liberating God hacked out a liberating space for themselves in the strangling midst of a lethal human jungle. In the protective shelter of this worshiping and praying space they came to believe—despite what their owners and white theologians, legislators, and scientists maintained—that they were God's children and that God demanded their freedom. John Hunter, a fugitive from Maryland, declared, "I have heard poor ignorant slaves, that did not know A from B, say that they did not believe the Lord ever intended they should be slaves, and that they did not see how it should be so." Lydia Adams makes a similar proclamation: "I've been wanting to be free ever since I was a little child. I said to them I didn't believe God ever meant me to be a slave" And Francis Henderson concluded from sermons he had heard "that God had made all men free and equal, and that I ought not to be a slave."[52] Not only were they reconfiguring their faith, but they were reconfiguring themselves as well. The "invisible institution" had this kind of effect.

> If sunup to sundown (time claimed by the slave system) marked the multiplicity of assaults to turn black workers from their divine created origin and intent (being created freely and created to be free), then from sundown to sunup (time claimed by the enslaved) indicated the black chattel's turn from the evil creation of the master to the original divine origin and intent.[53]

The result, from sundown to sunup *and* from sunup to sundown, was the genesis of a culture of resistance shored up by a completely reconfigured understanding of ethics. Even from an enslaved people, a liberating God demanded "liberated" behavior. No doubt Copeland is correct when she maintains that "from their aural appropriation of the Bible and critical reflection on their own condition, these men and women shaped and "fitted" Christian practices, ritual, and values to their own particular experiences, religio-cultural expectations, and personal needs."[54] In other words, they mated their space with their faith in such a creative, defiant way that the biblical ethics they hatched was completely contrary to the biblical ethics they were taught. It was in this new ethical world, where the secular and the sacred, the political and the spiritual were no longer separate, that believers could see worship and prayer as a space dedicated to the reflection upon and call for social and political liberation. Their reconfiguration of worship guaranteed a reconfigured ethics even as their reconfigured ethics demanded a new way of doing worship. All of it stemmed from a recognition that the biblical text was much more than the folk who introduced Christianity to them ever intended it to be. They saw that "much more," that liberating intent, because they "read" the foundational Christian book from the oppressive angle of their enslaved space.

In this new world, sin, Christianity's primary ethical antagonist, had a new look. Something important had shifted; the slaves, according to Raboteau, no longer understood moral propriety in the way the slave owners and the preachers they hired wanted them to. Sin was not defined only by the breaking of one's relationship with God; it was also, and perhaps more important, defined by the breaking of relationship with fellow sufferers of oppression. The communal component that distinguished their faith had also come to distinguish how one made a break with it. So Raboteau argues that "slaves viewed sin differently than did whites: what seemed antinomianism to white clergymen was in the slave's own system of moral judgment a primary value—to protect one another by not revealing the 'sins' of one's fellow slaves."[55]

And so the slaves maintained what was in effect a "code of silence" to protect others who had committed acts the owner or overseer considered unethical. Hiding the shelters of runaways or the identities of those who had stolen the master's property or the locations of the "hush harbors" where clandestine acts of independent worship took place or the identities of those who prayed and worshiped for freedom or the hostile and hateful feelings toward the master and mistress was expected, even if lying and subterfuge were necessary to do it. "The principle 'Us against them'—the in-group use of indirection and the development of masks to conceal true feelings—was essential to the slaves' own moral system."[56]

So were outright lying and deceit: "Normally considered moral vices, [they] were virtues to slaves in their dealings with whites."[57] So was theft; in their moral universe, if robbery targeted an owner or an overseer, it was described as "taking," and therefore was considered to be moral. "Nowhere is the slaves' rejection of the masters' religion clearer than in their refusal to obey the moral precepts held up to them by whites, especially commands against stealing." It was wrong to "steal" something from another slave; it was, however, not only appropriate but also moral to "take" from an owner. "While white preachers repeatedly urged 'Don't steal,' slaves just as persistently denied that this commandment applied to them, since they themselves were stolen property."[58] Because owners often fed their slaves as little as possible in order to increase their margins of profit, slaves had to find other means of assuaging the hunger of their children and kin. "Taking" was one such option. Still, as important a rationale as it was, this practical consideration was not the foundational element upon which the moral approval of "taking" from the owner was based. The underpinning came from their understanding of a God who could not tolerate the indignity of their oppression and who approved of whatever actions were necessary to survive it, even if human law and ethics understood such behavior to be immoral. In this ethical universe, sinning against God would have been the result of *refraining from* stealing from "fellow" human beings. Thus, ex-slave Henry Bibb could declare:

> I did not regard it as stealing then, I do not regard it as such now. I hold that a slave has a moral right to eat and drink and wear all that he needs, and that it would be a sin on his part to suffer and starve in a country where there is a plenty to eat and wear within his reach. I consider that I had a just right to what I took, because it was the labor of my hands.[59]

The ultimate form of stealing from the master was the taking of slave labor. Masters called it running away; the slaves called it escape. For the master, it was a crime; for the slave, it was an opportunity—a God-sanctioned opportunity at that. Joined together, these individual acts of defiance acted as a kind of corporate rejection and condemnation of the entire institution of slavery. The slaves were raising their own ethical ante; each flight away from an individual slave owner added to a growing sense of civil disobedience against the slave system that owner helped to support. "Thus individual runaways launched continual sorties against the very underpinnings of white societal well-being when they refused to remain chattel—and instruments of production for white profit." They were "speaking with their feet."[60]

They also, when pushed far enough, spoke directly and violently. Hopkins cites an illustrative example. After an overseer had lashed an old woman for what he perceived to be slow plowing in the field, the woman, once she perceived an opportunity, responded in kind. Sore from the whipping, she "took her hoe and chopped him right across his head, and, child, you should have seen how she chopped this man to a bloody death."[61] The recording of this event suggests that other slaves were witness to it. They did not intervene because, apparently, the actions were ethically appropriate given the circumstance in which the slaves had found themselves. While Hopkins points to other examples, this one suffices to make the point. The ethical world of the slave was different from the ethical world gerrymandered by the slave owner; in the slaves' world, liberation and God's care for their well-being, which ultimately mandated their liberation, were paramount. The slaves, therefore, felt morally justified to act accordingly.

Of course, most slaves could not hope to act in such a direct manner against the representative of the owner or the owner himself without expecting severely brutal repercussions. This is obviously why there are few accounts of such direct slave defiance on record, even though the treatment of slaves was very often extremely harsh. But there is still ample evidence that slaves sought forcible ways of resisting their lot. That evidence brings us face to face with the legacy of slave insurrection. Strikingly, the emphasis for these insurrections, planned from the start to be as violently bloody as necessary to secure freedom, came from the Christian faith and the biblical witness to it. Even more amazing was the fact that most of the insurrectionary leaders were preachers and leaders in their invisible slave churches. It was the biblical mandate of exodus coupled with the story of Jesus' life, death, and resurrection that not only prompted the violence but sanctioned it as well. Ethics, in this case, have been totally reconfigured. Space mattered *that* much.

Nat Turner is probably the best-known example of the slave insurrectionist. Leader of the bloodiest slave revolt in United States history in Southampton, Virginia, in 1831, Turner had "the reputation of being a seer, a prophet, and a preacher."[62] He was convinced that his actions were directed by God. Harding seems correct in his conclusion about the man and the revolt he fomented: "Even more important for our present concern is the central theme of Turner's *Confession*—the theme of a black, avenged Messiah, urged into action by nothing less than the repeated calling of God. Here was religion and resistance that would not be separated."[63]

Make no mistake, white folks knew what they were dealing with. They realized that their worst fears had come true; slaves had seen within the Christian religion the element of freedom the slave owners had tried their best to conceal. Even before Turner, the evidence was piling up alongside names like Denmark Vesey and Gabriel Prosser. Both of these men of the invisible slave church had planned what they understood to be biblically based and religiously oriented insurrections in 1822 in Charleston, South Carolina, and in 1800 in Richmond, Virginia, respectively. Against the weaponry of illiteracy and ignorance, and despite the slave owners' attempt to control the way the biblical stories were presented, the African slaves ferreted out a truth that white Southerners had desperately tried to conceal. They used that truth to concoct their own understanding of biblical ethics, an understanding that allowed for and even encouraged the spilling of blood. It was no doubt an acknowledgment of this circumstance that led one writer to the Richmond *Enquirer* to speak as he did: "The case of Nat Turner warns us. No black man ought to be permitted to turn a preacher through the country. The law must be enforced—or the tragedy of Southampton appeals to us in vain."[64]

Other, just as notable but, less violent, slaves and former slaves were no less resistant. They, too, viewed the biblical witness through the lens of liberation. But, as I will argue forcefully in the upcoming chapters, this lens already existed in the biblical story itself, providing a sense of constancy and connection for the variety of books and letters that make it up. It flourished in their enslaved context, giving them hope for a tomorrow filled with freedom. As the story and the context interacted, the lens mediated thought between them and enabled a new way of comprehending the world and operating within it. It enabled an ethics that was completely different from anything white American Christianity had seen, because it sprang from a space white Christianity had quarantined to African Americans alone—people like Harriet Tubman:

Like Turner she saw visions and dreamed dreams of struggle and conflict and searching for freedom. Like him she prayed and talked with God and became fully convinced that her God willed freedom. Indeed, one of her more radical biographers said that by the time

43

she escaped from her native Maryland in 1849, "she was ready to kill for freedom, if that was necessary, and defend the act as her religious right."[65]

And people like the great abolitionist Frederick Douglass. As Harding notes, "For Douglass, as for countless others, the requirements of God pointed in other directions, and black religion led them away from slavery. Often it led to protest, resistance and death."[66] Slaves and former slaves were willing to die for the cause of freedom. Clearly, though, many of them were also prepared to kill. The liberation lens on the biblical story, in both its Old and its New Testaments, made *this* kind of difference. Not just the acts of defiance, though, and not just the plans of insurrection or the running away or the "taking" and lying, but the religion itself, Christianity itself, had become an insubordinate entity encouraging seditious, liberative behavior. It was the kind of behavior that in the first century might have provoked one's execution on a Roman cross! "Slave rebelliousness should not be thought of exclusively in terms of acts such as arson, sabotage, flight or revolt, for religion itself, in a very real sense, could be an act of rebelliousness—an assertion of slave independence, which sometimes required outright defiance of the master's command."[67] The reconfigured slave faith had prompted both a new way of seeing the world and, more critically for us, a new way of acting in it. Their slave space, the space from which and in which their interaction with the biblical story took place, mattered *that* much!

CHAPTER THREE

The Synoptic Gospels: Kingdom Ethics

Right from the start of their involvement with Christianity, African Americans have been seduced by the Nazarene. They have been attracted to his power. To be sure, Moses was a kind of first love. He was the one who wielded the staff that powered Israel's liberation from bondage in Egypt. African American slaves longed for the day when his exodus would be recapitulated for them, when the freedom he engineered in his people's lives would be represented in theirs. But as great as he had been, as great as he still was, Moses was a man locked in the past. Even the man who stood the water on its sides and pressed his people through the resulting breach could not liberate himself from the bondage of death. And so his mortality separated him from them, isolated him from his idolizing African American slaves in their peculiar and bitter circumstance.

But Jesus was a liberator who overpowered even death. Here was a man whose ministry not only loosed the ill from their diseases, liberated the dead from their slumber, drove demonic forces from their human domiciles, and championed the cause of the poor, the outcast, and the oppressed; this man also held cosmic authority in his hands. If Moses' exodus provided the model for their hope, Jesus' person, and the kingdom of God power attached to it, offered the force that could transfigure that hope into contemporary reality. If death, as eternal as it seems, could be overcome, not just for Jesus but for all who would come to believe in him, what else could interminably enslave them? What could not be overcome? Jesus means freedom. What slave could possibly resist him? What slave would not want to be counted among his victorious number? What slave would not want to follow his teachings and emulate his life in the hope that his victory would one day be his or her own, in this world and the one to come? What slave would therefore not find in the narrative proclamation of Jesus' life an ethical guide for the living of his or her own?

And therein lies the problem: the narrative nature of the Jesus presentation in the Synoptic Gospels. Mark, Matthew, and Luke are not like Paul. Paul wrote letters that not only described the salvific meaning of Jesus' death and resurrection, but also exhorted the faithful to respond appropriately to that gift of God's grace. The synoptic writers rarely address their readers directly.[1] They depend on the story to make their ethical points. Whether their stories are read silently by an individual, read aloud to a community, or orally transmitted via sermon, song, and testimony by illiterate slaves, they make their ethical points by the way they shape the interactions and speeches that take place within these stories. The key, though, is that they *do* take ethical stands and they *do* suggest particular kinds of ethical behavior and particular ethical perspectives. But they do it as part of a story. "In order to grasp the moral vision of the evangelist, we must ask how Jesus' life and ministry are portrayed in the story and how his call to discipleship reshapes the lives of other characters."[2] The narrative presentation of Jesus, his followers, and his opponents creates an ethical world within the text that has dramatic implications for anyone in the "historical" world reading outside it.

Mark, Matthew, and Luke, then, offer narrative ethics. Their *stories* accomplish the task Eduard Lohse sets for a New Testament theological ethics; they "make clear the implications of confessing faith in Jesus as the crucified and resurrected Christ for the life and actions of the community of faith."[3] But the fact that they accomplish this task as part of a story addressed to a particular community of faith means that they do not combine together to offer a universal, systematic presentation of what a New Testament ethic should look like. Because Jesus is refracted through the contextual lens of their three different communal circumstances, he ends up looking different. What does this mean for New Testament ethics? Willi Marxsen has the right response. "If people drew different

Jesus images, did they also have different ethics? This would be the obvious conclusion."[4]

The ethical directives that develop from each unique Jesus presentation are specifically designed for and targeted toward the different communities in which the individual writers live. Each Gospel writer thus has his own unique understanding of what faith in Jesus means, and, therefore, what responsible behavior in light of that faith entails. The synoptic ethical portraits are developed and applied contextually.

Still, there is a unifying factor: the presence of Jesus as the incarnate revelation of God's will. Jesus, as contextually presented as he is, is the constant. The Jesus event is the key; it provides sufficient coherence to the various synoptic portraits so that they can be considered together.

The kingdom of God is the place to start. Jesus operates in each of the texts as a re-presentation of that future reality in the midst of his present ministry. His proclamation of the kingdom serves as the thesis statement for his ministry in Mark and Matthew; it is the foundation that undergirds his message of reversal in Luke. Jesus is the ultimate kingdom preacher. Ultimately, he is also equal to that kingdom. The evangelists incorporate into their narratives, right alongside their presentations of Jesus proclaiming the kingdom, the early church's consensus opinion that he was himself worthy of the same adulation and praise. That faith claim transformed the man who was one among many miracle workers into *the* messianic agent acting out the very kingdom that he claimed was just on edge of the human horizon.

All this activity—God's imminent breaking of the consummate kingdom into the corridors of human history, and Jesus' immediate presentation of that future reality in his present proclamation of it—aroused the desire for suitable human response.[5] After all, if God's judgment, which was a critical part of the kingdom reality, was already firing its earliest salvos in anticipation of an impending full scale assault, human beings needed to be about the business of taking proper cover. One could not hide, but one could respond. The point, of course, was to respond appropriately. But how, exactly, does one respond *appropriately* to the news that God's kingdom is on final approach?

It is exactly here that the distinct portraits of Jesus will propose different courses of ethical action. But once again there is an element of constancy. In all three synoptic presentations the expectation is for a kind of radical kingdom response that is in accord with the will of God. The motivational heart of synoptic ethics lies here. The pivot point for disclosing the content of God's will and provoking the motivation to follow it was no longer the exodus and its subsequent Sinai. With Jesus everything turned on the future. It was the future that demanded a return to the original will that God had set forth at the creation.[6] It was the future that empowered Jesus to interpret that will directly or to correct how its development should be tracked through the Torah. And it was the dawning of the future that encouraged residents of the present to lay claim to that will and live it. According to the evangelists, they could only do so by following the Jesus whose familiarity with the future allowed him to interpret it. New Testament ethics, then, at least the synoptic version, is apocalyptic, future, kingdom ethics.

It is this future orientation that gives the synoptic variety of New Testament ethics its potential for liberation. Surely, the African American slave could appreciate such an ethical perspective. Their past, lives anchored in the cultures and cults of Africa, had been stolen from them. Their present, lives lived according to the dictates of a slave institution, was not their own. Only in the future could they have realistic hope. Whether it was the immediate future of death and a new life with their Lord, the intermediary future of a land of escape perilously achieved, the long-range future of a coming war that would shatter the institution that bound them, or the imminent future of God's kingdom sweeping in from on high, the slave knew that his or her hope for freedom lay with the transformative power of King Jesus in God's highly anticipated coming day.

> Children, we shall be free,
> When the Lord [as Messiah] shall appear.
> Give ease to the sick, give sight to blind,
> Enable the cripple to walk;
> He'll raise the dead from under the earth,
> And give them permission to talk.[7]

For a people incarcerated in the present, a glorious past may encourage endurance and even foster the fight to resist, but it is in the future that the real hope for transformation will dwell. For that is where the Jesus who found liberation from even death now resides, waiting with an at-the-ready God to finish what his first century ministry started, the establishment of a liberation like his for all those who follow him, who live in response to that future now. The eighteenth and nineteenth century slaves understood this socially as well as spiritually. So, too, did the apocalyptic Jewish writers of the first century.[8]

> The Christians did not abandon a hope for this world. . . . When we recognize that the teaching in the New Testament, particularly that attributed to Jesus, is about the ideals applicable to God's reign *on earth*, the New Testament writings can certainly be seen as the struggles of those who looked forward to a new age but also recognized the obligation to live in the present *as if* they were living in the age to come.[9]

Now I am ready to ask directly the question that has been percolating in the background of this discussion. Jesus, as he is presented in the synoptic accounts, represents the future kingdom of God. But is he also representative of a future kingdom that drives the present and all those who live in it toward the kind of historical transformation that prefigures and therefore inspires the liberation of those who are oppressed? My answer is yes.

> In Jesus we find a figure whose activity is deeply disturbing within the political context of first-century Judaism. Although "the prophet does not physically change things by his actions . . . his actions may represent the change which God wills to bring about and which the prophet is charged to proclaim." Such prophetic activity and conviction challenged the status quo.[10]

Jesus was the ultimate kingdom preacher. And that kingdom symbol was pregnant with the potential for liberation. Or as Lohse puts it, "The coming of the Kingdom of God brings salvation to the lost. By associating with publicans and sinners, sharing a table with them, and speaking to them of the gracious compassion of God, he makes clear to all eyes that the coming of the kingdom of God means salvation for the suffering and freedom to those who are bound."[11]

I am suggesting, then, *that this lens of liberation is not only the access point that African Americans, operating from the foundational perspective of their slave forebears, might bring with them to the text, but that it exists in the synoptic texts through the symbolic imagery and implications of the kingdom.* A particular kind of "meaning" explodes from the text when that access point triggers a connection with this kingdom's meaning potential. This does not mean that liberation is the *only* ethical orientation of the synoptic texts. I am suggesting that, because of the kingdom's focus, it is a significant one. Indeed, before this chapter is through I want to press the case that it is so significant that it should be the lens through which the other ethical orientations in the synoptics are viewed. To be sure, Mark, Matthew, and Luke, by virtue of their determination to narrate toward the contextual situations of their reading audiences, developed that liberation imagery in different ways. But all three initiated their developments from the same kingdom starting point. Mark developed it through his narration of Jesus as a trespasser of societal boundaries. Matthew developed it through his narration of Jesus as the initiator of an alternative "visible institution." And Luke developed it through his narration of a Jesus who is the focal point of a God-directed program of societal reversal. The common denominator is the kingdom of God. And that kingdom lives itself out as a powerful force for liberation. It would seem only logical, then, that a disciple hoping to respond appropriately to the coming of that kingdom would want to incorporate liberation as a critical part of his or her ethical agenda.

The Gospel of Mark:
The Liberating Ethics of Boundary Breaking

Every narrative moment in Mark takes its cue from Jesus' keynote address in 1:15: " 'The time is fulfilled, and the kingdom of God has come near; repent, and believe in the good news.' " This programmatic utterance is the thesis statement that controls the direction and destiny of Jesus' Markan ministry. "In this scene, the Markan Evangelist identifies the essential content of Jesus' proclamation and the ethical response it requires."[12]

The kingdom of God, as Mark presents it, is both an expected future event and an accomplished present reality. Jesus' testimony that "it has come near" witnesses to its impending status. And yet, as the gospel unfolds, it also becomes clear that Jesus represents that future hope in his present ministry. Mark's chapter 3 celebrates Jesus as the one who has come into the strong man's (i.e., Satan's) house (i.e., this age) and, having bound him up, has retaken his realm for God's purposes and God's people. It is a clear indication that he sees in Jesus the reality of that kingdom. With his miracles, his exorcisms, and his authoritative teaching Jesus represents that "not yet" kingdom in the narrative's contemporary "now."

The future kingdom that he represents in the present is not a place, but a force—a powerful, sweeping indication of God's rule that cuts into the path of human time and overwhelms it.[13] In other words, Jesus does not construct a heavenly outpost, a divine space or mythological safe house where wearied disciples can escape the troubles of their first-century Palestinian world. He wields instead, through the language "repent and believe," a charismatic intensity that demands a responsive following into their most troubled arenas of tradition and ritual.

Matera is right to point out that, ethically speaking, we should maintain the connection Mark has made between repentance and belief. But Jack Sanders is also right to note the reluctance of many readers to qualify "repentance" as ethics. Surely, though, as he argues, it must. "It is clearly an action—more precisely a response—to a situation, which response may be evaluated "right" or "wrong": the right response to the gospel is repentance and belief, the "wrong" response is disbelief and rejection of the call to repentance."[14] Repentance, then, is the act preparatory to and for faith. Matera helpfully defines that act as "leaving everything behind." Its narrative partner, faith, is the resulting push forward in Jesus' wake. No wonder Mark immediately trails Jesus' kingdom proclamation with the showcase narration of four men doing exactly that, leaving everything they have, family as well as possessions, in order to follow (see also 10:28). We will come to see, of course, that their act of faith means much more than merely tracing Jesus' physical path throughout Galilee and Judea; they must also accept the tradition shattering demands that Jesus apparently believes God's in-breaking rule demands. Instead of clinging to biological family (the world's view), they will be called into a family connected by the will of God (3:31-35). Instead of saving their lives (the world's view), they will be called to surrender them (8:35). Instead of pushing to be first (the world's view), they will seek to be last (9:35). Instead of seeking to be great (the world's view), they must aspire to be the slave and servant of all (10:43-44).[15] They must no longer be bound by the world's expectations; the kingdom must instead be their discipleship guide.

The kingdom also becomes their story's ethical center. "The ethics of Jesus in Mark's Gospel are necessarily bound up with the story of Jesus. To know that story is to be shaped by a new ethical vision whose horizon is none other than the in-breaking kingdom of God."[16] It is an in-breaking vision with a boundary-breaking *modus operandi*. Mark sets the narrative stage by cracking God into the story just as Jesus is formally introduced. At 1:9, Jesus comes from Nazareth to be baptized by John in the Jordan River. Immediately, Mark cuts to the chase; as Jesus walks out of the water, the heavens are torn asunder and God's Spirit breaks out of its heavenly restraints and falls loose into human time. Mark will deploy this graphic verb of tearing one more time. At 15:38, as Jesus dies and the narrative anticipates its own closure, God seizes the moment and defies its despair by breaking through again. Targeted this time is the temple veil that segregated the area of the temple where allegedly God's presence was exclusively restricted. When the veil rips in two from top to bottom the reader is assured that the greatest boundary of all, the one that separates humans from God, has been definitively overturned. The empty tomb will merely seal a verdict that has already been narratively delivered: with Jesus, God broke defiantly and victoriously into human time. Jesus' preaching will explain the reason why.

This is not all *good* news! Don Juel is right: "If characters in the story find Jesus' ministry threatening, then they may have good reason."[17] The reason is that Jesus' preaching obliterates the traditional boundaries that have regulated the lives of God's people. It is not just that Mark connects the language of preaching with Jesus' activities of miracle and exorcism.[18] To be sure, Jesus' kingdom preaching liberates many from the shackles of illness, possession, and destructive nature. But Jesus does not stop there. He pushes on against human landmarks that were once established to regulate life, but are now, in Mark's opinion, destructively controlling it. The cultic and ritual traditions related to the Law are his first, and in the narrative, most provocative targets. Mark cannot even close the first chapter of his narrative before he unleashes Jesus' authoritative teaching against the ritual and cultic boundaries of the law. At 1:40-41, notably, just after Mark has recounted that Jesus' preaching has effected the healing of many diseases and the exorcising of many possessed persons in 1:38-39, a leper comes seeking Jesus' healing power. Jesus obliges him, but not before he pricks the consciences of both his sympathetic and hostile bystanders. Instead of healing him and then making contact with him, Jesus, against all the conventions of purity and holiness, touches and converses with him. Purity laws had set this man outside of the ritual boundaries of God's kingdom community. Jesus' troubling touch signals his re-entry. Only then does he heal him. It is no wonder that a cycle of controversy stories about just this kind of mistreatment of the law kicks off immediately after this episode concludes.

In 2:1-3:6, Jesus challenges laws regarding the Sabbath, laws regarding fasting, laws regarding holiness and purity (by eating at the table with tax collectors and sinners), and the authoritative understanding that God alone has the power to forgive sin. With a word, Jesus usurps even this ostensibly divine role, once again breaking down the dividing barriers between heaven and humanity. No longer must sinners endure the mechanics of the sacrificial temple system in order to obtain God's release; Jesus offers it just for the asking. He not only sets a man free of his individual sins; he sets an entire narrative audience free from their dependence on the temple state. No wonder representatives of that state already seek a way to destroy him (3:6).

Subsequent conflicts relate to Jesus' apparent disregard for the cultic and ritual traditions of the law. Mark 7:1-23 offers another key vignette. This time the food laws are so rigorously challenged by Jesus that Mark makes an astounding interpretative declaration. Jesus has rendered all foods clean (7:19b).

All of this is morally instructive in Mark's narrative presentation. If Jesus' preaching activities are the guide for human ethical behavior, and that is most certainly Mark's point, the members of both Mark's narrative *and reading* community are free from a scrupulous observance of the law. The community is free from regulations regarding withdrawal from sinners (2:15-17), from fasting (2:18-22), from the Sabbath (2:23-3:6), from purity (7:1-8), from oaths (7:9-13), and from kosher foods (7:14-23). Such regulations belong to the past, not to the new, eschatological, kingdom community of discipleship.[19] For moral discernment the precepts of the law are no longer primary. Jesus' kingdom ministry has usurped its place. The needs and conditions of human beings come first.[20] Here is Mark's transformative, liberative, kingdom-motivated moment. As was Jesus when he stood before the leper, humans have been freed from ritual and cultic restraints to be in service to and for one another.

Apparently, this transformative, liberative moment applies even to Jesus' teaching about love. One could certainly make the case that Mark had difficulty with the way the law was being interpreted because it set love of God at odds with love of other human beings. One could either love the laws of purity or one could consort with the likes of sinners and lepers. One could either love the Sabbath law and keep it unconditionally or one could love the hungry or distressed. One could either love the food laws that had been set forth to honor one's relationship with God or one could enter into table fellowship with others even though the food they ate or the cleansing practices they observed were disavowed. In Mark's narrative presentation, Jesus shatters this either/or dualism by connecting the love of God integrally with the love of humans such that one could not exist without the other. This, Schnackenberg argues, is what Mark sees uniquely happening in Jesus' teaching/preaching to the scribe at 12:28-34. Clearly, the love commandment was not new with Jesus. The command to love God before all else, of course, is the principle behind the Jewish *Shema* (Deuteronomy 6:5). The command to love others also predates Jesus (Leviticus 19:18). As early as 20 B.C.E. Rabbi Hillel (working with 613 commandments—248 positive and 365 negative) had tried to unify the commandments through a negative presentation of the Golden Rule (e.g., *"Don't* do to others what you would *not* have them do to you."). For Schnackenberg, Jesus' genius was in the novel connection of loving God with loving humans. "To Jesus, this was a two fold commandment; he put love of God and love of one's neighbor on an equal footing."[22] By breaking down the boundaries between the two kinds of love, he transformed the understanding of love and thereby fashioned it into a force that bore more weight, commanded more allegiance than even obligation to the law. Jesus' boundary-breaking preaching "liberated" even love.

These transformative, boundary-breaking, liberative moves inside the narrative also have dramatic implications for the world outside the narrative. What is only implied in the first controversy cycle of 2:1–3:6 becomes perfectly clear by the time Mark concludes the food discussion of 7:1-23. Mark's Jesus has toppled boundaries within Israel as a foundational prelude to the shattering of an even greater one, the one that separated Jew from Gentile. "By commenting that Jesus declared all foods clean, Mark makes explicit what is implicit in the feeding narratives: Jew and Gentile may now share table fellowship because Jesus, the Shepherd Messiah, has fed both. The kingdom of God is establishing a new reality that requires the rethinking of old traditions."[23]

Mark demands this rethinking by the way he drives his narrative. Not only does he offer the one feeding account on Jewish soil (6:35-44) in parallel with a similar miraculous feeding on Gentile soil (8:1-10); but he has peppered a full accounting of material in between these two bookend events which suggests the kingdom's imminent proximity has drawn Gentiles into God's liberative orbit. The food material in 7:1-23 is followed up immediately by Jesus' engagement with a Syrophonecian woman. Notably, the bread that was meant only for the "children" of Israel is delivered quite dramatically to Gentiles as well. Immediately afterward, Mark narrates Jesus' deliberate healing tour in the Gentile cities of the Decapolis. These activities act as a thematic preamble for the feeding of the four thousand in chapter 8. The narrative cobbling together of this "Gentile cycle" of materials offers the obvious presentation of God's kingdom power transgressing the once sacrosanct boundary that separated Gentiles and Jews. God was on the loose through Jesus, and in that frightening movement, two peoples have been liberated from their isolation from one another before God.

Mark climaxes this claim in his temple cleansing account of chapter 11: "Is it not written, 'My house shall be called a house of prayer for all the nations'?/ But you have made it a den of robbers" (v. 17). Jesus' Isaiah/Jeremiah quotation (Isa 56:7; Jer 7:11) pushes home the point: God has become so angered at the religious infrastructure's refusal to demolish the wall isolating Jews from Gentiles that God will demolish the temple that has borne little integrative fruit.[24] Indeed, if, as many commentators think, Mark's community had experienced an influx of Gentiles whose presence was causing both legal and ethnic turmoil, his narrative presentation of Jesus offers the ethical direction of integrative inclusion that was particularly relevant, even if incredibly controversial, for the moment. Jesus' boundary-breaking preaching in the narrative would have had its most potent ethical implications for those reading from outside the narrative.

Mark, then, has not, as some commentators would have it, presented an ethics of discipleship. He has offered instead an apocalyptically driven ethics of transformative boundary breaking that he believes should be the norm for discipleship. To be sure, as Verhey instructs, Mark places the theme of discipleship at key points in the narrative.[25] The earliest of these placements is 1:16-20, where Jesus calls his first four disciples. That act, however, is a consequence of a prior, and I would argue, more formative preaching moment: the programmatic declaration of 1:14,15. Here Mark sets his narrative standard. Discipleship—dramatic, life altering discipleship—is the appropriate response to the oddly paradoxical announcement that in Jesus' *present* ministry the imminently accessible *future* kingdom has already dawned. It is only *after* Mark has made it clear in both John the Baptist's forerunning and Jesus' introduction that God has torn His way into human time and history that Mark opens the narrative floor to the matter of discipleship discussion.

The second narrated call, that of Levi at 2:13-14, is given an even more striking placement. Mark puts it smack in the middle of the first two boundary-breaking controversy accounts. It even acts as the prelude to the second accounting, where Jesus gets into trouble for sitting at table with the socially and cultically dreaded tax collectors and sinners. He does this, of course, after he has, just prior to this troublesome stirring of the traditional sentiments, called one of those tax collectors to be his disciple. Even Jesus' classic discipleship statement of 8:34-37 gains its narrative weight from the apocalyptic realization that God is working through Jesus to overturn human expectations, even where those expectations concern the meaning of messiahship. The conclusion seems certain: for Mark, discipleship as a narrative theme follows from the realization of God's own boundary-breaking behavior around and in Jesus. The theme of discipleship is a narrative derivative; it derives from the apocalyptic activity of boundary breaking. It acts, for the characters within the narrative and, through them, for the readers outside, as an appropriate response to that kingdom behavior.

This becomes even more interesting when one realizes that Mark is asking for more than an automated response to Jesus' boundary-breaking kingdom activity. The evangelist is expecting much more than the proverbial jerk of the discipleship knee to Jesus' narrative knock. Discipleship in Mark's Gospel is not just following Jesus around; it is also, and perhaps more important, since it is narratively necessary that Jesus die on the cross and leave the human scene, that the disciples learn to do what Jesus himself has been doing. This is why, in the first eight chapters, before the disciples have a clue about Jesus' inevitable destiny, that Mark offers the reader a picture of Jesus *successfully* teaching them to do the powerful acts of transformative, liberating behavior that he himself has been doing.[26] "It is characteristic of all three discipleship pericopes that the statements about Jesus also for the most part apply to the disciples or the Twelve, so that they are included in the ministry of the earthly Jesus."[27] At 3:13-19, he appoints the twelve to go forth and preach. One can only presume that they, too, are to preach that the kingdom of God is at hand. Mark has introduced no other possible preaching topic. Not incidentally, they are also given the power to demonstrate the boundary-breaking, liberating reality of this kingdom. Armed with the weaponry of exorcism, they, too, will join God's apocalyptic battle with the powers of Satan.

The general thinking about the disciples in Mark is that they never measure up to Jesus' expectations. For the most part it is true that their deficiencies highly exercise the emotions of their teacher. But Mark also notes, at 6:7-13, 30, that, having gone out on their appointed kingdom rounds, they successfully preach, exorcise, heal, and teach. They do all that Jesus himself has been doing; they make real the transformative force of God's boundary-breaking kingdom. To be sure, things go downhill following Peter's confession in chapter 8. But Mark never lets the disciples go. Despite their failures it is clear that he believes that Jesus has not finished with them yet (14:28; 16:7). This apocalyptic story of teacher and disciple obviously has more to it than the narrative surface reveals.

What it *does* reveal is that these kingdom-authorized disciples are to form the nucleus of a community whose mode of being counters traditional cultic, legal, and social expectations. Right from the start the traditional expectations of familial responsibility are overturned. Peter makes clear at 10:28 what was already established as early as the first calling scene of 1:16-20; these disciples leave everything to follow and be like Jesus. They must surrender familial relationships that derive from blood (3:31-35) and communal ones that operate from nationality and/or geography (6:1-6a) and focus instead on becoming part of a community whose bond is Jesus' presentation of God's kingdom will (3:34-35).

It is Jesus who constructs the sense of communal formation. Before bestowing his own kingdom authority upon them, he chooses a mountain location, calls twelve, and then proceeds to rename some and refashion all into a unit focused on him.[28] Mark's choice of number and location, the same number and location so instrumental in the creation of Israel as a community, cannot have gone unnoticed, both in and outside the narrative. What God once did on Sinai, Jesus, acting as God's kingdom agent, is now restaging in Palestine. In this case, though, the community is being created as an opposition ministry. It is a force that will not only oppose Satan's dominion, but also traditional cultic, legal, and social boundaries. "Jesus' authority calls Mark's community into the uncompromising and uncomfortable status of a counterculture, a new covenant community standing in contrast to both the established religious authorities and the established civil authorities."[29]

This communal creation and disposition is prefigured in the illustrative first controversy cycle of materials. There, it is Jesus' corps of disciples who do not fast and who pluck and eat grain on the Sabbath. It is also they who, in chapter 7, eating with defiled hands, set up the controversy with the gathered Pharisees that culminates in Mark's understanding that Jesus has pronounced all foods clean. They not only follow Jesus on his forays into unclean Gentile territories, but it is they who act as assistants when Jesus recapitulates his feeding of the thousands on Gentile soil. It is they whom he evidently expects at 13:10 to take the point on a gospel sortie that will ferry the good news of the kingdom into *all* the world.

Indeed, this is where the counter-cultural status hits most effectively home, outside the narrative rather than within it. Clearly, Mark's Jesus has the expectation that the gospel will ultimately move beyond the people of Israel (14:9). No doubt this is precisely why Mark narrates a continuous cycle of material where Jesus seems to set up a discipleship ministry to the Gentiles with a protracted one of his own. While the disciples within the narrative may be clueless, it is hard to believe that disciples outside it could have been so. If they were, Mark makes it clear at 13:9-13. There, with the same kind of apocalyptic inevitability that Jesus had given to his own passion, Mark has Jesus explain that the gospel *will* be preached to all the nations. Since, by this time, Jesus has already forecasted that he does not have much longer on the scene, one can only surmise that some discipleship group will be responsible.

But this kind of universal preaching activity, as the narrative presents it, goes against all the traditional expectations of legal, cultic, and socio-political code. This is why the authorities, who feel the weight of a mandate to protect those traditions, have been so hot on Jesus' heels throughout his kingdom preaching tour. It is also why, at 13:9-13, Jesus anticipates that the same hostility will attend the work of any disciple who picks up with his boundary-breaking kingdom preaching and carries it on. The surrounding of this verse about preaching the kingdom to all the world, i.e., the Gentiles, with the stern notification of resulting persecution is a clear warning to any potential disciple. He or she will not only leave behind family and possessions; he or she will also leave behind any assurance of personal safety. In fact, he or she will *attract* the opposite of personal safety. Because of the kinds of transformative activity Jesus' kingdom preaching ministry demands, particularly in relationship to carrying the gospel beyond the boundaries of Israel, suffering will follow the activity of the disciple as inevitably as it followed Jesus' own activity.

Still, this kingdom-driven, boundary-breaking ethics that becomes the norm of discipleship for characters within and readers outside the narrative does not result in an ethics of suffering.

Suffering, even Jesus' suffering on the cross, is the consequence, not the goal of his boundary-breaking ministry. An exclusively "cross-eyed" approach, like the one that led Martin Kähler to allege that Mark's Gospel is a passion narrative with an extended introduction, denigrates Jesus' entire narrative ministry. It is as though his servanthood (10:45) as expressed in his transformative preaching career was completely disconnected from and discounted by the soteriological denouement that is his death on the cross. The man whose word was able to release humans from sin in chapter 2 must redundantly die in chapter 15 in order to procure this same release. Never mind that Mark never, even in the Supper recounting,[30] argues that Jesus must die in order to save humankind from sin. What he narrated instead was that this Jesus, whose transformative, liberative, boundary-breaking preaching caused reactionary resistance from the religious and civil authorities right from the start, must inevitably face the kind of end every dangerous reformer faced if he maintained his momentum on the kind of path he chose. "It becomes inevitable ("the Son of Man must undergo great suffering," as Jesus puts it in 8:31) that both the religious and political leaders must destroy Jesus as a threat to the tradition to law and order, and as an affront to common sense."[31] In an apocalyptic worldview those transforming activities get caught up in the larger cosmic battle between God and Satan. "Those who live God's lordship in the middle of the old aeon place themselves in opposition to the old aeon. Thus they must run the risk that the old aeon will rise up against them."[32]

What goes for Jesus follows for the disciple. Discipleship is not exemplified by suffering; suffering is the tragic outcome of following this kingdom-preaching Jesus. This is what makes Jesus discipleship heroic. Despite the probability that one will suffer if one persists in imaging the life of Jesus in his or her own life, the disciple goes ahead and images that life anyway. The ethical call is to preach and live the kingdom as Jesus preached and lived it, transformatively, in a boundary-breaking way. The price for such preaching will be paid in blood. The cross stands as a monument to this inevitable truth.

After the cross, in the proclaimed word of an empty tomb, stands the hope that Jesus' kingdom vision, like Jesus himself, did not die. Both survived, and even demolished the cosmic boundary of death, perhaps the greatest apocalyptic adversary there is. Only the hope of such an envisioned victory could possibly sustain a disciple in the kind of transformative, boundary-breaking ministry that would invite such an inevitably tragic end.

Surely, this is how the African American slave would have apprehended Mark's narrative meaning potential if he or she had had the training and leisure to make such a study. A people who must endure a life of constant suffering would be less likely to romanticize it into a sought after goal of daily living and discipleship. Suffering is what suffering simply is: tragedy. It should be avoided; it must be transformed. One only endures it *if* it is somehow to be seen as the way toward a boundary-breaking transformation and liberation that will ultimately destroy both it and the circumstances that impose it.

> And, if the makers of the spirituals gloried in singing of the cross of Jesus, it was not because they were masochistic and enjoyed suffering. Rather, the enslaved Africans sang because they saw on the rugged wooden planks One who had endured what was their daily portion. The cross was treasured because it enthroned the One who went all the way with them and for them. The enslaved Africans sang because they saw the result of the cross—triumph over the principalities and powers of death, triumph over evil in this world.[33]

Running away and the threat of suffering associated with it provide a potent case in point. One of the few publicly demonstrative methods of boundary breaking available to someone incarcerated in a life of slavery was running away. Both slave and slave owner understood this fact and appreciated its connotations. Each successful escape was as damaging to the system of institutionalized slavery as each one of Jesus' successful exorcisms or healings had been to the continued dominance of the realm of the "strong man." Successful escape identified a weakness; it suggested transformative possibility. It illustrated in the life of one oppressed individual or group of individuals a glimpse of what could become a corporate reality for all. That is why, just as the authorities had to do everything, even to the point of enlisting the cross, to stop Jesus, so the slave owner had to do everything within his or her power, even to the point of enlisting their theological interpretation of Scripture, to impress upon his or her slaves that running away could not be tolerated. Such an act would inevitably, and *justifiably*, lead to suffering. Dwight Hopkins points to the theological justifications rendered by some Baptists and Anglicans.

> And if lawful to buy them 'tis lawful to keep them in order, and under government; and for self-preservation, punish them to prevent further mischief that may ensue by their running away and rebelling against their master, Exodus 21:20,21.[34]

So justified, masters could wield the most brutal forms of punishment imaginable to deter future attempts of escape. This kind of suffering could not possibly have been sought. Still, having considered the boundary-breaking goal, slaves very often risked and, subsequently, endured it.

> Considering the likelihood of punishment and a harder life in case of failure, ridicule from the other slaves, his ignorance of the world and geography, his penniless condition, his viewing every white man as his enemy, and his memory of his master's tales of the horrible fate which befell fugitives who succeeded in reaching the North, a slave had to think a long time before he took the first step toward permanent freedom.[35]

> Moses Roper, an incorrigible runaway, regularly received 100 to 200 lashes from his owner. Once his master poured tar on his head and set it afire. On another occasion Roper had escaped from leg irons, his master had the nails of his fingers and toes beaten off.[36]

> In another instance, Lilburn and Isham Lewis, two nephews of Thomas Jefferson, slowly chopped up the body of a live slave as a lesson to deter other chattel from running away. In a deliberate manner, one of the nephews hacked off the feet, paused to lecture the other slaves in attendance, continued by chopping off the legs below the knees, cast these into a ferocious fire, and proceeded slowly with intermittent lectures while the victim howled in pain, with finally nothing remaining except the bodiless head, which was likewise tossed in the flames.[37]

Despite such dire, almost apocalyptic premonitions and punitive presentations of retaliatory torture, slaves continued to run. Even the threat of such brutal retribution, meant to prevent further recidivism in the perpetrator and discourage others from following suit, did not quash the enduring dashes for freedom. The slave understood what Jesus' kingdom preaching had taught: the liberative, boundary-breaking goal was worth the price an individual might have to pay to obtain it. It is the same understanding that drove the African American civil rights leaders of the 1960s and 1970s and, I would argue, should be driving African Americans still. African Americans are not called as a people to suffer. They are, however, called to the kinds of transformative, boundary-breaking behavior on behalf of an already suffering people that may, in the end, make their own suffering as inevitable as Jesus' cross. This, I think, is what Markan ethics looks like through an African American slave lens.

The Gospel of Matthew: The Liberating Ethics of a "Visible Institution"

On first glance it would appear that the Gospel of Matthew is a poor candidate for viewing ethics through an African American slave lens of liberation. Marxsen echoes the thoughts of many when he argues that any social concern in Matthew is mostly accidental; the second evangelist is preoccupied primarily with the believer's future salvation.

> The admission requirements for heaven will be fulfilled in the present, and if many people fulfill them, that will change the present as well as people's living and working together in the present. But for Matthew the accent does not lie on this "social component." Rather, for him it is on people being concerned about their *future* salvation. If the world they live in thereby becomes a better world, that is naturally a welcome side-effect—but only a side-effect. It does not get Matthew's immediate attention.[38]

Interestingly enough, Marxsen's devaluation of Matthew's social concern demonstrates its presence in the narrative's meaning potential. It operates through Matthew's interest in community—an interest now understood to be one of the driving forces in the development of the evangelist's plot. Marxsen can disconnect this interest in a spiritually oriented community focused on salvation from any direct interest in social concern because for him the sacred and secular apparently are separate spheres; what happens in the spiritual world has little, and only coincidental meaning for the social and political world.

It is exactly here, of course, that the African American slave would have disagreed with Marxsen's Matthean assessment. For the slave the secular and the sacred were intimately bound together; what happened in one had dramatic effect for the circumstances of the other. One of the most pertinent points of such convergence was the surreptitious slave worship service. The "invisible institution" of the "brush harbors" was, to be sure, a religious gathering. Its requirement for "invisibility," however, was strictly social and political. The slaves understood very well how upset their masters were at the prospect of the slaves worshiping without proper, which is to say white, supervision. More important, they knew *why*. The owners did not want the slaves to do exactly what the slaves were in fact doing. They were reconfiguring the owners' presentation of the Christian faith as reconcilable with their enslavement. The praying, singing, preaching, and, most important, independent gathering, may not have had an overt political agenda; but these actions did have overt social and political connotations for the institutional infrastructure of slavery. Every slave and every slave owner knew it. This is why slave owners sought to curtail such activities and slaves did everything in their power and risked everything in their masters' cruel arsenal of punishment to continue them.

Matthew, too, has institutional concerns. His stress on the language (16:18; 18:17) and foundational matters (chapters 16 and 18) of *ecclesia* is unique among all the Gospel writers. In fact, I want to press the point that Matthew's narrative attempts to establish a "visible institution"—an identifiable, alternative worship community in an environment that he believed was hostile to its reconfiguration of the faith of God's people. This Matthean attempt is historically analogous to what the slaves were doing in the American South. What the slave had to do in secret, Matthew felt in his own context had to be done in the open. He, too, however, anticipated that his risky endeavor would invite suffering for those who joined his cause and the community that would institutionalize it. In other words, he also knew that his spiritual endeavor had dramatic social and political ramifications. I would contend that those ramifications were liberative.

Matthew's interest in the social and political is on narrative display right at the start of a story that is a dramatic transfiguration of its Markan source "the story of Jesus' infancy in chapters 1 and 2. When Matthew adds his infancy narrative he also adds a political connotation whose meaning potential is rife with liberative themes. Jesus' coming is a fulfillment of Old Testament expectations (1:22-23; 2:15; 2:17; 2:23; 3:15; 4:14). The particularities of those expectations suggest to the narrative King Herod that the helpless babe is also a social and political threat.

When Herod's wrath forces Joseph to flee with Jesus and Mary into Egypt, Matthew understands this to be at the direction of God's will (2:15) so as to fulfill the prophecy of Hosea 11:1: "Out of Egypt I called my son." Certainly, the reader is reminded here of the fact that Israel was also seen as God's son. But Matthew has given us a picture of Jesus that indicates something more is at work, and at stake. Jesus is son in a sense that is completely unique. He is the prophesied messianic Son.

The discussion at 2:16 and the explicit quotation at 2:5 that Jesus was born at Bethlehem conjures up the Son of David motif that Matthew had already established (1:1-17, 20). His birthplace is a fulfillment of messianic expectations. Then, there is the star! This miraculous celestial appearance not only celebrates Jesus' birth; it also directs the Magi to him. It cannot be simply coincidental for Matthew that in both Jewish (see Num 24:17) and Greco-Roman[39] legend the birth of epochal human beings was often so heavenly heralded. Complicating matters further, prominent voices of the time were hopefully expecting the arrival of God's divine agent who would take all political as well as spiritual control unto himself. Appealing to Josephus, Richard Horsley writes:

> Some of the Pharisees, who had always refused to take the loyalty oath to Caesar and Herod, prophesied that the kingdom would be taken from Herod by a new king who would bring the restoration of wholeness in some manner or form. The visionary Pharisees were executed, of course.[40]

The narrative Herod, maniacally possessive of his own claims to the leadership of the people, was understandably shaken. While such a prophesied arrival implied liberation for much of the Jewish population, it was a portent of dethronement for him. This very religious prophecy, thereby, initiates a brutal social and political crackdown that results in the murders of scores of innocent male infants (2:16-18). Already prefiguring the suffering that will dog Jesus relentlessly in the passion narrative, Matthew is painting a portrait that realistically recognizes the risks that attend the kind of liberative effort Jesus has, even as an infant, been sent to engage.

This scenario, I think, points us towards the climactic verse 15 in the second chapter of Matthew's narrative. Now, we can appreciate that Hosea 11:1 quotation more completely. We recognize that it also indicates a connection to Israel's exodus, that is to say, liberation, from Egypt. Matthew sees Jesus as the true Israel, recapitulating in himself the experience of the old Israel, particularly, the experience of exodus.[41] Just as Israel was called by God for a salvific purpose, to lead the nations to God, so Jesus now, it appears, is shown being led by God in the midst of messianic expectations of liberation.

Certainly, the Moses-Jesus comparison that many scholars recognize is also significant. The parallels are striking. Pharaoh decrees that Moses and all the male children should die. Moses is saved in a miraculous way by the intervention of Pharaoh's daughter. In Matthew's context it is the guidance of an angelic dream that saves Jesus. Moses flees to Midian just as Joseph must flee with Jesus to Egypt. After Pharaoh's death God directs Moses to return with the same language used to counsel Joseph's return from Egypt, "for those who were seeking the child's life are dead" (2:20). As Harrington explains, "We can assume that Matthew's readers would have heard echoes of the Moses story in Matthew 2."[42] But to what end? What was Moses' purpose? It was to lead the exodus of the people. This, I would suggest, is how Jesus' own birth was viewed in the recounting given by Matthew. Clearly, it is how it was viewed by the narrative Herod.

> The infancy narratives are about liberation. The birth of the Christ-child means that God has inaugurated the long-awaited deliverance of the people of Israel from their enemies. The people's liberation evokes brutal repression and involves suffering, but the dominant tone is one of relief and excitement as the people respond readily to God's initiative.[43]

The potential for a Matthean liberative meaning, and ethics, starts right here.

Matthew cranks up that potential in his portrayal of the kingdom language that he thrusts into the text immediately after the birth narrative closes. As soon as John the Baptist is introduced in 3:1, he opens his ministry in 3:2 with the exact same message that Jesus will use in 4:17 to direct his own: "Repent, for the kingdom of heaven has come near."

The kingdom of heaven is, as Leander Keck argues, Matthew's controlling "master image."[44] Therefore, like Mark's, Matthew's ethical portrait is very kingdom driven; perhaps even more so. First, he contends that even John the Baptist's ministry was guided by this recognition of God's imminent proximity. Second, he alters the first evangelist's construction of the proclamation so that the ethical imperative of repentance, without its Markan companion of belief, is voiced prior to the indicative realization upon which that imperative is based in Mark's Gospel. For Matthew, proper ethical behavior, repentance, and the expectation of the kingdom are shown right from the outset to be integrally tied together. They are tied in such a way that one's ethics, or, one would presume, one's lack thereof, determine one's standing in relationship to God's kingdom.[45] Third, he connects the ethical directives of his parables to the language of the kingdom in a way that is, quantitatively at least, even more noticeable in his narrative than it is in Mark's. As Matera points out, while Mark has fourteen references to the kingdom of God/heaven, Matthew has fifty, and thirty-two of those are peculiar to him. Many of those are found in the ethically oriented parables. "These parables provide readers with an insight into the moral universe, created by the kingdom of heaven, in which Jesus' disciples live. In effect, they describe what it means to live in light of the kingdom of heaven."[46]

Even more important, the parables describe the kind of ethical behavior necessary for entrance into the kingdom (e.g., 13:43; 21:43). To be sure, the kingdom is God's gift. But "to enter it one must do God's will, produce the fruit of righteousness worthy of the kingdom, be vigilant, enterprising, compassionate, and merciful."[47] Matthew had already intimated this, of course, in John's and Jesus' opening, repentance-laced, kingdom statements. In the parables, over and over again, the message becomes concrete.

It becomes so concrete, in fact, that many would argue that Matthew's narrative offers a program of ethics that is as directly applicable for readers outside the narrative as it is for the characters within it. The Beatitudes, the *apparent* statements of blessing (macarisms) that open the Sermon on the Mount at the beginning of chapter 5, are clearly directed as much to Matthew's readers as to Jesus' narrative listeners. Verhey believes that these macarisms represent the "quintessence" of Matthew's ethics. He argues that Matthew, as opposed to Luke, ethicizes the tradition so that the emphasis falls on the exhortation to develop certain "blessed" behavioral patterns in response to Jesus' proclamation of the kingdom. "The reign of God that Jesus is announcing and already manifesting shapes and requires certain character traits: submissiveness to his reign, humility, the longing for the vindication of the right, mercy, sincerity, and the disposition for peace."[48] The Beatitudes are not, therefore, indicative statements celebrating folk who already demonstrate such behavior. They are, instead, as I have argued elsewhere, apocalyptic macarisms that act as imperative calls to kingdom responsive behavior.[49] Be poor in Spirit! Mourn! Be meek! Hunger and thirst for righteousness! Be merciful! Be pure in heart! Be peacemakers! These are operational, ethical encouragements for the present and future, not self-satisfied reflections on the past.

Matthew closes his narrative with the same kind of ethical emphasis that opened his Jesus Sermon. Jesus' final words at 28:19-20 charge his disciples to teach an ethical mandate for living to all those who would become his future followers.[50] And, significantly enough, as Hays points out, it is an ethical word meant for a visibly emerging community. "Matthew is not interested merely in soliciting converts; the gospel, according to Matthew, summons people to join a disciplined community of Jesus followers who put his teachings into practice."[51] Matthew has envisioned a "visible community," and he wants to teach the believers who make it up how they must live. And so he focuses on an ethical concept he puts into play early on, the concept of "righteousness." At 3:15, Jesus interprets his own obedient behavior, his submission to John's baptism, as an act of righteousness. At 5:6, 10, Jesus' followers and Matthew's readers are counseled to respond to the imminent arrival of the kingdom by yearning for it and acting according to it in ways that encourage their own persecution. In other words, Matthew focuses on the kind of righteousness that he understands is necessary for entrance into the kingdom of heaven.[52]

To gain a sharper ethical understanding of what Matthew means by that righteousness, we must access it culturally. The second evangelist is writing in the context of what can only be described as a sectarian war. In the post 70, post-temple Palestine in which he operates, there are many different Jewish groups fighting to become the voice that best represents the history and tradition of the people.[53] Matthew's text gives evidence of at least three. There is, of course, the group represented by Matthew's own emerging community, the Jewish believers who maintain that Jesus Christ was the true representative, representation, and interpreter of God's will as that will is institutionalized in the Torah. Harrington terms this group "Jewish Christians."[54] Many scholars have argued that a second group, which focused on the leadership and teaching of John the Baptist, and apparently questioned and perhaps even contested Jesus' messianic identity and role, provides the contextual motivation for the narrative scene at 11:2-6.[55] But clearly the primary Matthean rival existed in the text as the scribal and Pharisaic contingent that many scholars later came to connect with the emerging Rabbinic wing of Judaism that would ultimately become the faith's orthodox core. J. Andrew Overman terms this group "formative Judaism." Matthew's narrative, then, bears the thematic evidence of being the literary representation for one Jewish sectarian community in deep struggle with another.

> I believe what the reader encounters in Matthew's Gospel is a Jewish community, which claims to follow Jesus the Messiah, discovering that they are now different from what is emerging as the dominant form of Judaism in their setting. The defensive posture of the Gospel and strident attacks on the Jewish authorities represented by Matthew by "the scribes and Pharisees," comprise all the emotion and tension of a family falling apart.[56]

Certainly, disagreement over the proper way to interpret the Torah was one of the principal reasons for this falling out. "The law emerged as both the common ground and the battleground between the competing factions and communities during this period."[57] Unlike Mark, whose narrative presentation gives one the sense that Jesus sees the law as an oppressive boundary whose chokehold on the people must be broken, Matthew gives his readers the sense that the law was a gracious gift from God to the people of faith.[58] His key text in the Sermon on the Mount, 5:17-20, states in very clear terms that Jesus saw the law as a permanent fixture whose demand for righteousness had to be filled. Righteousness was necessary for entrance into salvation as represented by the symbol of the kingdom. Righteousness became the communal code word for Matthean ethics.

Righteousness, though, was defined and determined by proper interpretation of and, thus, obedience to the Torah. Matthew demanded that such obedience be radical. And therein lies the problem. Matthew defined radicality oppositionally. Radical obedience of the law, his "better righteousness," meant doing the law in a way that was "better" than the way the scribes and Pharisees observed it (5:20). In other words, according to Matthew, the community that represented "formative Judaism" was observing the Jewish Torah improperly.

The primary problem was the legalistic mutation of God's gift. Concentrating only on its external demands, the scribes and Pharisees gleefully acknowledged the letter of the law, while they ignored the spirit of its original, God-directed intent. The end result: they had the cognitive capacity to teach the law, but not the internal commitment to live it. For this reason Jesus counseled his followers and Matthew's readers to attend to what they said, but to ignore what they did (23:1-7). Their teaching was not the problem; the problem was their showiness and self-righteous elitism. They did what was legally necessary, not what was kingdom required. It was this ostentatious, empty display of legal fidelity devoid of interior commitment that drew the Matthean Jesus' ire and subsequent charge of hypocrisy.

Jesus looks for more than an obedience that is a mere external observance of the Torah obligations. When he says "better" in 5:20, he therefore means *qualitatively*, not quantitatively "better." He is not looking for more acts of legalistic piety; he is not counseling a contest of dueling righteousness. He is also not talking about a different *kind* of activity; the behavior expected in Matthew was already expected in rival communities.[59] He is also not talking about behavior that is "better" because it is reform oriented; the Pharisees were themselves noted for their efforts of legal reform.[60] "Better" righteousness begins from the inside; it is integrally linked to an interior disposition wholly subservient to God's will as that will is authoritatively presented in Jesus' person and ministry.[61] It is this reality that makes Matthean sermon ethics qualitatively different from those of the Pharisaic leadership; it is not a legalism that requires external commitment to human legislation, but rather one that requires an internal orientation of gratitude that motivates visible acts of righteousness (cf., 5:22,28,43-44; 6:1-23; chap 23). The expectation of the imminent sovereignty of God demands a response from the whole person. The kind of reaction that seeks human wholeness and transformation, like mercy, rather than legalistic, cultic performance, like sacrifice, is now required (9:13; 12:7).

This does not mean, however, that Matthew's "better" righteousness remains internal. Even before Jesus' ministry officially begins, Matthew sets the groundwork in the proclamations of John the Baptist. At 3:7-10, he demands that the repentant response to the approaching kingdom is one that bears visible fruit. Clearly, throughout the entire Gospel, Jesus demands a similar, observable yield. Speaking, for example, of the parable of the five foolish virgins at 25:1-13, Matera counsels: "To be wise is to *do* Jesus' words; that is, to produce the fruit of righteousness."[62] Matera goes on to point out how very important "doing" righteousness is in Matthew's text. Jesus will judge according to one's deeds (16:27); actions are deemed more important than words (7:21); what a person does or does not do will be decisive as regards his or her kingdom standing (25:31-46). To be sure, "In Matthew's Gospel, Jesus places a premium upon doing God's will by practicing righteousness."[63] In the Sermon on the Mount the emphasis is just as striking at key places like 5:13-16; 7:15-20; 7:21-23; and 7:24-27, where Jesus emphasizes the importance of behavioral fruit. The antitheses of 5:21-48 demonstrate that he expects a radical kind of kingdom driven, ethical behavior. Matthew, then, has internalized, or, some would say *spiritualized* the law, not as an end, but as the means to the goal of better ethical, *and not simply legal*, performance.

The key performance, I will say again, is the creation of a new and distinct community that is distinguishable from its sectarian rivals because the things they do (exterior) are directly connected to the thing they believe (interior). "The law of Jesus provides a model *for* community as well as a model *of* community. It is precisely in doing the commandments that community existence and the meaning of community are realized."[64] The people of "better" righteousness have, by being and, therefore, by doing "better," created a "better" community.

It is their better righteousness that can make them "perfect." Here, we must be careful. Perfection, as Jesus seems to understand it here at the close of the antitheses section at 5:48, is not a blessed state of existence. Jesus has not been up to this point crafting the walls of a metaphorical sanctuary in which a human believer could step and joyously thrive. Jesus is not talking about a place where one can become; he's talking instead about the kind of ethical behavior one must display. When he says that believers must be perfect as God in heaven is perfect, context demands that we read the statement as saying that we must do the "better" kind of "perfecting" righteousness. Perfection is a kinetic reality, not a static one. We are talking, then, not of a community of people who have become something; we are talking instead of a community that is continually *doing* the kind of internally oriented ethics the radical antitheses espouse. Perfection should be accessed not as a state of being, but as the "blessed" active existence that derives from an engagement of radical activity that is internally driven and realizes divine rather than human legal intent.

This action orientation continues throughout the final two sections of the Sermon. In 6:1-18, Jesus defines piety as a kind of action orientation (alms giving, prayer, and fasting) that takes its cue from the kingdom's proximity and demands that are on full display in the Lord's Prayer (6:9-10). The final section of the Sermon, 6:19-7:27, picks up on these earlier themes and exploits them. The stress on the kinds of ethical demands that make up "better" righteousness continues, as does the challenge to the rival, hypocritical community whose righteousness operates from human rather than divine initiative and concern. "The central theme of the entire section, then, is the urgency of seeking the kingdom of God and the righteous behavior that is appropriate to it."[65] What becomes clear is that "better" righteousness in

Matthew's narrative and sectarian cultural contexts was viewed as radical, transformative human activity. It was not, as it will most certainly be in Paul, God's gift to humans, but rather it is human ethical behavior in response to the gift of God's kingdom. Indeed, as Mohrlang points out, Matthew heightens the stakes for this *doing* of the "better" righteousness by connecting it to kingdom entrance (3:7-10; 5:29-30; 7:19). Doing "better" righteousness is not only how one responds to what God is doing; it is also what makes one acceptable in that new kingdom reality that God's activity is crafting. It is what builds the "better" kingdom community. "Here Matthew's free and unabashed use of the threat of judgment attests his conviction of its value in inciting the Christian community to live up to the high moral standards of Jesus."[66]

But why? Why does Matthew so stress the component of ethical *doing* in response to and in fear of the kingdom that he comes dangerously close to re-creating the very same kind of scribal and Pharisaic legalism that he clearly wants to debunk? I would argue that in the end his approach is fundamentally different. After all, he does stress that the doing must operate from a transformed interior being and focus. The fact that Matthean "better" righteousness is righteousness from the inside mitigates against the conclusion that it is surface legalism. The fact that it is also ethical activity operating in response to what God has done, rather than in the hope of provoking God's action or currying God's favor, also suggests against such a conclusion.

> Like Paul, Matthew understands that the ethical imperative is related to the salvific indicative, for the call to a greater righteousness is part of Jesus' proclamation about the kingdom of heaven. . . . Whereas Paul emphasizes that the indicative makes the imperative possible, Matthew stresses that "the fulfillment of the imperative is a prerequisite for the ultimate, full and final expression of the indicative."[67]

But why, still, does Matthew allow the question to be raised in the first place? Why does he stress *doing* so emphatically? It is because the doing creates, or, in the language of many African American slaves and their progeny, *conjures* something. The "better" doing that the Matthean Jesus describes and demands identifies its doers as the connected citizens of a visible community. It is made "visible" by the righteousness that establishes its interior, spiritual parameters and thereby characterizes its exterior, behavioral ethics. The "better" righteousness concretizes a community which in turn conjures God. This is not the God witnessed to by the scribal and Pharisaic ranks of "formative Judaism"; it is instead the apocalyptic God whose kingdom is prefigured in the person, work, and interpretative will of Jesus the Christ.

Theophus Smith argues that conjurational spirituality is the hermeneutical approach that African Americans bring to the biblical text.[68] His work shows how powerful an impact the religious tradition of conjure had upon the leading thinkers of African America right up through and beyond the key civil rights movement of the 1960s and 1970s. As Smith and others point out, its influence was already powerful in the lives of the African American slaves. The syncretistic African American slave Christianity absorbed and sometimes simply attached African folk magical practices like conjure to its core beliefs and practices. Vincent Harding points out, for example, that the insurrectionist associate of Denmark Vesey in South Carolina, a certain Jack Pritchard, also known as Gullah Jack, operating with communal support, summoned the powers of conjure for the planning of their violently liberative effort with as much "faithfulness" as Vesey called upon the liberative imagery of the Christian tradition.[69]

This conjure is more than hostile magic associated with the likes of voodoo, wielded as an attack agent against suspecting and unsuspecting enemies. It is also, and perhaps more important, a transformational force whose portfolio of potions, sayings, incantations, rituals, and performative acts relies upon powers within and exterior to humankind. In such a mind-set, even the Bible can become a tool of conjure, "a book of ritual prescriptions for reenvisioning and, therein, transforming history and culture."[70] African American leaders have, for example, acted out the Mosaic image of liberation or the Jesus image of triumph over victimization. In other words, they performed the language of the Bible typologically in order to conjure, that is to say, prepare, the communal ground and the people who occupied it for cultural transformation; biblical figures became part of a unique conjure strategy. But there was something even more important than using such biblical typology to foment aspirations of liberation. There was also the conjurational expectation that God could be invoked to initiate the powerful typology of, for example, exodus, or, perhaps even kingdom, in the contemporary life of the people. "From this perspective I propose the hypothesis that black North American experience features a development from designating or 'summoning" God in worship, to an intention to conjure God for freedom."[71] Human conduct, in this way, according to Smith, could conjure the presence of God for the purpose of establishing a new cultural reality. Smith is careful to note that such actions do not create God, but instead "collectively create the phenomenal conditions conducive to their subjective apprehension of the divine."[72]

> Henceforth more than a minority of believers and converts would be convinced of the possibility that through prayer and expectation, through *acts* of obedience, and *righteousness*, black folk could inherit divine promises of prosperity and freedom.[73]

Given such a hermeneutic perspective, acts of "better" righteousness, like those found in the Sermon on the Mount—meekness, purity of heart, love, forgiveness, prayer, etc.—could be understood as actions designed to "conjure" God. Doing the imperatives of the Sermon thereby becomes a conjure act. The acts are unimportant in and of themselves. One does not do the imperatives because they are law, but because the actions create something powerfully unique, a "blessed" reality, a transformed, *alternative* God community that stands apart from all others. Through its fulfillment of the Sermon imperatives, through its successful presentation of "better" righteousness, the transformed community mimics the reality of the kingdom. In Matthew's sectarian world, then, Matthew's community, not the community of "formative Judaism," would be the one that conjures, that is to say, that provides access to the kingdom of God. The social and political ramifications are as significant as they are explosive. Because of its "better" righteousness, Matthew's community becomes a "better" community of faith.

Matthew has, in effect, created a counter-community of faith, a "visible" institution that sets a new agenda and incorporates new options that are radically different from those espoused by the communal witness of a "formative Judaism" that will ultimately become the mainline faith tradition. The mere existence of an alternative—a working, active, confrontational alternative—provides transformative and, I would argue, liberative potential.

The Jewish sectarian community that formed at Qumran provides a working, first century example. Clearly the devotees of Qumran had no intentional social and political aspirations. They withdrew into the desert especially to separate themselves from what they perceived to be corrupt spiritual and socio-political practices in Jerusalem. And yet, because they chose to form a community, their very existence would have had social and political ramifications. The Matthean community is also an alternative community. Only, it refuses to withdraw. It intentionally establishes itself as a visible, working, involved, and evangelical alternative to the more "formative" tradition. It sets up camp within the boundaries of Israel, on "formative Judaism's" home court, just as the slave "invisible institution" would set up shop in the slave South centuries later. It, too, would visibly tout its alternative Jesus principles, its alternative religious ethics, as the more appropriate manner of doing God's will. This community is not only socially and politically challenging, it has a social and political liberative potential. The liberating potential exists specifically for those seeking an alternative to the "formative" traditions. I would describe that potential in two ways. One is negative; the other, though linked, and more important, is positive.

The negative potential exists as a liberation "from." Matthew's alternative perspective on doing a "better" righteousness frees up its followers, not from the law, but from Matthew's perceived legalistic and surface interpretation of it. The literalist interpretation that attends to the letter of the law alone actually diminishes the followers' ability to do God's will, to do the kind of righteousness necessary for entrance into the kingdom of God. This is because it is aimed only at the satisfaction of exterior requirements and limits itself to meeting those requirements. The person himself or herself, the inner moral agent, remains unchanged. The Matthean Jesus calls for much more: an interior reorientation that reconfigures one's understanding of God's will in a radical way. No longer looking to please human beings with a demonstrable devotion to the letter, the Matthean communicant devotes himself or herself to ascertaining the original will of God that spawned the legal letter in the first place. That means, of course, looking to Jesus' interpretation of that will in his life and ministry. Matthew offers illustrative testimony to this claim at 9:10-13, where he is following Mark 2:15-17. Jesus is sitting at table with tax collectors and sinners. The Pharisaic interpreters of the law call him on his very odd behavior. The ethics that results from Jesus' confrontational explanation of his conduct operates not from the cultic and purity codes of the humanly interpreted Torah, but from God's original intent for it. As in Mark, Jesus explains that those who are well have no need of a physician. But then, by grounding his behavior in the Hebrew Scriptures, he gives an authoritative weight to his controversial actions that in Mark he did not. In essence, Matthew, at this point at least, "out Marks Mark." Jesus' boundary breaking is directly tied to, and therefore legitimated by, God's prophetic will. In Matthew, Jesus therefore quotes Hosea 6:6: "I desire mercy, not sacrifice" Richard Hays, depending on the work of John Meier, notes that something incredibly transformative has just occurred. "Mercy, not sacrifice, is God's will. And if mercy replaces the chief act of cult, how much more does it take precedence over Pharisaic rules of purity."[74]

In Matthew's sectarian world this is religious transformation that would have had powerful social and political ramifications. Wayne Meeks certainly seems to think so. "The sectarian character of the ethic consists in the demand that prudential and publicly enforceable rules be set aside altogether. The only valid standard is 'the will of the Father in heaven.' "[75] The liberation in Matthew seems, then, to be a liberation from cultism, from purity boundaries, from the legalities of ceremonial law, and even from the Torah itself when it is interpreted to be a mechanism that institutes ceremonial and social difference. The law, as it has come to be interpreted in "formative Judaism," limits the potential for a believer to do God's will. This is why righteousness must be transformed; it must become "better."

This transformative understanding of righteousness also means that one no longer hopes to "conjure" God with one's deeds of righteousness in the same way as before. God, according to Jesus, is already present. The kingdom has already arrived. Proper response to that divine activity, kingdom conjuring "better" righteousness, was what was required. Kingdom "conjuring" behavior created the kind of communal circumstance where God's presence, already dawning in Jesus and imminently on the horizon in consummate form, could be found, not created. The difference is subtle, but substantial. The Matthean believer is freed from using the law as a mechanism for earning salvation, and instead finds himself or herself "doing" the will of God as a response to the salvific kingdom that has already arrived. "Doing" remains important, but it has become a responsive rather than a causal agent. The believer is no longer trying to earn righteousness by doing the law; the Matthean believer is doing righteousness to conjure in their local arena the kind of communal reality that allows the already dawning, universal kingdom to become "visible."

The positive ethics, which draws directly from this freedom "from," exists as a liberative inclusion of people even further outside the boundaries of acceptability than tax collectors and sinners. Not only is this a liberation from the principles of "formative Judaism" as Matthew understood them from his sectarian perspective, but it is also a liberation from the very ministry expectations that Matthew's own narrative espouses right up until the closing commission in chapter 28. The evangelical, and I would argue in this case political ethics that Matthew's Jesus held for his own ministry and the ministry of his immediate disciples is overturned and radically opened up at the conclusion of the narrative. Here the Matthean Jesus establishes an ethics for the readers of the narrative that is not only different from but apparently contradictory to the evangelical thrust of the characters in the narrative, even the character of Jesus himself. Jesus' narrative ministry is directed at the people of Israel (10:5-6). Matthew, in his fight with the people who would become "formative" Israel, frees the people who populate his community not only "from" an adherence to the surface legalities of the Law, but also "for" a push beyond his own ethnic boundaries (an act against which the cultic and purity codes would have objected) into all the world (28:19). The community that organizes around Matthew's narrative will therefore do a different kind of "better" righteousness than the community of Jesus' followers who populated the narrative. They are freed to push Jesus' interpretation of God's will to the people of all the nations. They are not only liberated to move out beyond their own social and political circles, they are given this transformative possibility in the form of a directive from the risen Jesus with the same kind of authority (28:18) that he possessed in the Sermon on the Mount. As Meeks notes, it is almost as if the risen Lord says, "In my earthly existence I *said*, but now, as risen Lord, I *say*."[76] "Jewish Christians" are freed to call Gentiles, and Gentiles, by the order of the risen Christ, are now freed to become part of the company of kingdom believers. In Matthew's world, this is what his very visible community stands for. This is the alternative it represents. This is the "better" righteousness the members of the community *do*. This is the vision of God they conjure. In Matthew's world, it is not only religiously transformative, it is socially and politically liberating. What a liberating, and incredibly threatening, communal alternative this *ecclesia*, this "visible institution" must have represented!

The Gospel of Luke:
The Liberating Ethics of Reversal

In the Gospel of Luke, the potential for liberation becomes fully realized right on the surface of the text, and right from the beginning of it. Opening with a clarifying prologue, the third evangelist tells his targeted reader, the most excellent Theophilus, that he has intended to write the kind of account that will enable a reader to perceive the orderliness of God's historical plan. The objective of that plan, ethically speaking, is social and political reversal. Luke's Jesus, playing out the characterization God has scripted for him, offers this liberating message to anyone who is oppressed.

Luke's ethical presentation has two primary thrusts: "He modified [Mark's narrative] and added to it yet another ethical perspective, a perspective that is distinguished by its solicitude for the poor and oppressed and by its concern for the mutual respect of Jewish and Gentile Christians."[77] To be sure, the latter is important, but it is the former that I want to stress. Unlike Matthew, where the community was composed primarily of "Jewish Christians," Luke's community, it is rather universally agreed, was composed primarily of Gentiles.[78] Jesus' Matthean commission to push beyond the ethnically limiting constraints of the Torah as it was pharisaically interpreted was therefore liberating in the Second

Gospel. However, Jesus' desire in Luke for a community that has already breached those boundaries to get along better together strikes one as more a message of ethical maintenance than liberation. The liberative theme hits home in the narrative demonstration of God's care for the poor and oppressed. In Luke, God actually shows social preference. Jesus lives and acts throughout his ministry in solidarity with the poor and oppressed—living as one of them, taking sides with them. Indeed, to hear him tell it in this Lukan rendition of the Beatitudes at the Sermon on the Plain, the kingdom of God even belongs to them (6:20). Luke rejects Matthew's spiritualization toward a poverty of spirit; he's talking about the historical poor, the socially and economically destitute, and he's handing them the proverbial keys to God's kingdom. "The servant's vocation is to proclaim good news to the poor, the blind, the captives, and the oppressed. Thus, for Luke, Jesus' messianic activity is the work of *liberation*, and the direct link of the gospel to the message of the prophets is to be found in the prophetic call for justice."[79]

Before pushing forward to demonstrate how Luke sets up his text with this ethical emphasis of justice oriented towards the poor, I want to consider two preliminary matters: Luke's narrative definition of "poor," and Luke's understanding of the kingdom's ethical role. First, Sharon Ringe makes a crucial observation that will have potent ethical ramifications. In the synoptic accounts, the evangelists use the language "poor" as a descriptive whose range extends well beyond the matter of economics. "These [synoptic] contexts [where the poor are mentioned] underline the importance of 'the poor' in Jesus' ministry and in his identity as the Christ. They also expand the meaning of 'the poor' to include people who are socially outcast or physically disabled, as well as people who are economically disadvantaged."[80] Joel Green applies such a recognition specifically to Luke and draws out the implications. He points out that even though Jesus opens his ministry with the programmatic statement in 4:16-21 where he defines his ministry as one of speaking good news to the poor, he does not seem actually to preach directly to poor people per se. Do L. Schotroff and W. Stegemann have any grounds for their musing that Luke's Jesus might therefore be better described as "pastor of the wealthy"?[81] Of course not. Green explains that the problem is the limited understanding of the term "poor" that many researchers bring with them to the text. It is clear that Luke prefers the Greek word for "poor," πτωχός, a word that the Septuagint uses to translate a variety of Hebrew forms.[82] The key, though, is that the semantic focus of the form does not key on economics. "That is, the emphasis falls on the relationship between God and the poor, with the former extending grace to the latter, who find themselves increasingly at the periphery of society."[83]

As with Matthew, so now with Luke, cultural location becomes critical for understanding. Green notes that in the Greco-Roman world, wealth and poverty were elements of relationship rather than exclusively matters of money. One would therefore think in terms of status, which turns the discussion in the thematic direction of power. "Status honor is a measure of social standing that embraces wealth, but also other factors, including access to education, family heritage, ethnicity, vocation, religious purity, and gender. In the Greco-Roman world, then, poverty is too narrowly defined when understood solely in economic terms."[84] Here we are at the heart of the matter when looking at Luke's understanding of "the poor." Luke uses "poor" in lists with other key terms like captive, blind, oppressed, hungry, weeping, excluded, reviled, maimed, lame, and leper at 4:18; 6:20; 7:22; 14:13, 21; and 16:20, 22.[85] In each case "poor" stands at the head of the list, except for 7:22 where it is in the final climactic position. Green's assessment of what Luke is doing seems correct: "The impression with which one is left is that Luke is concerned above all with a class of people defined by their dishonorable status, their positions outside circles of power and prestige, their being excluded."[86] Jesus' message in Luke's Gospel is more than a message about enriching those who are presently destitute; it is a message about empowering those who are powerless. It is a message that reverses social, economic, and political status, a message that proclaims the kind of societal transformation that makes those who were formerly cast to the oppressed margins of society the ones around whom the new God-directed society will revolve. I will describe below how Luke develops this thought.

Before I do, I must also evaluate Luke's presentation of the kingdom, because, in Luke, too, though in a different way, ethics are kingdom driven. In Mark and Matthew the expectation for the kingdom's imminent arrival provided potent ethical inducement. That expectation remains a factor in Luke. Like Matthew, Luke picks up on the apocalyptic theme and quantitatively exploits it. To Mark's fourteen references, he offers thirty-nine, twenty-one of which are peculiar to him.[87] And even though, unlike Matthew, Luke does not offer Jesus' proclamation of the kingdom as the programmatic statement for his ministry, his Jesus does contend at 4:42-44 that he was sent for the express purpose of preaching this kingdom.[88] Clearly, then, his programmatic statement about preaching good news to the poor is directly related to his kingdom expectation. The man who was anointed *to preach good news to the poor* was likewise sent *to preach the good news of God's kingdom.*[89] Preaching the kingdom and preaching reversal apparently go hand in hand. That certainly appears to be Jesus' point in the parable of the great banquet (14:15-24). In the kingdom, societal insiders who dismiss God's call will find themselves on the margins; those who have been societally marginalized, but who respond to God's call and commands, will find themselves at the center of God's consummate kingdom. God's kingdom, according to the parable, attends to obedience, not status.

This time, though, there is a kingdom wrinkle. And it is a substantial one. In Luke, the influence of the kingdom's coming is not as great because the kingdom is not thought to be coming quite as soon. Writing much later than his synoptic colleagues, Luke is dealing with the problem of a delay. He uses his narrative to apprise his readers of the situation. Operating carefully on his Markan source (Mark 9:1) at Luke 9:27, his Jesus, while still prophesying that there are some standing with him who would not die before seeing the kingdom of God, stops short of echoing the Markan claim that they will see this kingdom *come with power.* Also, as Matera notes, at 17:20-21, in an effort to refocus attention away from the cataclysmic future, Jesus proclaims that the kingdom is already operating among them.[90] To be sure, this does not negate the future kingdom orientation that remains a vital part of his text (eg., 9:27; 22:18; 23:51), but it does reflect a growing awareness that devoting all one's ethical energies to that future is misguided. Delay is real. Ethical reflection must therefore be crafted in light of its troubling pause. And so, as is widely noted, in the parable of the pounds at 19:11-27, Jesus uses the example of a traveling nobleman and his servants to teach an ethics of responsible living in the interim between Jesus' going and his kingdom coming. Nowhere is this emphasis on more powerful display than in Luke's subtle and yet simultaneously dramatic revision of Jesus' key discipleship statement of Mark 8:34: "If any want to become my followers, let them deny themselves and take up their cross and follow me." At 9:23, Luke adds an additional thought with a single word: "If any want to become my followers, let them deny themselves and take up their cross *daily* and follow me" (italics added). Jesus' apocalyptic mandate for radical, end-time discipleship has now become an expectation of continual ethics in a continuing world.

That ethics, it is time to say again, is an ethics of reversal. Luke drafts a narrative whose leading characters and pivotal moments echo the centrality of this theme. Jesus, of course, is Luke's prime exemplar, both in his person and his actions. Jesus himself represents the very nature of reversal that Luke's narrative espouses as the grounds for the reading disciple's own ethical activity. With the parable of the vineyard (20:9-19), for example, Jesus offers a scenario where unethical tenants punish the servants of a vineyard owner and subsequently kill his son. The scribes and chief priests recognize accurately that Jesus has told the parable against them. He is the Son whom God, the cosmic owner of human life and human history, has sent to extract from the leading earthly tenants of Israel the obedient yield that God is due. Instead of paying up, the leaders would rather destroy the Son and lay claim to his lordship than submit to his representation of God's will. Jesus therefore expects that the same thing that happened to the parabolic son will happen to him; the leaders will cast him out and kill him (9:22; cf., also 9:44; 18:31-34). Their victory, however, will be a short-lived mirage. God will engineer an astoundingly improbable reversal. Because Jesus has obediently complied with the mission upon which he had been sent, the one whom the leaders reject and banish into the very margins of existence will, as the psalmist prophesied (118:22), become the cornerstone upon which God's salvific work will be built. Jesus' presentation of God's person and God's will will be vindicated. The foundation for the Lukan ethics of reversal in favor of the "poor" starts right here.[91]

It pushes forward with Luke's narrative positioning of Jesus in the continual company of social and political misfits. Without saying a word, Jesus, whom Luke narrates as the very presence and power of God's kingdom, actualizes the theme of reversal by the way he behaves. He attaches himself to sinners (5:30-32; 7:33-34, 39; 15:1-2; 23:39-43); he touches lepers (5:12-16; 17:11-19); he embraces children (18:15-17); he stays with Zacchaeus, a chief tax collector (19:1-10); and he cavorts with women (7:11-15, 36-50; 8:1-3, 40-56; 10:38-42; 13:10-17). Surely, Matera's assessment of this kind of textual evidence is correct. "By associating freely with sinners, lepers, women, and those on the margin of society, Jesus acts out the reversal of fortunes that the kingdom of God is effecting in his ministry."[92]

If Jesus does not make the message plain with his person and his associations, he does so with his unequivocal preached word. According to 4:16-21, Luke's noticeable choice for the programmatic statement of the messianic ministry, Jesus claims that he has been anointed with the specific task of reversing the social and political fortunes of the dispossessed. Conflating the transformative message of justice as reversal from the Isaiah texts at 61:1-2 and 58:6, Luke removes the Markan kingdom pronouncement as the symbolic representation of Jesus' teaching and inserts this Jubilee thought in its place. This, according to Luke, is the kind of message Jesus could be counted on to be preaching wherever and whenever his ministry took him. "As in the Book of Acts, the reader is probably meant to infer that Jesus' teaching on subsequent occasions resembled this sermon. The fact that this teaching is put in such a prominent position within the whole gospel strongly suggests that it is intended to set the tone of the ministry which is to follow."[93]

And, as suggested above, it follows along the thematic lines of Jubilee. No doubt, as Ringe asserts, this is why Luke's Jesus appeals so dramatically to Isaiah 61 and 58. "At its very root, the Jubilee is about liberty."[94] The surface language makes that clear. But there is more. Jubilee is not only about liberty, it is also about *liberation*. The Isaiah texts envision an explicit social and political reversal of historical fortunes, as does Jesus' reference to them in his own opening sermon. Those who are societally oppressed will, by the anointing and empowerment of the Holy Spirit, be lifted up. There can be no more dramatic a claim to societal transformation than that. Except one perhaps. And Jesus had the audacity to make it. He claimed that with the inauguration of his ministry Isaiah's prophecy had actually been fulfilled (4:21). In him and his ministry the time of Jubilee had arrived.

If all this were not controversial enough, Jesus irritates his listeners even further with a preemptive rebuttal to what he perceives would be their most likely argument against his claims. Why does he not demonstrate his avowed capabilities by performing his liberating exploits in his own hometown? Jesus' response adds fuel to a fire already igniting against him. By appealing to the story of the prophet Elijah who fed a starving widow in Sidon when there were plenty of starving widows in Israel, and then Elisha who cleansed a Syrian leper when there were plenty of lepers to go around in Israel, Jesus suggests that God's Jubilee empowerment is as accessible to people outside of Israel as within.

> The Jubilee images found in the text from Isaiah were understood by Jesus' contemporaries as referring to blessings promised particularly to Israel at the time of God's eschatological reign. The prophetic reading of that text represented in the Nazareth pericope challenged that assumption of privilege, but left the socially, revolutionary implications of the Jubilee imagery intact. In that way, the text of promise was turned into a threat: the poor to whom the good news would come and the captives who would be set free might be any of God's children.[95]

Right at the start of Luke's narrative, then, Jesus does what Matthew only sees happening at the end, and then only from the risen Christ; Jesus opens the doors of kingdom participation to people from all nations. Just as important, he does it in a way that suggests reversal. The outsiders come in, the insiders, because of their inattentiveness to what God is doing through Jesus, are left out. It is a provocative message. Predictably, the insiders do not respond well to it. Rising up in anger, they intend to kill Jesus before his reversing ministry can get under way. Jesus, however, slips mysteriously away. The Jubilee ministry of liberation is off.

Like Elijah and Elisha, Jesus goes off seeking the outsiders. As I have already noted, Luke's ethical example par excellence populates his kingdom with all sorts of societal riffraff from the highways and hedges of life. With the parable of the great banquet at 14:12-24, Jesus makes his message unmistakably clear; the socially ostracized (the poor, the maimed, the lame, and the blind) will find a place at the kingdom table. The wealthy and powerful who have tended more to their own wealth and power than to God's word, and have thus contributed to societal oppression, will not.

The Sermon on the Plain presses the point that the parable has pictorially crafted. In Luke's Beatitudes, poverty and hunger are no longer the character traits they were in Matthew's Sermon on the Mount. Here they are literal social and political evils that will be overturned. The "poor" will obtain the power and glory of the kingdom; the hungry will be filled to satisfaction; the weeping will laugh; the ones hated and persecuted on earth because of their allegiance to Jesus will find the human verdict and sentence overturned in the heavenly court.

Luke's Jesus also takes the opportunity of this Sermon to teach his disciples that this imagery of God's reversal affects how they are to live their lives as disciples. The language of reversal in this way becomes a part of the ethics of discipleship. This is why Matera can point to the command to love one's enemies at 6:27-36 as a reversal of the common expectations for human relationship. The implications are wide ranging. Love itself is now seen through the liberating lens of reversal—not only in the case of loving those that act against you, but also in the more general sense of love that operates as a kind of grace that extends mercy even where the normal rules of human judgment rule that mercy is not deserved (6:35-36, 37-42).

> Jesus has promised his disciples that they will be the beneficiaries of a reversal of fortunes, but if they do not act upon his words they will experience God's judgment. There is an intimate connection, then, in Jesus' preaching between the reversal of fortunes that the kingdom of God is effecting and the ethical life. God graciously extends salvation to Jesus' disciples who, in turn, must act upon Jesus' word.[96]

The travel narrative picks up on these themes and rides them all the way into Jerusalem. Many of the unique Lukan parables, like the good Samaritan, the great banquet, the rich man and Lazarus, the publican and the sinner, demonstrate a profound concern for the poor and the defenseless. Other key ethical themes for kingdom discipleship are also tied directly into this reversal imagery. Whether Jesus is speaking to issues as diverse in scope as proper treatment of possessions, relationship with strangers, the need for prayer, the hope for humility, the power of persistence, or the expectation of repentance, there is a link to the Jubilee theme that launched Jesus' fateful preaching tour. "Speaking to his disciples, he exhorts them to be as vigilant as servants who await the return of their master from a wedding feast (Luke 12:35-40). Then, in a remarkable description of a reversal of fortunes, he promises that the master himself will wait on those servants whom he finds prepared (12:37)."[97] Reversal is in the air. It is a part of the fabric of kingdom life; it becomes the modeling mandate for the kind of life expected of kingdom followers.

But it is not, for Luke, something espoused only by Jesus. It is a narrative fixture that settles into key characterizations and, indeed, into the plot structure itself. A consideration of Luke's opening narration, before the adult Jesus even arrives on the scene, is a good case in point. The magnificent Magnificat sets a tone for the Gospel that is as overwhelming as it is thematically centered in the concept of "overturning." Mary's statement of praise looks both backward and forward in the text and celebrates God's powerful transformative activity. The language she uses of God lifting the lowly and casting down the mighty is not only picked up in Jesus' words and actions, it has already been previewed in the way God acts with Mary herself and her cousin Elizabeth (1:25, 48). "In effect, Elizabeth and Mary exemplify the reversal of fortunes that the Savior God is effecting by the birth of his Son."[98]

The infancy story resonates with the same reversing effect. The powerful Lord and God of all creation extends God's divine reality into the human sphere not in the form of a great king, but in the form of a helpless infant child. But Luke does not leave his point here. In his account this child is not greeted with the same kind of fanfare that he receives in Matthew. There Magi shower him with treasures when they find him with Mary and Joseph in the house where they are lodged. Not so in Luke. This infant is one with the commoners, part and parcel of the community of outsiders. Poor shepherds are his attendants. His lodging place is a stable, his bed an animal's manger. Right from the start, everything in Luke's world is turned upside down.

John the Baptist realizes the ethical potential in this inside-out world view. Luke allows him the privilege of preaching a sermon, and he makes the most of it. He requires his listeners to do with their own resources what God has been doing with God's, that is, to empower those who are powerless. So at 3:10-14, he exhorts his listeners to do the unexpected, to reverse their own principles of living by living according to the principle God has exhibited in the sending of God's Son to the "poor." He begs everyone to share their food and clothing with those who have none; he demands that tax collectors and soldiers, known for their abusive tendencies, treat their charges with care and respect. Here, just before Jesus begins his ministry, John prefigures it by doing what Jesus will himself later do; he draws a strong connection between God's divine activity of liberation and the kind of ethics humans should craft for their transformative living with one another.

The religious demand is for repentance. Struck in the face by God's transformative kingdom movement into the world in the form of Jesus as Messiah, Luke's readers are offered the opportunity to take part in doing God's business. They are offered the opportunity to turn around, to reverse their tracks and realign themselves with God's kingdom agenda. John starts it off at 3:3 and 3:8, preaching a baptism of repentance that clearly draws both its mandate and its sense of urgency from the recognition of God's kingdom movement through the expected coming of God's Christ. Jesus picks up on the theme and carries it to its fruition. Hart is right to point out that of all the synoptic writers, Luke is the only one who has explicit instances where Jesus either directly calls sinners to repentance or touts the importance of repentance through his parable teachings (5:32; 7:36-50; 13:3, 5; 15:11-32; 18:9-14; 19:1-10; 24:46-8).[99] Repentance becomes the appropriate spiritual response to God's activity in the world. "The sinful woman, the prodigal son, the publican, and the condemned criminal [23:40-43] are people on the margin of society, but in each case they repent because they experience or trust in the love and forgiveness of God."[100]

In Luke's hands, though, this spiritual response is acutely ethical in the way it is lived out in the life of discipleship. Personal, spiritual reversal has a corporate, social twist. The spiritual about-face must have an ethical parallel. Luke draws this out in two steps, the second and climactic of which we have already discussed. First, though, he connects repentance with "doing." It is not simply an internal spiritual matter; the spiritual turn must act out in demonstrable discipleship ways. Luke narrates this theme by repetitively placing a key question in the mouth of his characters who are trying to understand how they might become better respondents to God's kingdom move: "what shall (I) we do?" John's listeners ask it at 3:10 and 3:12. It is asked of Jesus by a lawyer prior to the parable of the good Samaritan at 10:25; by a steward in the parable of the dishonest steward at 16:3; and by a young ruler who wants to know what he should be doing to inherit eternal life at 18:18. In each case the question prefaces a key discussion by Jesus on the kind of ethics a kingdom aspirant should live by. And in each case, Jesus makes the case by means of a story or saying that reverses the expectations that the characters in the text and the readers outside it have brought with them to the narrative circumstance.

That hint of reversal opens the way back into the Luke's primary ethical agenda. Yes, repentance means doing. But, as the Gospel has been demonstrating all along, reversal is the kingdom "doing" of choice. This is the kind of activity the narrative espouses and Mary, John the Baptist, and Jesus display. Here is where the mandate for discipleship finds its narrative and thus its historical footing. What would a community oriented toward such an understanding of repentant, reversing ethics look like? What kind of impact would it have on the surrounding communities and culture? Though Luke is not as institutionally motivated as Matthew, he does offer this narrative with what appears to be a clear intent to affect the way his reading community lives its life of discipleship in response to what God has done through Jesus of Nazareth. That living response, thematically symbolized by the prophetic imagery of Jubilee, would clearly have much more than an internal, spiritual effect. To live the kind of reversal Jesus lived would bring about societal transformation at the most fundamental social and political levels. Empowering the oppressed and humbling the mighty is more than a call for spiritual repentance; it is a bid for social repentance that will have concrete historical impact if it is lived out in the way that Jesus and John the Baptist, and the narrative that Luke placed them within, demanded.

Oh how the African American slave would have cherished such transformative imagery. Even if the specific language is not always there, the theme of liberating Jubilee is potent in the slaves' narrative expressions. So is the expectation of reversal—that God would lift the oppressed and bring down the oppressor. These are images that need no interpretative introduction. They sit on the surface in the slave narratives just as they sit on the surface of Luke's Gospel story. The point James Cone makes from the spirituals could have been made with the vast majority of slave narrative materials. "The divine *liberation* of the oppressed from slavery is the central theological concept in the Black spirituals. . . . Just as God delivered the Children of Israel from Egyptian slavery, drowning Pharaoh and his army in the Red Sea, he would also deliver Black people from American slavery."[101] Examples of this liberating motif are legion.

> Oh Mary, don't you weep, don't you moan,
> Oh Mary, don't you weep, don't you moan,
> Pharaoh's Army got drowned,
> Oh Mary, don't you weep.[102]

> O my Lord delivered Daniel,
> O why not deliver me too?[103]

It is the language of reversal swept up by the hope and promise of a messianically driven Jubilee.

> Arise O Zion! rise and shine.
> Behold thy light is come;
> Thy glorious conq'ring King is near
> To take his exiles home;
> His spirit now is pouring out
> To set poor captives free
> The day of wonder now is come
> The year of Jubilee.[104]

With Luke there is no need for hermeneutical translation. Luke's story is one the slave would have a natural and easy affinity toward, and a slave owner would have needed to reconfigure if and when his slaves took hold of it. For here the language of the

Gospel has every bit an overtly doubled (spiritual *and* political) meaning as the coded language of the slave spirituals that sang of the Jordan River when they really meant the Ohio, or talked of Satan being overthrown when they really meant the slave owner and his slave system, or talked of heaven when they really looked to the North and freedom.[105] In Luke, repentance is surely repentance, just as heaven in the slave spiritual is surely heaven. It is only when you really know the story and understand it in its total narrative and cultural context that you also realize that there is something else.

A Concluding Thought

Several months ago I was walking across the Princeton Seminary campus with a colleague. After hearing my pitch about the pivotal role that the kingdom of God plays in developing the message for discipleship in the Gospel of Mark, he opined that perhaps the church needs today to return to an emphasis upon the kingdom. That, of course, is precisely what I believe, not only in regard to the matter of discipleship, but in terms of ethics as a whole. Clearly, the kingdom was the foundational cornerstone in the ethical presentations constructed in the synoptic narratives. In Mark, it provided the urgent license for radical, boundary-breaking behavior. In Matthew, it offered the theoretical brick and mortar for the erecting of a visible, alternative, faith institution with the spiritual force to counter the predominant communal ethical norms of the day. In Luke, it was the wheel upon which an emphasis and energy for continual, daily acts of radical, transformative behavior would turn the world upside down and inside out. Over and over again the kingdom symbol offered an objective, future orientation whose present impact on believers' ethics was formidable. Each of the evangelists offered us a narrative portrait where this objective, future reality was the key to Jesus' own kingdom-driven behavior. The ethical key for Jesus was subsequently offered in the narrative progressions as the behavioral axis for those who would follow him. I want to make the argument that wherever the foundational source of our ethical reflection moves away from the objective reality of the kingdom, as located historically in the ministry of Jesus and as eschatologically anticipated in the coming of God's reign, that we are, as followers of Jesus, in danger of losing our bearing. There is something crucial to our identity as biblical and ethical entities that is intricately and irrevocably tied to the reality of that coming kingdom, so much so that one might make the audacious claim that an ethics constructed on any basis other than the expectation of that kingdom is not an ethics derived from the portrait of Jesus painted in the synoptic accounts.

This does not mean, however, that the ethical focus operates exclusively from Jesus' past as it is re-presented in the synoptic accounts. Even though the focus may begin here, even within the synoptic narratives themselves, it did not end there. The kingdom remains a future reality. It is the same kind of eschatological expectation for contemporary believers as it was for those in Jesus' own time. This is the beauty of the kingdom symbol as ethical foundation. Ever grounded in Jesus' past, it always operates out of the future, and so never becomes outdated or inappropriate to the new circumstances that arise with each new and passing day. Jesus' life provides the model for using the kingdom as an ethical guide; but Jesus' fervent orientation toward the kingdom as a future reality gives it a newness of life whose potency is as living and viable as is the presence of the resurrected Christ.

Of course, there are always dangers in trying to apply an apocalyptic symbol to a time that clearly envisions, and should envision after two millennia, an ongoing history. But Luke shows us that the kingdom emphasis can be ethically applicable even, and perhaps especially, in such a reality. It is the only foundation that can retain its ethical meaningfulness into an ongoing and apparently boundless future. That is because its existence is itself part and parcel of that future.

CHAPTER FOUR

John: The Christology of Active Resistance

John does not do ethics. Or so it seems. That is pretty much the way most New Testament ethicists begin their work on the Fourth Gospel. Frank Matera's comments are representative:

> For anyone interested in the study of New Testament ethics, the Gospel according to John is a major challenge . . . there are remarkably few references to moral conduct. . . . Moreover, the most explicitly ethical teaching of the Fourth Gospel—that Jesus' disciples should love one another as he has loved them—raises a series of questions . . . has love become exclusive and sectarian?[1]

Wolfgang Schrage is more blunt. He counsels that "we may ask whether a chapter on the Johannine writings even belongs in a book on the ethics of the New Testament."[2] Of course, by going ahead and including such a chapter, he betrays his thought that it does. His thinking is sound. In fact, the Fourth Gospel not only belongs in a work on New Testament ethics, but it also rests comfortably at home in a work on New Testament ethics that operates through a liberation lens.

At first glance, such an assertion sounds absurd. However, further reflection will demonstrate that John's social and historical setting provides a firm foundation for making it. When we carefully read John's work in the light of its first-century context, we find his language and symbolism to be the stuff of active, counter-cultural, communal resistance. If this is, indeed, the case, one need not read the circumstance of African slaves back into John's narrative. One can instead read John's narrative in the light of its own social location. Such a reading will encourage the realization that there is a correspondence of relationships between his context and the more contemporary African American ones.[3] John's readers were engaged in a social, religious, and political conflict that corresponds in many ways to the battles Africans and their descendants have waged on American soil. Because of that correspondence, John's first-century story has an ethical word that is on target for twenty-first century African Americans.

The seed of this correspondence germinates with John's christological assertion that Jesus is the Son of God. His glorious descent into the human arena inaugurates a new age, a present reality of salvation. Humans can participate in that salvation by believing in Jesus' divinity. But such belief pushes against the grain of both Jewish and Roman thought; it invites almost universal scorn. John's Christology and the salvation that develops from it are thus by definition countercultural. Any human belief or action based on that Christology must therefore also be countercultural; it must resist the worldviews upon which John's contemporary society is constructed.

In Johannine language, the primary way to foster that resistance is to show demonstrable love for those who champion the Evangelist's contrary, christological assertions. This intramural "love for one another" guarantees the viability and sustenance of a community whose very existence is counter to the cultural, religious, and political sensibilities of the time. Exclusive allegiance to this one community breeds a sense of alienation from all the others. Loving one another, widely recognized as the premier, and perhaps exclusive, Johannine ethical exhortation, thus becomes the foundation for an ethics of active resistance. In this resistance lies the correspondence with contemporary communities of liberation, like those of the African slaves.

Shucking Corn: A Slave Perspective on Countercultural, Active Resistance

In his excellent work, *Down, Up, and Over: Slave Religion and Black Theology*, Dwight N. Hopkins discusses the uncanny ability of shackled African slaves to seize sacred domains of pleasure, word power, and resource redistribution.[4] According to Hopkins, the slaves stole pleasure, co-opted power, and appropriated resources in an effort to foster self-respect and engineer a sense of communal belonging and pride. In a social economy that outlawed their access to such fundamental human rights, they were trafficking in the black market of resistance. Even activities that on the surface appeared to be innocuous, "fun" events of escapist pleasure had their way of seeding spiritual and, quite often, physical dissent.

Caught up in a spiritual ecstasy ignited by the fervor of physical play and emotional heat, these slaves who knew of no separation between the sacred and the secular *played their way* into a reality where the injustices that presently plagued them were "in truth" no more. It was in this very *present* realization of a freedom that did not yet exist that a counter to their contemporary culture was contrived.

> Indeed, the pleasures and amusements of fun times literally hoisted African Americans up into a novel spiritual current and sped them far away from the life-denying and time-controlling power of the plantation system and sensibilities. In enjoyment, blacks liberated themselves by merely having fun in a situation that allowed relatively few openings for free breathing by slaves. . . . The simple control of fun times in the theology of pleasure . . . marked one form of rebellion and re-creation of the African American self.[5]

In those controlled "fun times" slaves dreamed the counter dreams of resistance and liberty.

One such countercultural "fun" moment was what Hopkins calls "the disputed dynamic of the corn-shucking." For the masters it was an efficient way to close out the harvest and prepare its fruits. According to slave narratives, hundreds of slaves would often gather, sometimes from different plantations, before mountains of raw corn ears waiting to be stripped of their outer husks. The slaves generally picked two generals who in turn selected two teams. In the playful competition that ensued, they finished the harvest while they enjoyed the privilege and power of their own assembled company. It was the kind of assemblage that was otherwise forbidden. In song, laughter, joking, and reverie, they did their work. At the same time they worked out their senses of self and identity in language and symbol that the master and overseer neither appreciated nor truly understood. "What the master hoped would be a spectacle of buffoons and a theater of fools was seized by African Americans and re-imaged into a novel world of self-knowledge and self-care."[6] They laughed before their masters. Under the guise of fun, they even laughed *at* their masters. Sometimes they even went so far as to deploy the language of ridicule and derision. It was all accepted as a part of the ritual reality. For the master it remained just that: ritual play. Only for the slave did it ever become something more: the conjure of resistance.

> They talked back to the master in their joking and "roasting" of him, his mistress, and their way of life. They claimed the master's space in front of the master's face. They usurped the power of decision making by choosing teammates in the corn-shucking context. They regulated the time needed to finish the shucking in order to take time to enjoy one another. They experienced a rare event: the power to eat from a massive menu, the right to choose which foods to eat, and the pleasure of having a feast cooked by someone else. . . . They employed a rhythmic call and response way of being in the world when they sang throughout the ritual act. . . . Movement and sound became acts of freedom.[7]

For a precious moment in time they were transported. Still *in* the world, they were no longer *of* the world, no longer shackled by it, no longer dehumanized because of it. For a precious moment there was spiritual, linguistic, and ritual resistance. For a moment who they were was counter to everything the slave owner knew them to be.

The corn-shucking as a moment of seizing a sacred domain is a glimpse of the future in the midst of the present. The slaves' future comes alive in the coded language, symbolism, and actions of disrespect of the corn-shucking, and in their camaraderie. A new reality—one that has possibilities—explodes in the midst of the old and, by its very existence, encourages the promise that what is now only anticipatory shall be consummated. Indeed, already, in the resistance itself, the new thing, in the common, coded, connected exhilaration and concern for one another over against a common evil, the future has dawned.

Review the themes: Realized eschatology. Dualistic worldview. Alien, oppressed, and estranged status. Ecstatic joy and care for one another. A belief in something or someone greater than the oppressive circumstances. Hope that comes from outside. Hope that starts as belief in something spiritual but groundswells into active social and historical resistance. It is through such a slave lens that I initiated my look into the christological ethics of the Gospel of John. Then something wonderful happened. In my attempt to search John's world through such a lens, I found that a corresponding lens was already there, in John, waiting to be appreciated and developed.

Johannine Christology: The Potential for Ethics

Everything in John begins with Christ. What the prologue establishes, the rest of the narrative carries out; Jesus Christ is the pre-existent Son of God who has been sent by God into the world for the express purpose of saving humankind from sin. As in Mark, the narration clues the reader in to Jesus' identity right from the start. "In the beginning was the Word" (1:1); "the Word became flesh and dwelt among us" (1:14); and that Word is Jesus, the Christ (1:17-18). John, however, would not have been satisfied with Mark's communicative capabilities. In Mark, this revelation was a secret. In John, everybody knows who Jesus is. On first sight, John the Baptist announces that Jesus is the Lamb of God come to remove the sins of the world (1:29). The first followers know right away that they are following the Messiah (1:35-51). And Jesus' teachings are no longer opaque parables cloaking a kingdom mystery that most hearers are unable to fathom. When Jesus teaches in John, he does so plainly. He says who he is, and he says why he has come (3:16, 31; 4:26; 6:35, 41, 48, 51-58; 8:12, 23, 28, 58; 10:7, 9, 11, 14; 11:25; 14:6; 15:1, 5; 17:1-5). All this he does quite openly, before friend and foe alike (18:20).

There is also no kingdom confusion. In the synoptic plots Jesus comes preaching the kingdom of God, as if it is the appropriate object of belief and the proper motivator of behavior. At the same time, the narratives proclaim Jesus as the Christ who ushers in and represents the glory and power of that kingdom. No wonder historical critics of the Synoptic Gospels have argued rather contentiously as to whether the proper object of faith is the kingdom, the Jesus who preaches it, or both. To be sure, Jesus preached the kingdom. But did he also consider himself to be the Son of Man who would usher in that kingdom? Or was that connection a contrivance of the early church? How are we finally to identify Jesus in the light of his relationship with the kingdom of God?

John simplifies matters; his focus is on Jesus alone. John's Jesus does not proclaim the kingdom. John's Jesus proclaims himself.[8] The narrative problem in John, then, lies not in identifying Jesus, but in believing that his identified status is the truth. Do Jesus' claims and the protestations of his followers and narrator truly represent how and through whom the God of creation and history is acting in the world? The matter is not one of identification, but one of belief. John writes his story to market the claim that Jesus is the Son of God and therefore the appropriate object of human faith (20:30-31).[9]

This faith is critical because it leads to life. Even a cursory reading of the ninety-eight citations where the verb "to believe" occurs in the Gospel of John confirms this contention. At 1:12-13, those who believe are given the power to become children of God. At 3:15-16, 36; 5:24; and 6:40, 47, the one who believes will have eternal life. At 12:46-47, the one who believes shall be saved. At 20:30-31, John confides that his fundamental purpose for writing this gospel is that people might believe that Jesus is the Son of God, and that, having believed, they might also have life.

Unfortunately, though, Jesus' signs, identity, and teachings are not enough to provoke faith. Some indeed do believe, but many, characterized by John with labels like "the Jews" and ."the world," do not (12:37). God's act of sending the Son does not overpower human initiative and responsibility. The incarnation provides an opportunity, not an accomplished fact. Humans are not made to believe; they are invited to do so. They have a choice. Johannine ethics begins here, with the choice and the consequences that follow from it. "The fundamental ethical demand of the Book of Signs [chapters 1-12] consists of faith *in* Jesus and faith *that* Jesus comes from God."[10] Jesus' identity as Son of God is the truth to which the signs in the Gospel and the Gospel itself testifies. The opportunity to believe in that truth is John's initial ethical invitation. "Faith is an ethical action, then, because it requires those who believe to alter the fundamental way in which they know and understand themselves."[11] They must come to believe that in Jesus the impossible has occurred; the Word of God has become human flesh. Christology has founded ethics; ethics has become Christology.

The level of ethical intensity rises in John's eschatological format. Unlike the synoptic evangelists, John does not await the future coming of God's salvific presence in the form of the kingdom. Since Jesus is God's Son and Jesus is already in the world, so, too, is the salvific presence of eternal life already in the world (6:35; 11:25; 14:6; 17:3). To believe that Jesus is God's Son is to have access to that salvation right now (3:18; 6:46-47). All one has to do is believe. Likewise, those who refuse to believe will experience right now the separation from God that is the judgment of eternal death (3:18).

A crisis has occurred. Humans must choose. Are we with Jesus or against him? In John's world there can be no middle ground. It is as though Moses' challenge to the band of Hebrews following him to the Land of Promise (Deut. 30:19) has been rekeyed in a new eschatological light: In the incarnational reality of Jesus' coming, God has set before the people belief and unbelief, life and death. Only this time it is *eternal* life and *eternal* death. Jesus acts and John writes so that they might choose life.

Johannine Love: Christological Ethics

Of course the perceptive critic will recognize a problem; in the Johannine framework, it appears that ethics has been reduced to mere belief. Indeed, ethics has been integrally connected with belief, but it has hardly been reduced. Johannine belief, by its very nature, must bear behavioral fruit. The new life it conjures will be lived concretely. It will be lived in love.

In Johannine thought, faith and love share an indissoluble bond. Having examined Jesus' saying that he is the true vine in 15:1-17, Johannes Nissen and Raymond Collins arrive separately at a very similar conclusion. "The basic moral stance is not just a *consequence* of the faith; it is a *constitutive* part of Christian existence. Faith and love are one. Our being shapes our doing."[12] John 15:5 establishes the case; Jesus declares that those who abide in him will naturally bear fruit. John 15:9 closes it; that natural fruit is love.

From an African American perspective this link makes perfect sense. "The Bible is concerned with religious questions, but their questions are never separate from physical ones. A person is a totality. Blacks have seen this instinctively because of their struggle to survive in American society."[13] In the African American worldview, faith and doing have always been natural allies. What one believed had powerful implications for what one did and how one lived as a social, political, and even enslaved being. Consider the ruminations of ex-slave Thomas Likers. What he came to believe he also went on to enact. "But as soon as I came to the age of maturity, and could think for myself, I came to the conclusion [belief] that God never meant me for a slave, & that I should be a fool if I didn't take my liberty [fruit] if I got the chance."[14] Faith and doing were one.

As one might expect, the link that binds faith and love together for John is Jesus. To believe Jesus is to love Jesus. Love is the appropriate response to one's realization that in Jesus God has descended into human history in order to rescue humans from the judgment of sin. But this love is insufficient if it exists only as an internalized emotion or spiritual connection. In John, to love Jesus is to do his commandments, to work the works of faith, even those works that God had sent Jesus to do, and more (14:12-24, esp. vv. 15, 21,23; 15:10). Jesus cannot be any clearer: "If you love me, you will keep my commandments" (John 14:15).

That clarity still leaves room for two critical questions. First, can we keep Jesus' commandments? In the Johannine worldview the answer is "yes." The realization of salvific potential in the person and presence of Jesus as Son of God means that the powerful possibilities of the end time reside in the present time. Since the salvific moment has already occurred, we can be born *now* to new life. We therefore have the capability *now* of actually living the ethics, of doing the commandments of that new life. In John's world there is no excuse.

But there is a second question. What exactly are Jesus' commandments? Interestingly enough, at the three places where Jesus specifically mentions his commandments (14:15, 21; 15:10) he does not define them. Unlike the Exodus accounting, John has no listing in prioritized order. In John one must divine the commandments from the narrative presentation. One must read and discern. What one perceives is that Jesus really offers only one command expectation: love one another. And, as Matera points out, this expectation "is undoubtedly the focal point of his ethical teaching."[15] It is an expectation come full circle. Faith in the Sonship of Jesus comes first. To believe him, though, is to love him. To love him is to do his commandments. His one Johannine commandment is that they love one another. John's ethical expectation has grown directly out of his christological assertion.

But the cycle is still not fully complete. A piece is yet missing. John must also explain *how* a love for Jesus mandates a love for one another. Once again, the answer lies in the Fourth Gospel's Christology. Jesus declares rather oddly that his one commandment is a *new* commandment (13:34). Whether his contemporary critics agreed or not, latter-day commentators have maintained that a proposition to love was not new at all. Love was already a preeminent ethical expectation long before Jesus descended onto the historical scene (cf. Lev 19:18, 34). So why did Jesus call it new? According to John, he did so because his was the first love command to draw the warrant for its being and expression from the person and activity of Jesus himself.

First, there is the connection to Jesus' person. Love never stands alone in the Gospel of John; it draws its identity and its intensity from Jesus. Faith in Jesus leads to love for Jesus. The foundational premise is that God's love in the sending of Jesus (3:16) and Jesus' love for the believer (13:1; 15:9) come first. It is this incarnational expression of divine love that in turn draws out the human response of love. The love command, then, does not operate as a legal code but as a personal relationship. Believers love him because he has first loved them (3:16; 1 John 4:19).

More important from a communal standpoint, as Jesus loved them, so they are to love one another (13:34; 15:12). A pattern of reciprocal relationships establishes itself. The love between Father (God) and Son (Jesus) creates the paradigm for the Son's love for his disciples (14:21-31; 15:9-10; 17:23-24, 26). That christological standard becomes the exemplar for the disciples' love for each other. They love as he loved them. "The new commandment rests on a new reality; the new imperative is based on a new indicative, the love of God in Christ and the love of Christ in his own."[16]

Because this paradigm of Jesus' love is so critical for the ethical life of the community of faith, John gives two concrete examples of how it plays out in Jesus' own life. How does Jesus love? Jesus washes his disciples' feet (13:1-20).[17] A menial task of the lowest order, the washing of feet in a land of sandals worn in dust and desert was a thankless job imposed upon servants and slaves, not volunteered for by friends or, most certainly, by teachers and leaders.[18] And yet, Jesus sets the standard for their love for one another by absolving himself of his status as their teacher and Lord. Perhaps there is a better way to put it: Jesus redefines that identity.

As the temper of christological identity shifts, so also does the ethical expectation that is based upon it. The glorious Son of God in whom they had invested their faith demonstrated his love through this example of self-debasing and, therefore, self-sacrificing service (13:12-17, esp., 13:15). Hays and Matera are perceptive in noting that John's placement of this episode right at the door of the passion narrative was not coincidental. This self-debasing act is symbolic of a larger act of love that Jesus will soon demonstrate for his believers. His washing of their feet is anticipatory of his bleeding on behalf of their entire persons and beings. This is the kind of love Jesus has for them, the kind of love they must likewise have for one another.[19]

"No one has greater love than this, to lay down one's life for one's friends" (15:13). This is the meaning of the cross in John's narrative. As many scholars have pointed out, the cross in John does not have redemptive significance.[20] The redemption has already occurred in the sending of God's Son (3:16). The cross is instead the final illustration of the love that motivated God to send the Son, and the ultimate exemplar of the kind of love Jesus' disciples were to manifest to and for one another.[21] Just as Jesus is lifted up on the cross, so also does the cross lift up Jesus' love so that it can become a visible reminder to all who would follow him; this "lifting," as John 15:12-17 explains, is the way of love. *This* is the kind of love believers are to show one another. "From the love of Jesus manifest in his passion, one can point to the intensity and extent of the love which ought to be characteristic of Jesus' disciples. In effect, Jesus' laying down of his life for his friends is not only an example of great love; it ultimately constitutes the love of [one another] as Christian love."[22] The cross may not be the foundation for redemption in John, but it certainly is the foundation for ethics.

And given that this cross event occurs not in the metaphysical reality of literary or philosophical thought, but in the physical, historical world of first-century Palestine, John's christological cross ethics is a very material ethics. While the historical emphasis may have been summoned as a theological means to combat the docetic idea that Jesus' death was only apparent, and, therefore, not physically real, it functions quite nicely as an indicator of Jesus' material ethical agenda. "John stresses, however, that the one who really became flesh, who really became human, died visibly on the cross. Only from there can he then also establish ethics for the disciples: ethics must really be done in the world."[23] Love was not exclusively a matter of the spirit; it involved the entire human person in all the rich and dirty dimensions of soul *and* body. Furthermore, love was not exclusively personal; it was interpersonal, even communal, directing an image of self-sacrifice for others on a corporate, social scale. The interpersonal reciprocity between Father and Son generates a very public love between the Son and his followers and between those followers and one another.

The first reason, then, why Jesus calls this "love one another" charge a new commandment is that it is directly linked to his person. This is, indeed, quite new. The second reason has to do with Jesus' activity. "Love one another" is a new commandment because it occurs in this "new" time in which Jesus acts, and it occurs on behalf of the "new" people with and for whom Jesus acts.

Time comes first. Jesus' commandment "to love one another" is new precisely because it has been crafted as the ethical cornerstone of this new, salvific age. Perhaps it is John's way of declaring that new wine is meant for new wineskins. A new time requires and receives, through the teaching of the Son of God, a new command.

Even more exciting is the fact that in their execution of this "new" commandment, the disciples participate in this eschatological reality and simultaneously witness it to the world around them. The sign that they are indeed included in the new age is their love for one another. One of the earliest commentaries on the theology of the Gospel of John certainly thought this to be the case.

The author of 1 John writes at 3:14 of his letter, "We know that we have passed from death to life because we love one another." Hays comments: "The love within the community is the sign and guarantee that those who belong to Jesus are free from the grip of death."[24]

The disciples will also make this "new" age visible when they do the works of love that Jesus has himself done. The new age he has initiated has empowered them (14:12-14; 15:16-17). "He draws his own into loving community with the Father (17:26), but also expects that they will produce the fruits of this communion with God bestowed by him (15:8f., 16f.)."[25] The very visibility of this loving communion, like the visible lifting up on the cross, guarantees that its impact will not be solely intramural. Just as the "invisible institution" of slave churches in the brush harbors of the Southern plantations directly impacted the social and political climate around them, so also, one would think, would the visible practice of such noticeable, self-sacrificing, *communal* love influence the world in which the Johannine community was located. It is at this point that Johannine intracommunal ethics stands on the verge of becoming intercommunal "social" ethics.

It stands so because of the sociopolitical context in which John's recitation of Jesus' "new" commandment occurs. John's love is narrowly focused because of the historical situation that J. Louis Martyn and many others after him understood to be the circumstance of John's work.[26] To be sure, as many critics have noted, in the Gospel of John Jesus does not proclaim a universal love for one's neighbor or for one's enemies.[27] This does not mean that John takes the opposite view of the sectarians at Qumran and counsels hatred toward those outside his own community. He does not. But he also does not include them within the scope of Jesus' "new" commandment. Like the African slaves who were bound to a world where their love was neither expected nor accepted by those outside their own quarters, Martyn argues, John's community felt itself oppressed by and alienated from the world outside. For this reason, apparently, love was targeted to the place where it could have its more important spiritual and communal effect, the Johannine community itself.

Martyn theorizes that the Johannine narrative reflects a two-level drama. On the first level there is the Jesus story several decades prior to the actual writing/compilation of what we have come to know as the Fourth Gospel. The antagonists in the Jesus story are the Jewish and Roman leaders who throughout the work exhibit a high degree of enmity toward the Son of God and his followers. Needless to say, they do not believe in his christological claims. John uses this conflict to speak to issues percolating in his own time toward the end of the first century CE. This is the drama's second level. Jerusalem has been destroyed; the Second Temple of Herod the Great has been laid waste. At this point, the actual identity of Jewish leadership has shifted. Most of the groups who composed the Jewish Sanhedrin, which took up residence in the Temple of Jesus' time, went the way of the Temple itself. But the Pharisaic grouping, clustered around a rabbinic leadership devoted to the interpretation and reverence of the Torah, survived. Because their identity was not moored to the Temple, they were able to withstand the consequences of its destruction. It is this community and those who follow it that played the role of antagonist on this second level.

During this second-level time of John's writing, the Jews who believed in Jesus' divinity were becoming a more identifiable phenomenon. Tensions were high. A rupture was developing within the synagogue communities. Martyn even believes that a particular benediction against heresy in the Eighteen Benedictions was written specifically to ferret out and expel these Jesus followers. While many now debate that notion,[28] the overwhelming bulk of scholarship does appear to be in agreement that Jews who did confess faith in Jesus as God's Messiah were expelled from the synagogues and that the resulting creation of two separate and identifiable Jewish communities ignited a great deal of social friction (see John 9:22; 12:42; 16:2). "Under these circumstances, the community necessarily defined itself sharply against the synagogue and against 'the world,' which came to be seen as a hostile and untrustworthy place."[29]

This is why John warns his readers in advance that their commitment to Christ will bring them grief just as Jesus assured those who followed him that they would be persecuted because of their faith in him. Jesus exhorts his followers to love one another as he has loved them, and to do so demonstrably at 15:12-17. It is no mistake that this text is followed up with one where Jesus then explains what will happen when these believers live out their faith in him by concretely loving one another. At 15:18–16:4, he warns that they will be persecuted by those who refuse to believe. "Thus the juxtaposition . . . can be seen as both natural and deliberate within the framework of intensified opposition from the synagogue authorities."[30]

Christology, then, is the corresponding key for both settings. Whether one lives in the time of Jesus' ministry or in the time of John's writing, a profession of faith in Christ will bring with it certain abuse. And since the Jewish community that disbelieves is much larger than the "believing" community, this abuse will be oppressive. "Believers" will be excommunicated and isolated into an identifiable, sectarian community whose faith and practices are counter to everything that is acceptable in the Jewish traditions. The establishment of their own "ways," most notably their identifiable and exclusivistic "love for one another," will set them apart even further. But they must, as John's Gospel counsels again and again, continue to do this work as a way of illustrating their devotion to their Lord's identity as the One sent by God and as their way of concretely living out that faith in the world. It is in this very social way that they, like Nicodemus in John 3, must be "born again." "Coming to faith in Jesus is for the Johannine group a change in social location. Mere belief without joining the Johannine community, without making the decisive break with 'the world,' particularly the world of Judaism, is a diabolical lie."[31] They are, in other words, to become a countercommunity with an attitude.

Contemporary members of oppressed communities would, no doubt, certainly understand John's social predicament and the narrative way in which he sought to address it. The correspondences run forward to African Americans as well as backward to Jesus. The sense of the slave community, as discussed in chapters 1 and 2, was that love was directed toward those in the community itself. It was for this reason that activities considered unethical in the white "world" were considered ethical within the slave community, activities like stealing from the owner, or running away, or inciting rebellion. A different understanding of what composed ethics existed between slave and owner because the owner created the life circumstance that way. Love within slave communities was often "sectarian" in its own way, where love for one another often lived itself out in countercultural ways like the code of silence that protected fellow slaves, or the shared interest in coded language and song that encouraged one's fellow chattel while lashing out at the owner and his minion. Indeed, in such a historical scenario, what J. L. Houlden says about John in his context sounds very applicable for the slave in his or hers. There is correspondence.

> Yet, it is unfair to disparage this [view of love] as a regrettable narrowing of the broad generosity of Paul and the other Gospels. (Who has ever read it thus?) Looked at in John's perspective, it could not be otherwise: his ethics followed straight from his theological convictions. In the world which he saw, a world in which salvation was hard to find, a world in itself the object of near despair, a man's moral duty could only lie within the Christian circle [re: slave community], where alone "meaning" was to be found [cf., for example, the corn shucking experience]. Society at large had no moral claims; the question of general obligations simply did not arise. It is not that such obligations are willfully refused: they do not enter within the writer's purview.[32]

A similar correspondence exists with the African American led civil rights movement. Once again, with love as a pressing theme throughout the movement, the focus was on the ostracism imposed on the black community by the larger white community in America. In this case that oppression lived itself out as racial segregation, the sociopolitical progeny of slavery. The Bus Boycott of Montgomery, Alabama, that in many ways provided the movement's initial spark was an active attempt by African Americans to support their own for the purpose of enduring and overcoming the outside oppression arrayed against them. To be sure, this effort was one of internal love, where love for one another led to momentous sacrifices of walking to work and school, supplying cars and time to aid those who had long distances to travel, enduring outside hostility through shared moments of worship and prayer. This, too, was resistant, community centered love that not only enabled the black community in the United States to survive, but, through the force field of change it energized, helped transform the larger American community in a positive direction of civil reform. One wonders if John's community, whether it had this goal of larger societal transformation in mind or not, did not also realize that a by-product of its communal resistance would be the transformation of the very oppressive world that tortured it. Could this be the lens through which we should read passages like John 1:29; 3:16; 4:42; 6:33? These texts indicate an interest in the salvation and transformation of the entire world, not just the Johannine community itself. However, scholarship generally considers them to be the exceptions that prove the Johannine rule; John's interest is intra-, not inter-communal. Perhaps if we read those "exceptional" texts through the kind of African American lens just suggested, we would have a better understanding of their placement in the text. Perhaps they are not aberrations at all, but fit quite well within John's social-historical understanding. Perhaps John already understood that the "love for one another" that enabled his believing community to sustain itself and simultaneously resist the hostile world around it would also, by energizing an alternative reality and a competing force for change, transform that world. If the sacred and the spiritual are not separate, perhaps this "sending" for the redemption from sin could have been thought to have exactly this tranformative impact as well. "For God so loved the world that he gave his only Son, so that *everyone* who believes in him may not perish but may have eternal life" (3:16).

Johannine Dualism: An Ethics of Resistance

It is this sectarian sense of estrangement from the world that drives the potential for an ethics of resistance in John's Gospel.[33] The mixing of the Evangelist's sociological circumstance and his christological thought in a narrative stew already stocked with a dualistic worldview yields an ethics whose operational premise is "resist."

John operates from a theological perspective of cosmological dualism. His worldview is dualistic because he envisions two great and significant, competing realities. He assigns them qualitative value. One is good. The other is evil. Each wants to be the reality that lays claim to the cosmos. Each wants to be the power that receives human allegiance. John knows these two powers as God and Satan. Satan is the devil, the evil one who fights against God's plans for humankind, and infiltrates humans themselves, hoping to influence their thoughts and win their favor (8:44; 12:31; 13:2; 13:27; 14:30; 16:11; 17:15). God is the one Jesus calls Father, the one who expresses great love for the world and thus sends Jesus as his Son in order to save it.

On the level of the narrative story, the war waged between these two powers is symbolized by the contrast between competing conceptualities like light and darkness (1:5-10; 3:19-21), life and death (3:36; 5:21), spirit and flesh (3:6-8), truth and lie (1:14; 8:44-46), and, above all, above and below (3:31; 8:23).[34] It is this last category that separates Johannine cosmological dualism from the kind of eschatological dualism more prevalent in the synoptic and Pauline portraits. There the distinction is one of time, between the now of human separation from God and the not yet of kingdom salvation. Since that moment of salvation, of life lived in relationship with God, has already occurred in John with Jesus' coming from the Father, the future has no salvific priority. "Hence eternal life for him is not the anticipation of a future life at the consummation; rather, eternal life is life determined "from above.""[35] John's focus is on the present. In the present, the primary contrast is spatial. What belongs to "above" is of God; what belongs to "below" is of the devil.

Jesus, of course, as the pre-existent Logos who was with God at the creation of the physical world, is the first citizen of the above. Thus, the Evangelist connects him with all of the positively valued symbols which represent the above; he is light (8:12; 9:5), life (11:25; 14:6), spirit (3:34-35; 6:63), and truth (14:6). The narrative crisis occurs because Jesus has been sent from above to save those who live below. But, of course, Jesus does not fit in below; inhabitants of the above belong above. He is therefore a misfit and is treated as such (cf. 1:10; 3:19). His christological identity does not, can not fit in. It, therefore, *must* cause a crisis. Anyone who holds to this identity, which a Johannine believer is called to do, will be caught up in the alienation that Jesus himself suffers. By identifying themselves with the agent from "above" they will no longer fit in with the way life is orchestrated from "below."

To be sure, John is not very specific when he talks about the reality "from below." The symbolic language of darkness, death, lie, and flesh lacks sufficient detail. Apparently, though, John knows that it is difficult to choose against something, to resist its way of life, unless one has a handle on exactly what it is. That is why he symbolizes "below" as the human world into which Jesus descends (8:23). This world, though, must not be confused with the physical universe inhabited by humans. "Since all things were created by the divine *Logos* (1:3) and since the Word (*Logos*) itself became flesh (1:4) and came into the world as 'to its own home' (1:11), the physical universe cannot simply be identified with sin."[36] More particularly, the world represents the occupants of this physical universe who are resistant to the "truth" that Jesus Christ is God's Son sent to save humankind from sin. The world in this sense is more than an individual nonbeliever or even an aggregate of non believers who have allied themselves into some form of communal recalcitrance. It is instead the systemic defiance of God's lordship over the world through the person of Jesus as Christ. It is the structural refusal by human authority, both Jewish and Roman, to "see" Jesus as the medium through which God is operating in the world (9:35-41).[37] This is why John describes the world symbolically as being wrapped up in darkness. Ruled by Satan, it is controlled by the power of sin (1:10-11; 7:7). That is why John refers to it so pejoratively as "this" world (8:23; 9:39; 12:31; 16:11; 18:36).[38]

It is important to reemphasize the point, though, that "this world" is not inherently evil. Since everything in the human sphere was created through the guidance and person of the very Christ who has now descended into it, its ontological state is not darkness. It chooses darkness. The world is not a lie; it chooses the lie when it reifies human authority and human thinking and rejects the lordship of Jesus as God's Son. The world makes an ethical choice and then threatens others to choose with it. In this sense, *this* world is extremely active; it recruits persons to its cause through fear just as John is himself recruiting persons to the cause of Jesus' lordship through the telling of his story. It threatens loss of status and societal standing. John narrates this loss with the language of hatred and synagogue expulsion.

This is why John populates his story with the likes of the blind man of John 9, the lame man of John 5, Nicodemus, and Joseph of Arimathea. They are characterizations of choice for the world below or the world above. The blind man is the community exemplar. Even though he knows the consequences, he chooses to support the christological confession that Jesus is the Christ sent from God. John 5 chronicles the more dubious escapade of a healed lame mane betraying the very Jesus who healed him so he can protect his status in the community. Like Nicodemus (3:1-21; 7:50-53; 19:39), Joseph of Arimathea (19:38), and the parents of the healed blind man of chapter 5, he fears that an open profession of faith in Jesus will invite the hostility and excommunicative force of the synagogue leaders and Pharisees. In the characterization of these illustrative options, John encourages his readers, just as Jesus was in the story encouraging his listeners, to choose the path of faith in his Sonship, and thereby ally themselves with the things from above.

Nicodemus, as a negative example, is a good case in point:

> Nicodemus endeavors not to choose, or not to declare his choice, until it is too late to matter. That is why he is confronted with the birth from *water* and spirit: the water of baptism symbolizes and embodies the act of choice and declaration. Since it is this act which stands between the Johannine community and the secret Christians, the water, and the rite of baptism to which it refers, is immovably rooted in the dialogue with Nicodemus, not as a sacramental ritual but as the social boundary that confronts Nicodemus and that he is challenged to cross.[39]

This is the language of shifting social realities, not ignoring them. John's charge is that his followers see the alternatives and make a conscious faith declaration that implies a concrete and confrontational life choice. "Birth from above is not an invisible event, unknown to anyone but the individual in question. It alters that person's place in the world and stance toward the world, or it has not taken place at all, and it aligns him or her with others who have become equally unfamiliar to the world."[40]

The narrative knows that the forces and people who have been coopted by the power from below will persecute, ostracize, excommunicate, and oppress anyone who testifies to the christological identity of Jesus as the one who has been sent by God from above. It knows that the choice it asks of believers like Nicodemus is a hard one. And yet it asks its readers and hearers to do so anyway. There is no middle ground. One must choose either "to continue to dwell in the darkness or to come into the light."[41] This "choice," I can now say more definitively, is the stuff of a Johannine ethics of active resistance.[42]

It is active because it advocates the creation of a visible community whose intramural love sets it apart and makes it a viable, recognizable alternative to the traditional ways of being and living in the world. Just as Jesus was sent into the world by God as a beacon slicing through the darkness, lighting the only true path to God and salvation, so too are the disciples sent into the world by Jesus with the same confrontational agenda in mind (17:18; 20:21). Where God sent Jesus as an alien individual, Jesus sends his disciples as an foreign community bound together by their love for one another. In this dualistic worldview this community's very survival, its defiant existence guarantees that a choice for the "things" that are from above (light, life, truth, etc.) will always be available to all those who dwell in this physical universe and are therefore susceptible to the machinations of the rulers and leaders of "this world" below. It is a community called to go forth and live in the world like light driven into the midst of darkness or truth thrust into the midst of a great lie, just as Jesus was sent to sojourn in the world but never to became a part of it. This is what John means when he exhorts the community to resist being "of the world" even though they live "in the world" (17:14-19). This community's faith in Jesus, which results in a love for one another, will continually identify it as something different, a misfit, and thus set apart.

Love, in such a narrative scenario, is the ultimate countercultural force. It is their love for one another that makes them a visible and viable alternative to the prevailing thought of their surrounding, hostile world. Love holds them together when the persecutions come. Love keeps them together and thus guarantees that more persecution will come. As long as the community based on faith in Jesus as the one sent by God endures it will be hurt; as long as they love one another, they will endure. The world's goal is to extinguish them in the same way that darkness wants to overcome the light. By continuing to love one another they exist; that is, they continue to resist. This love, then, is the primary social method of that resistance. No doubt this is what Nissen has in mind when he writes, "In my estimation the meaning of the Johannine sectarianism is that because it was sectarian it *challenged* the world on the basis of the love of God and the word of God."[43] Like the "invisible" slave worshiping institutions that met in the secluded brush arbors of southern plantations despite the express forbiddance of their owners, this Johannine community, by continuing to exist, defied the mandates of the world. By existing "visibly," this community smacked that attitude of resistance right up against the world's face.

The problem with John's dualistic rendering, of course, is that, in the end, his narrative connects the structural intransigence of "the world" with the characterization that he names "the Jews." The exchange in 8:39-47 where Jesus identifies "the Jews" as children of the devil is particularly striking. The Christian anti-Judaism that has operated from this literary connection has led to tragic historical consequences. Many have made the case (correctly) that John's ultimate intent was not to castigate Judaism as a faith or "the Jews" as an entire people.[44] As Matera points out, even at John 8, the case is not as clear-cut as it first seems. "Jesus' statement does not mean that the Jewish race is physically or spiritually descended from Satan [no more than Peter really is Satan in Mark 8]. Were that the case, it would be impossible to explain why he continues to speak with the Jews."[45] John more likely used the language "the Jews" to refer to that part of the Jewish people who refused to believe that Jesus was the Son sent by God into the world to redeem the world from its sin. This refusal had a structural-political component that John narrated by connecting "the Jews" with the Pharisees and other officers who took the lead in rebuffing Jesus' christological claims.

> In the Fourth Gospel, the root meaning of the Greek word *Ioudaioi* is probably not simply "Jews" but "the Jews who lived in Judea (as opposed in the gospel to *Galilaioi*, "the Jews who lived in Galilee"). Judea was the economic center of Palestine. In John's gospel, therefore, "Judeans" are perhaps especially Jerusalem's priestly aristocracy, who collaborated with Rome and controlled the religious-economic center of Judea, the Jerusalem temple. In other words, in John, the "Judeans" embody *ho kosmos*, the system.[46]

If the understanding about Johannine sociology that has been in vogue since Martyn's groundbreaking work is correct, then we have a clearer picture of what probably motivated the Evangelist to write about "the Jews" in the way that he did. Given that the community felt itself alienated from and oppressed by the larger Jewish community of which it had once been a part, the Johannine community initiated a very intramural, sectarian struggle. The characterizations of Nicodemus, Joseph of Arimathea, the healed lame man of John 5, and the parents of the healed blind man of John 9 symbolize what was probably a very credible historical desire on the part of many during the time of John's writing. Many wanted to remain within the synagogue communities even with their profession of faith in Jesus' lordship. The problem, at least in John's view, was that the traditional leadership forces in Judaism would not allow the continued infestation of the synagogue with such Christ believers. John's negative portrayal of the aforementioned characterizations suggests that he possessed the same either/or attitude. But John's community was in the numerical minority. It lacked the power to protect its adherents who, once they publicly confessed their faith, as John's narrative counsels them to do, were excommunicated, ostracized, hated, and persecuted. It is this oppressive circumstance that drives the harshness of his language about "the Jews."

Unfortunately, interpreters have often held on to the harsh language and either forgotten or simply ignored the context in which the language took its initial shape. Christ believers later assumed the role of the societal majority and assumed the religious and political power that went with such status. In the hands of such believers, John's language became a license to oppress and ostracize the "alien" Jewish communities in their midst in the same way that John felt that his once "alien" communities were persecuted by the majority in theirs. Judaism was identified uncritically with "the world," seen as negative and hostile, and therefore threatened and harmed. John's language of resistance mutated into a language of terror. For this, the Christian community has much to repent.

Still, I would maintain that the language is, in John's historical and literary context, the language of resistance, not terror. It is important to note, for example, that the countercultural thrust in John is targeted as clearly at Roman as Jewish leadership. John makes it clear in the arrest and trial scenes that Roman authority finds Jesus and the movement he heads to be a legitimate threat.

Only in John is Jesus arrested in the garden by a *speira* (18:3, a "detachment" in the NRSV, the Greek word for a Roman cohort made up of 600 soldiers) and its *chiliarchos* (18:12, "officer" in the NRSV, the word for a tribune commanding that number of men), together with "police from the chief priests of the Pharisees" (18:3). Why would the powers-that-be send 600 soldiers and temple police to arrest one man, Jesus?[47]

Clearly, the Roman authorities were, at least in John, equally concerned about the impact this man could have. And if John's two-level narrative uses Jesus' confrontations with the leaders of his time to speak meaningfully to the Johannine community's confrontations with the synagogue leadership of John's time, why should we suspect that the case would be any different concerning Roman leadership and authority? Indeed, in a very striking testimony later on in the Gospel, Jesus, standing before Pilate, makes a declaration about Roman authority that would have had the same countercultural ring of resistance in John's time as it did in Jesus'. At 19:1-11, when Jesus challenges Pilate's assertion that he has power over Jesus, John's Gospel is challenging the entire Roman view of power and authority over the world. Indeed, Rome may control "the world," but it does not control the power of the Son that has come into the world, or the people who are faithful to him. "The whole dialogue subverts Roman claims of sovereignty and subordinates Roman power to the power of God."[48]

It does so in spite of the way many commentators have interpreted the other key phrase in the Pilate/Jesus discussion that occurs at 18:33-38. Pilate wants to know if Jesus is "King of the Jews." He wants to know because, as he mockingly explains, his own constituents are the ones who have turned him in. Jesus explains that his kingship is not of this world. This does not mean that it is a sectarian kingship that has nothing to do with the world. It means just what it says, what I have been arguing all along, that though "in" the world, his kingship, like he himself, is not "of" the world. In fact, in John's narrative scenario, the leaders who have turned him in are not of his constituency precisely because they represent that world in which Jesus is an alien sojourner. His kingship is in the world and confronts the world precisely because it is not "of" the world. Its refusal to be "of" the world is the stuff of its resistance and therefore the problem of its continued existence as far as the world is concerned. It is because his kingship is so stubbornly and so successfully not "of" the world that the world must retaliate with every weapon, even the Roman "cross," at its disposal. The world's reaction to this resistance demonstrates just how powerful the countercultural social and political implications of Jesus' kingship really are.

This discussion of John's ethic as a Christology of active resistance has led me to a renewed appreciation for the manner in which he ends what apparently was the conclusion to the first rendering of his Gospel, 20:30-31. The debates about the actual Greek formulation in the different manuscripts is so well worn that it need not be reintroduced here. In doing my research for this chapter I came across many finely tuned arguments for both reading the key verb "believe" in the present tense (which suggests that John was writing to believers encouraging them to continue believing) and in the aorist (which suggests that John was writing to nonbelievers encouraging them to start believing). Many have even rightly challenged whether it really makes that much of a difference which tense John initially rendered the verb since either tense allows for an interpretation opposite to the one traditionally attached to it. My own reading tends to suggest that John was more than likely writing to fellow believers and encouraging them to stand fast as a community that actively resisted "the world." But this does not mean that I think the Gospel does not have a strong evangelistic thrust. Indeed, precisely because of its ethical agenda of active resistance, I would argue that by speaking to his community of believers in the way that he does, he sets up the possibility for the most potent form of evangelism there is. Interpreters miss John's impact here because of the limited way in which we think of evangelism. Most would define evangelism as a moving out into communities and inviting them to join whatever movement is being represented. John's Gospel does not appear to have that kind of mandate in mind. What it does have in mind, however, is the maintenance of a community whose foundation is the countercultural belief that Jesus is the Son sent by God to save the world from its sins. This community sustains itself and perpetuates itself through the love its members show toward one another. It is by way of this love that the community can be identified, but also by way of this love that the community stands out visibly as separate and unique from every other community that surrounds it. It sees itself "as presenting, by its own very existence and its own countercultural form of life, 'testimony' to the world."[49] Through its love, it is recognizable to people outside of it, to those who would tend to be hostile toward it, and to those who might find it an appealing alternative. Through its love, then, this community becomes a kind of alien light shining in the darkness, an attraction pointing to something outside of itself. Or, as Nissen puts it, referencing 17:20-26, "By this mutual love of the community, 'the world may believe.' "[50] In this way it is sent into the world even as it steadfastly refuses to become a part of the world. It is, I would argue, in this way that it becomes an attraction to people in the world seeking a lighted path to God and God's love. In this oddly ironic way, by being visibly sectarian, it is actually reaching out to those who are lost in the world, and encouraging them to participate in the love that sustains it.

A Contemporary Correspondence of Resistance

There is no question for me that John's Gospel has a potent message for contemporary communities struggling with oppression. The correspondences between John's social circumstance and that of contemporary oppressed peoples suggests that the Fourth Evangelist's counsel to his own first-century world has abiding ethical implications. The viewing of his text from a perspective influenced by the situation and circumstance of African American slaves not only renders visible the liberative potential in the Gospel narrative itself, it enables the person who perceives that potential to apply it appropriately to present ethical quandaries. I think in this case most particularly about the situation of contemporary African Americans who still struggle with a sense of separateness and isolation from their surrounding American "world." The African American existence is still very tragically marked by a dangerous degree of dualism, still, as W. E. B. Dubois recognized at the beginning of the twentieth century, caught up and caught in the struggle of two worlds. The institutionalized racism against which African Americans continue to struggle corresponds in many ways to the systemic hostility of "the world" that John felt was pervasive in his own time. I would agree with Rensberger when he argues, "And the result of this understanding is to provide location and validation to a community disenfranchised by the "world" and its authorities. For John's community as for black Christians, the world is wrong because Jesus is right. They are not what the world says they are; their true identity is to be found in the presence of Jesus."[51]

This christological affirmation must, as John understood, lead to an attentiveness to the people whose allegiance to it makes them an identifiable community. The love for one another which Jesus believed was a natural outgrowth out of love for him must be for the African American community the same kind of priority John felt that it was for his. For a community in struggle that cannot count on the assistance of the world that surrounds it, it is imperative that it find ways to support and maintain itself, to make of itself a viable, self sustaining entity whose future endurance lies in its own hands. This is what the love John espoused as the "stuff" of countercultural resistance was all about. Love, as a force that sustains even as it resists the destructive and hostile tendencies of a surrounding, oppressive "world," can be as potent a constructive force for African American Christians as it was for Johannine believers. This kind of love calls for social as well as spiritual transformation and looks for the tranformative fruits of that love even as it celebrates its spiritual Jesus connection. John's Gospel should be a reminder for the African American community and all oppressed minority communities like it that true change begins with faith, the kind of faith that leads to love, the kind of love that builds a community, protects that community's present, and guarantees its future even as and probably because it challenges, counters, and resists the hostilities of the world around it. This is the kind of community that witnesses to the truth that in Jesus Christ God has broken into the world. It is the kind of community that remembers what its slave forebears already knew, that even the most spiritual faith in Jesus has an ethical edge to it, an edge that breeds hope, sustains life, and counsels resistance. This is the kind of faith that must be sheltered and nurtured. This is the kind of faith that witnesses to the lordship of Christ in the world and all the countercultural possibilities that such a witness implies.

CHAPTER FIVE

Paul: Theology Enabling Liberating Ethics—Sometimes

I opened the previous chapter by acknowledging the allegation that the Gospel of John does not do ethics. Paul courts an even more devastating charge. In the judgment of many liberation critics, he renders *bad* ethics. Neil Elliott summarizes a representative ruling: *"The usefulness of the Pauline letters to systems of domination and oppression is nevertheless clear and palpable."*[1] African American slaves swore out countless corroborations to this testimony. Amos Jones records that "they held the apostle in righteous contempt."[2] They believed that Paul religiously took away the freedom God and Jesus had so graciously offered.

> Interestingly enough, blacks in American slavery, though pitifully but understandably illiterate because of the prohibitions placed upon them by the white oppressor, discovered forceful themes of liberation in the Old Testament and New Testament; but they did not find these themes in Paul's writings.[3]

In fact, they found the opposite. They found themes so supportive of the slave status quo that many vowed never to listen to Paul preached or, when and if they were so able, never to read Paul for themselves. The classic recollection of African American spiritualist Howard Thurman is characteristic.

> During much of my boyhood I was cared for by my grandmother, who was born a slave and lived until the Civil War on a plantation

near Madison, Florida. My regular chore was to do all of the reading for my grandmother—she could neither read nor write. . . .
When I was older and was half through college, I chanced to be
spending a few days at home near the end of summer vacation.
With a feeling of great temerity I asked her one day why it was that
she would not let me read any of the Pauline letters. What she told
me I shall never forget. "During the days of slavery", she said, "the
master's minister would occasionally hold services for the slaves.
Old man McGhee was so mean that he would not let a Negro minister preach to his slaves. Always the white minister used as his text
something from Paul. At least three or four times a year he used as
a text: "Slaves be obedient to them that are your masters . . . as unto
Christ." Then he would go on to show how, if we were good and
happy slaves, God would bless us. I promised my Maker that if I
ever learned to read and if freedom ever came, I would not read that
part of the Bible.[4]

Paul's letters, as the words of Thurman's grandmother suggest,
have had an interesting history in the hands of African American
readers. In this particular case, Thurman's grandmother is actually
referring to a text, Col 3:22, that is not from one of the undisputed
seven letters of Paul (Romans, Galatians, 1 and 2 Corinthians, 1
Thessalonians, Philippians, and Philemon). A similar saying is
found in material that has earned the predominantly undisputed
recognition of not being written by Paul: the pastorals. The particular reference is Titus 2:9. Still, there are places in the undisputed
letters where Thurman's grandmother could have pointed. The
difficult text at 1 Corinthians 7:20-22 comes immediately to mind.
As Raboteau records, the missionaries to slaves strove "to uphold
the doctrine expressed in an oft-quoted passage: The Scripture, far
from making any Alteration in Civil Rights, expressly directs, that
*every man abide in the condition wherein he is called, with great
Indifference of Mind* concerning outward circumstances."[5] The
Philemon letter is apparently clearer; there Paul records his return
of the runaway slave Onesimus to his master.

It is not difficult to understand why a slave or an ex-slave like
Thurman's grandmother would have felt the same antipathy for
Paul's writings as she felt for the letters written in imitation of
them. The slaves and ex-slaves refused to respect texts that justified their exploitation. In other words, they did not simply inter-

pret the biblical texts out of their experience; they also *critiqued* them out of and because of that experience.

The reaction of worshiping slaves in 1833 Georgia to a sermon based on Paul's letter to Philemon is illustrative. In this case a white preacher clearly intends to connect Paul's return of Philemon's slave to the right of American plantation owners to hold and maintain human chattel. The listening slaves were certain the Bible could not contain such a tacit endorsement of the institution of slavery because the being and reality of the God who was the moving force behind the Bible was a God of liberation.

> In Liberty County a group of slaves were listening to a white minister hold forth on a staple topic—the escaped slave, Onesimus, and his return to his master. According to the report from Georgia, half of the Negro group walked out when the point of the sermon became clear, and the "other half stayed mostly for the purpose of telling [the preacher] that they were sure there was no such passage in the Bible."[6]

That secondhand report is verified by the firsthand account of the Reverend Charles Colcock Jones, the white Methodist missionary to slaves who was the preacher of record:

> I was preaching to a large congregation on the *Epistle of Philemon*: and when I insisted upon fidelity and obedience as Christian virtues in servants and upon the authority of Paul, condemned the practice of *running away*, one half of my audience deliberately rose up and walked off with themselves, and those that remained looked any thing but satisfied, either with the preacher or his doctrine. After dismission, there was no small stir among them; some solemnly declared "that there was no such an Epistle in the Bible"; others, "that they did not care if they ever heard me preach again!"[7]

Contemporary African American religious leaders have often followed the lead of their ancestral forebears. "Very few black theologians have given the apostle serious consideration when they have sought to spin out their theologies of liberation from the Bible. . . . There was a deeply engrained antipathy within the ranks of black theologians for the apostle Paul."[8]

Pauline ethics, at least on the count of slavery, seemed *bad*. It certainly did not appear to be liberating. How, then, do I come up with a chapter title that has "Pauline theology" sitting side by side with "liberating ethics"? Even sometimes?

I do so very carefully. And I start with that model condemnation of Howard Thurman's grandmother. The appeal for a liberating Pauline ethics makes its case right there. I have already noted that the scriptural words she quotes do not come from one of Paul's undisputed works. In making his case for a liberating Pauline ethics in an African American context, Amos Jones lays a great deal of weight on this historical observation. Paul's own writings, he claims, have a liberating intent. Proslavery forces were only able to use him as their ally in promoting slavery because they appealed to the Pauline school of writings as though those materials were written by Paul himself. But Paul, Jones argues, held a very different opinion on such matters from those who wrote later in his name.

> The failure of the church to sort out Paul's genuine letters from those attributed to him caused the proslavery position of the deutero-Pauline epistles, the Pastorals, and the catholic epistles to become mixed with and attributed to be the same as the position of Paul, although Paul's position would be diametrically opposed to the subsequent positions.[9]

Ten years later, Neil Elliott, writing with the specific intent to demonstrate the liberating character of Paul's letters, built his own case from Jones's observational foundation. Calling the later epistles "forgeries" that distorted Paul's position on many critical issues, he issued a challenge to evaluate Paul's ethics from Paul, not from the disputed words of those who, pretending to write in his name, soiled it. "I am convinced," he writes, "and mean to convince my reader, that Paul himself is far more an advocate of human liberation than the inherited theological tradition has led us to think."[10]

Writing through the liberation lens of Latin America, Elsa Tamez had already reached a similar conclusion with regard to the key Pauline claim of justification by faith. Even this most spiritual of indicative statements, she argues, implies a liberating ethical imperative. "One is justified by grace in order to be able to do the true works of justice that are also accomplished by grace."[11]

If nothing else, the works of these three scholars warrant a second "liberation" look at *Paul's* theology and the ethics that are a part of it. To be sure, Paul's letters do not present us with anything like a systematic ethics. His are occasional writings addressed to the specific needs of the communities he was pastoring. But they do establish a tendency. I want to make the case that it is a boundary-breaking theological tendency, and that the liberative quality in his ethics issues from it.

Paul's theology has as one of its primary goals the breaking down of religious, social, and political boundaries between Jews and Gentiles in the first-century believing communities. In his attempt to demonstrate the viability of Gentile presence in the people of God, Paul challenged the Jewish legal barriers that would have prevented such inclusion, and the Gentile sense of superiority that could have sabotaged it. His, then, was a boundary-breaking motivation. Sometimes. For the apostle, it seems to me, does not in the end always maintain the courage of his own somewhat shocking convictions. The liberating ethics his theology enables on the one hand is often disabled on the other by less egalitarian theological and practical considerations.

A Boundary-Breaking Paul

Did Paul intend to shatter the ethnic, religious, and social boundaries separating first-century Jews and Gentiles? I think so. In fact, I believe this intention drives his epistolary counsel. Much as African American scholar W. E. B. Dubois identified the color line as one of the most powerfully devastating realities in the life of twentieth century America and wrote to challenge it, so Paul realizes that the ethnic divide between Jew and Gentile threatens the very survival of his and other Christian faith communities. This is why Paul directed his comments in the overall sweep of his letters to *both* Jewish and Gentile believing communities. It is why, as Richard Longenecker argues, he claims no difference between Jew and Gentile in the one body of Christ.[12] It is why Elisabeth Schüssler Fiorenza can claim that "one could show that Paul's work centered around the abolition of the religious distinctions between Jew and Gentile."[13]

This boundary-breaking emphasis appears to be an integral by product of Paul's conversion. To understand the conversion, we must go back to Paul's accounting of himself before it took place. At Gal 1:13-14 and Phil 3:6, 9, he declares that he was a great and successful persecutor of the church because of his zeal for the traditions of his fathers. I agree with Willi Marxsen's assertion that Paul already knew the content of the Christian faith when he was a Pharisee persecuting it. Indeed, he persecuted the faith precisely because there was something problematic about that content. It was not the church's belief in Jesus as the crucified Messiah; "that would not even have been a crime worthy of persecution."[14] Such a belief would have earned derision instead.

No, if the Galatians and Philippians citations are to be a guide, the criminal Christian content was the infant faith's dismissive position on the Jewish Law. For Jews, the Law was the spiritual mechanism that provided access to salvation. Disregarding it "made them blasphemers in the eyes of Paul, who still considered them Jews."[15] The Law was also a socio-political gift from God that acted as the cornerstone of the people's creation as a people. To attack it, then, was not only to attack the God who had given it; it was also to attack the entire infrastructure of Israel's corporate and religious existence.

The Hellenistic Christians would have been the most irksome for Paul in this regard since it was they who most forcefully proclaimed that the law had become obsolete. While the Aramaic-speaking Jewish Christians would have practiced their faith in concert with their allegiance to the Law, as Paul's skirmishes with them would later indicate (e.g., Galatians 2), the Hellenist Christians "could not be tolerated because they overstepped the boundaries of what was possible within Judaism. They expressly stated that they rejected the law."[16] This meant that they also rejected the ritual standards the law imposed. Many of these (circumcision, dietary regulations, etc.) had long formed an inviolate dividing line between Jew and Gentile.

According to Marxsen, evangelistic Jews in the Diaspora had already recognized this problem. In their attempt to convert Gentiles to the faith, they found that while many became enamored of the synagogues because of its monotheism and ethics, potential proselytes chafed at the prospect of circumcision and other ritual requirements for keeping of the Law. "For in the coexistence of a minority of Greek-speaking Jews and a majority of

Gentiles there was always a latent question: Do people really need the law in order to stay with God or come to God fully?"[17] Hellenist Christians operating in the Diaspora were tending more and more to answer with a definitive "no." That negation brought the "legal" boundary separating Jew and Gentile tumbling down.

The shocking nature of Paul's conversion lies in the fact that it is just this negation that he would later so successfully affirm. The consequence of the metamorphosis is clear: he ended up tearing down the very boundary that he had done everything in his former life to uphold. It was he now who claimed that righteousness was no longer a legal reality, but a theological one; it came not from the Law, but through what God had done in Christ Jesus. This proclamation opened the possibility of righteousness to *anyone* who would believe in that Christ. "Paul's basic interest was to extend to everyone, without exception, the message that the gospel is the power of God for the salvation of all, because in it is revealed the justice of God."[18] Indeed, Marxsen's redemptive recognition is, in fact, much more than he seemed to comprehend. In Christ Jesus, God had displaced the Law as redemptive yardstick *and* sociopolitical marker. The separating boundary that the Law had raised between the ethnicities Jew and Gentile had fallen, or, better said, in Christ Jesus, had been shattered.

Theology Enables Ethics

In Paul, theology and ethics always go together. "There is no meaningful distinction between theology and ethics in Paul's thought, because Paul's theology is fundamentally an account of God's work of transforming his people into the image of Christ."[19] Rudolf Bultmann set up a classic discussion on the matter in his article "Das Problem der Ethik bei Paulus."[20] There, using the terms, "indicative" and "imperative," he attempted to demonstrate how the two were so integrally related that logic could not define the relationship between them. "In positive terms, Bultmann declares that the imperative is grounded in the fact of justification and derives from the indicative."[21] According to many, Bultmann's attempt to decipher the Pauline relationship between the imperative and the indicative foundered on his attempt at an interpretative slogan: "Become what you are." Jack Sanders points, for example, to Victor Furnish's complaint that such an observation makes Paul's imperative too much the result of his indicative, and so, not integral to it.[22] Sanders argues that Furnish has misread Bultmann; that in the end Bultmann and Furnish press the same understanding that "the Pauline imperative is not just the result of the indicative but fully integral to it."[23] Well before Furnish, though, as Wolfgang Schrage notes, Bultmann had come under attack from Ernst Käsemann.[24] He identified Bultmann's fixation on Pauline anthropology as the culprit. It suggested a particular ethical focus: justified humans ought to become what they had been created to be. The scholar's sound bite ("become what you are") implied that, following God's act, humans should respond. Focusing instead on God's eschatological righteousness, Käsemann argued that what God does enables human activity. All human activity, then, starts with God, not with humans themselves. It is only at this point of understanding that one could appeal successfully to key Pauline texts like Galatians 5:25 ("If we live by the Spirit, let us also be guided by the Spirit") as indicative of the relationship between theology and ethics in Paul (see also Rom 6:2, 12-14; 1 Cor 5:7). Marxsen's reading is a helpful summary: "The Pauline imperatives are not intended just to invite people to act; they are addressed to *changed* people. Therefore they do not simply presuppose a 'known' indicative; they presuppose an indicative that has *affected* people."[25] In Paul, then, ethics do not stand alone as a separate theoretical category. They presuppose a relationship where the one is an integral part of the other. *Theology enables ethics.* Ethics establishes theology in the living reality of a community's loving and liberating existence. Sometimes.

Theology

For Paul, everything starts and ends with God, particularly with what God is doing in and through Jesus Christ. Paul makes his case at 1 Cor 2:2: "For I decided to know nothing among you except Jesus Christ, and him crucified." First Corinthians is an excellent example precisely because Paul's counsel is so directly related to the ethical concerns raised by the Corinthians themselves. As Hays and Houlden point out, what is clear in this correspondence is evident everywhere else, "The singular message of

Christ crucified is made to address all the particular problems of conduct faced by his infant communities."[26] Here is the point: what God does through Jesus Christ is foundational for ethics because God's action in Christ meets the requirement of justification that the law previously had tried to fulfill. It is through the sending, death, and resurrection of Jesus Christ that believers are justified before God. The tenses, and thus the timing, are key. Through God's Christ act, the future judgment of God has become a present reality, and a favorable one at that. Humans are not just judged; through Christ's death and resurrection they are redeemed.[27] They are saved, which is to say, brought into right relationship with God. So transformed, they are *enabled* to live a transformed existence.[28]

Justification, instead of being a legal act that focused on anthropological capabilities under the law, became a christological one that operated as a gift from God. "In the death of Jesus, God demonstrates his righteousness, which also benefits and claims every human being. This saving act is the basis for justification and reconciliation."[29] That means, of course, that there is no real separation for Paul between justification and sanctification. Sanctification, usually identified with ethics, is not a follow up to justification, but is an integral part of it. And thus, with Lohse, we can argue, pointing to 1 Thess 4:3, that God enables Christians to live holy lives. "Because they through baptism have become the property of God and the Lord, so that they now belong to him and are therefore 'holy,' their lives should correspond to this 'sanctification' that they have already experienced."[30]

This "enabling" is also boundary breaking. Paul himself makes the case at Rom 3:24-26:

> They are now justified by his grace as a gift, through the redemption that is in Christ Jesus, whom God put forward as a sacrifice of atonement by his blood, effective through faith. He did this to show his righteousness, because in his divine forbearance he had passed over the sins previously committed; it was to prove at the present time that he himself is righteous and that he justifies the one who has faith in Jesus.

Jesus is the *hilasterion* that the NRSV translates as a "sacrifice of atonement." Whether that definition is completely accurate or not, the editors have grasped the key point that it is through Christ's sacrifice that the debt of human sin has been paid, that the justification of humankind has been achieved. Humans have not obtained that status on their own lawful capabilities; God has done it for them. And, in so doing, God has also leveled the redemptive and social playing fields. Jews and Gentiles stand before God together; equal partners in sin *and* equal recipients of God's grace. In God's Christ act of redemptive atonement that brought humans back into right relationship with God, the social boundaries of ethnic divisiveness were also torn down. This, Tamez is right to say, is what Jesus as *hilasterion* fully means. "It thus expresses God's expiation by God's own deed, once and for all, of the sins of all humanity. In that way the expiatory role of the temple functionaries was annulled, and with it the ritual law, and salvation was thereby extended to all nations."[31]

The problem, of course, is that the present often looks like anything but an existence where humans are reconciled with God, and thereby brought into right relationship with one another. Paul's own letter to the Romans is a testament to the fact that the ethnic divide has not been bridged socially or theologically. Here, once again, Pauline theology offers a point of helpful clarification. This time the theological focus is on eschatology. As Lohse notes, the apostle's "ethical teaching was unfolded under the eschatological perspective of Paul's theology, which is closely related to Christology."[32]

The coming, death, and resurrection of Christ are now commonly acknowledged as apocalyptic events in Paul. Jesus' transition into human history sets off a chain of confrontational interactions between God's salvific intentions and the destructive intentions of the rulers and supernatural powers of the present age who back them. It is, of course, because of the recalcitrance and hostility of those ruling powers that Jesus is ultimately crucified. In their attempt to stop God's salvation bid, they vainly attempt to crush the man sent to implement it. Ironically, as 1 Corinthians 2 makes clear, it is the Christ act on the cross that anchors God's run at reconciliation, and thereby dooms the rulers and powers who had deployed it as their ultimate weapon. For, as 1 Corinthians 15 clears up, Jesus' resurrection is not an isolated event. When God raised Jesus from the dead God did not only demonstrate that the forces of this age have been unsuccessful in their attempts to throttle Jesus. God also foreshadowed through the hope of the general resurrection of all believers the divine promise that their attempts to shackle humankind to sin and death would fail as well.

This sense of foreshadowing in 1 Corinthians 15 is important because it maintains the force of future expectation in Paul that operates in tension with his understanding that in Christ's death and resurrection the power of the present rulers and the forces of sin and death that back them have been destroyed. As Elliott points out, Paul does not spiritualize matters by completely collapsing God's victory into the present. The Corinthians, of course, had done exactly this, and this is why their ethical predicament was so precarious. Believing themselves already spiritually safe and presently saved, they felt that their bodily behavior was no longer of any consequence and therefore no longer needed to be regulated. Paul's attempt to correct their theology is therefore also a stab at reforming their ethics. The present, in Jesus' resurrection, is only a foreshadowing of the future promise (which is the general resurrection of all believers) that God's plan of salvation will triumph. In the current time that triumph is only anticipatory; it is an eschatological, not a literal reality. Presently, the apocalyptic struggle between God and the forces that rule this age goes on. "It is precisely Paul's own insistence that the powers remain unconquered until 'the end,' when they meet their decisive defeat at God's hands, that resists any narrowly spiritual interpretation of the Powers. Paul interprets Jesus' death *as the beginning of God's final 'war of liberation' against all the Powers that hold creation in thrall* through the instruments of earthly oppression."[33]

Ethically, this recognition of Paul's apocalyptic theology has two important consequences. First, it once again demonstrates Paul's boundary-breaking intentions. His understanding of the cross brings people of all cultures, nationalities, and ethnicities together in the same God directed struggle for the justification of humankind. What Elliott says about the connection of the Corinthians with the circumstances in Judea applies to all who give credence to the apostle's apocalyptic scenario. In the cross, God has taken a mighty, and ultimately decisive, swing against the powers on behalf of *anyone anywhere* who casts his or her lot with what to the world appears to be a foolish and stumbling act of divine assistance.

Far from "denationalizing" the cross, Paul has, so to speak, interna-
tionalized it. He insists that the Roman colonists of Corinth, thousands of miles from the trouble in Judea, must mold their lives into
a constant remembrance of one particular crucifixion in Judea,
because through that crucifixion God has revealed the imminent
end of the Powers and has begun to bring "the scheme of this
world" to an end (1 Cor 7:31).[34]

The cross has become a redemptive marker that extends beyond all
social, cultural, geographical, political, and even temporal divides.
It has not only broken the back of the powers who would keep
humans separate from God; it has decimated the boundaries they
set up to divide humans from each other.

The second ethical consequence applies particularly to Paul's
communicants at Corinth but extends to believers everywhere. Even
though in Christ's death and resurrection God's positive judgment
has already occurred and justification has already been effected,
Paul realizes that believers must still be challenged and exhorted to
proper ethical living. What appears on the surface to be a contradic-
tion (why should a transformed people constantly require the challenge to live transformed lives?) becomes clear eschatologically. As
Paul understands it, humans are caught up in a reality of two ages.
In Christ, there is the breakthrough of a new creation (2 Cor 5:17);
the day of salvation has arrived (2 Cor 6:2). According to Romans 8,
believers participate through the Holy Spirit with Christ in this
promised inheritance.[35] And yet, the old age persists. Believers are
caught between the two, living partially in both, fully in neither.[36]
Tossed and turned, pushed and pulled, they require guidance. This
eschatological tension is the theological grounding for Paul's constant ethical exhortations. The people who are justified (Rom 8:1-4),
freed from sin (Rom 6:22), transformed into a new being in Christ
(Rom 12:2; 2 Cor 3:18), and are, therefore, theologically enabled to
live transformed lives are themselves caught up in an only partially
transformed existence. Because, though justified, they are not yet
saved (Rom 5:9-10), they are always vulnerable, always in need of
the kind of encouragement that Paul's letters faithfully bring (Rom
6:12; 13:11-14). They are capable of meeting Paul's high ethical
expectations, though, because, through God's Christ act, they are
dead to sin, and therefore as vulnerable to God as they are to the
powers that oppose God (Rom 6:11).

Enabling

Saying this, of course, moves us from Pauline theology into Pauline anthropology. In other words, we are now at the point of clarifying exactly how Paul's understanding of God and God's actions through Christ Jesus enable human ethical activity. The key is baptism. Baptism gives human beings citizenship in the new age even as they continue living in the old. It does so metaphorically. That is to say, Jesus' death becomes a metaphor for our own. To be sure, as many critics have observed with regard to the Philippians Christ hymn (Phil 2:5-11), humans cannot imitate the degree of Christ's self-emptying. Clearly, Paul cannot be asking humans to relinquish the kind of status that Jesus himself relinquished; we cannot give up what we do not have, divinity. But Jesus' action can become a metaphor for our own; we can empty ourselves of what we hold most dear in the same way that Jesus emptied himself of his heavenly identity and status. In so doing, we can participate in Christ's obedience.

In a similar, metaphorical way, we can, through faith, in the act of baptism, participate even in Christ's death. Romans 6:2-10 is as clear as crystal; in baptism we are crucified, we are killed, and we are buried with Christ. His death becomes our own. And just as his death projected him not into destruction, as the rulers of this age would have hoped, but into the future promise of a resurrected age, so, too, as Rom 6:5 and 1 Corinthians 15 confirm, does our death with him give us a share in the future to which he was raised. It is at this point in Romans 6 that Paul demonstrates precisely how theology enables humans to live ethically. At Rom 6:4, he makes the connection in a telling proclamation: "Therefore we have been buried with him by baptism into death, so that, just as Christ was raised from the dead by the glory of the Father, so we too might walk in newness of life."

Baptismal theology enables a new, "baptized" ethic. The old self, the one connected to the power of sin, has been crucified in the sacramental act; a new self freed from sin has been enabled. "Therefore," the apostle exhorts, "do not let sin exercise dominion in your mortal bodies, to make you obey their passions" (Rom 6:12); for "those who belong to Christ Jesus have crucified the flesh with its passions and desires" (Gal 5:24). Through baptism the believer has been set free, released from bondage to sin, enabled to serve the Lordship of Christ. This is why it is incomprehensible for Paul that a believer would want to take advantage of his or her salvific circumstance and sin all the more so that grace would have an opportunity to abound (Rom 6:1). Grace is to be lived, not abused.[37]

Clearly, Paul's understanding of God has a direct bearing on his expectations for human living. Dead in Christ, humans are therefore dead to sin, and, thus, no longer enslaved to its power. But, as flesh-and-blood creations caught in the squeeze between two competing aeons, they do remain vulnerable. This is not to say that Paul understands that the human body and human flesh are inherently evil. The apostle does not share the Greek dualistic understanding that envisioned a good spirit trapped in an evil biological frame. Indeed, his sense of creation theology would have mitigated against such a view; God created the physical body and the human flesh. It would have been unthinkable to Paul that God had created an evil reality.

This theological discussion also had a direct bearing on the way in which Paul understood ethics. Marxsen points, for example, to the very dualistic anthropology evident in Paul's Corinthian congregants. The Corinthians believed that the soul was locked in the body. The soul was the arena of salvation and the body the arena of ethics. But since only the soul mattered, ethics became inconsequential. When Paul fought such an understanding by appealing to creation theology, he also re-enabled the possibility for Corinthian ethics. "Thus in contrast to the Corinthian anthropology, he tries to upgrade the body. In so doing Paul brings in the concept of creation, which is unknown in the context of dualistic anthropology. It is required, however, by Paul's concept of God. There is nothing that is not from God. In this way body and soul can be treated together. Ethics becomes possible again."[38]

In addition, Paul's incarnational and resurrection thinking would never have jibed with Greek skepticism about the body. Jesus, of course, in emptying himself took on the form of a human body. And, as White points out, the body that is dignified by the incarnation is also sanctified as the temple of the indwelling Spirit. It can be yielded to God so that its members can become instruments of righteousness; it is destined to be raised incorruptible.[39]

As 1 Corinthians 15 makes clear, Paul expected a bodily resurrection. The resurrected body would have been spiritual, yes, but it was most certainly and unashamedly a body. "Therefore the person before faith is not only a sinner but also a sinful body" (Rom 6:6). And therefore Christians do not look forward to redemption *from* the body, but redemption *of* the body (Rom 8:23; cf. Phil 3:21).[40]

For Paul, then, flesh and body do not equal sinful and evil. Indeed, the apostle often uses both terms in neutral (1 Cor 5:3; 13:3; Gal 1:16) and even positive (1 Cor 6:17; 12:27; Gal 2:20; 6:17) ways. A comprehensive review of his use of the terms indicates instead that for him flesh and body indicate the "humanness" of the created nature.[41] Flesh is the human being in his or her physical totality, and body is the frame that incorporates and gives it shape and substance. Flesh, then, is not evil; it is simply human, or to be more precise, "humanness." The problem is that it is this very "humanness" that makes a person vulnerable to the power of sin (cf., Gal 5:13,16,17, 19, 24; 6:8). "To yield to these powers, thus rejecting the sovereignty of God's claim, is to live 'according to the flesh' rather than 'according to the Spirit,' and to allow 'sin' and 'death' to take over."[42] It is this vulnerability that dying with Christ in the act of baptism intends to overcome, not by refashioning flesh into spirit, but by making flesh as vulnerable to the power and force of God's Spirit as it is to the power and force of sin. Through a believer's dying with Christ, God breaks him/her loose from enslavement to sin so that the opportunity to be attached to an other, competing power becomes possible instead. In baptism, the believer is given just such an opportunity to be as vulnerable to God as he or she once was to sin. In other words, the believer is ethically enabled.

That is to say, through God's Christ act of death and resurrection, and the believer's participation in that act through baptism, believers are ethically enabled to yield their fleshly bodies to the work of Christ. Faithfully empowered, they are physically enabled to live the spiritual life that Christ himself modeled. Certainly, this is what Paul means when he declares at Rom 6:10-13 that

> The death he died, he died to sin, once for all; but the life he lives, he lives to God. So you also must consider yourselves dead to sin and alive to God in Christ Jesus. Therefore, do not let sin exercise dominion in your mortal bodies, to make you obey their passions.

No longer present your members to sin as instruments of wicked-
ness, but present yourselves to God as those who have been brought
from death to life, and present your members to God as instruments
of righteousness.

Why can Paul realistically expect a positive response to his ethical exhortation even from fleshly humans living in a sinful age?
Because those humans have been transformed *in the flesh* through
Christ. This is how Pauline theology slides safely home into
Pauline anthropology. We have already learned that humans are
too caught up in a sinful age, too vulnerable to the powers of sin
to engineer their own salvation. Paul himself, as a loyal Pharisee,
once thought such a human orchestrated turn of righteousness
could be accomplished through the Torah. "In the teaching of the
synagogue, the reminder of future judgment was bound up with
the exhortation to a pious life corresponding to the conditions of
the law."[43] But the Law, he came to see, could not do the very
thing its adherents desired; it could not justify human beings. It,
therefore, could not enable ethical living. From God's perspective,
its rightful place had always been as a disciplinarian, a gift to keep
human wrongdoing in check until such time that a righteous God
acted to bring humans into right relationship with God, and thus
enabled them to live ethically before God and with one another.
Humans, though, came to misread the code. Over time, from their
perspective, the law's goal became justification, this bringing of
humans into right relationship with God. But the law's power was
limited because the law's efficacy rested upon human responsibility. The law could only justify if humans were capable of living
up to the demands that the law had set forth. But sinful humans
living in a sinful age found themselves incapable of living up to
the law's demands (Rom 3:9-10, 23; 7:14-21; Gal 3:10, 21-22). The
more they tried to meet its legal requirements, the more they
found themselves distanced from its difficult goals. The law suc-
ceeded not in justifying humans but in demonstrating to them just
how far from justification they were. They were so incapable of
meeting the requirements of the law, so sinful, that any hope of
obtaining a right relationship with God for most was impossible.
In fact, those who continued to press the cause ended up with
destruction instead. "For, since humanity had been misled by the
false hope that they could attain life by works of the law, they

were in fact not led to life, but inescapably delivered over to death."[44] Even those who, like Paul himself evidently, somehow found it possible to overcome their sinful proclivities and meet every demand that the law required (Phil 3:6) found that they had achieved a legal status of superiority but not a realization of right relationship with God (Phil 3:7-14). This is what Paul came to see as the problem of the law. Though it had been given as a disciplinary tool by God (Gal 3:19, 24), it was received by humans as a medium of salvation. But it could not accomplish the goal humans had set for it. And therein lay the crisis in which Paul himself was caught up as he pushed himself past his Damascus Road experience and turned toward a belief in Christ Jesus. Christ Jesus, he came to understand, did what the law could not. Christ Jesus fulfilled the goal humans had given the law; thus in Christ Jesus the law was fulfilled. In Christ Jesus the goal of the law had been accomplished (Rom 10:4). But humans had not earned that goal. God had given it freely (Rom 1:17; Gal 5:5). Humans could only appropriate it faithfully.

The role of the law, at least from God's perspective, then, need not change (see Rom 3:31: "Do we then overthrow the law by this faith? By no means! On the contrary, we uphold the law"). The law remained a disciplinarian. In such a role the law is good (Rom 7:12: "So the law is holy, and the commandment is holy and just and good"; Paul points out further in this text that sin used the law as a tool of death. It is sin, a key power in this sinful realm, that is evil, not the law). Its realm remains that of the flesh; its task continues to be that of checking the tendencies of the flesh, because the flesh is so susceptible to the power of sin. But those who had been transformed by God, those who had been justified by God's actions in Christ, no longer needed a disciplinarian (Gal 3:25-26). Though still living in the flesh, they did not have to be forced into living ethically; they were enabled to live ethically because they had been transformed. They were freed from using the law as an ill fated means of salvation, and even freed from needing to use it as a disciplinarian.[45] They operated on a higher standard, that of faith. They were re-shaped. Brought into right relationship with God, justified through God's Christ-act, they were recut into spiritual beings. Their enslavement to sin was shaved away. The possibility of living for God was empowered so that they were now able to present their bodies as instruments for righteousness (Rom 6:15-18, 22; 14:8; Phil 2:12-13).[46] The people of God had been enabled.

And with their enablement, the people of God were also broadened. The boundary that the law helped impose between ethnicities crumbled alongside the belief that it could effect salvation. No where is this boundary-crossing emphasis on clearer display than in Paul's brief correspondence to the church at Galatia. Here the Jewish/Gentile issue takes center stage. The letter opens with the immediate presumption of a grave crisis (1:6-9); people have entered the community teaching a radically different gospel. Paul's work of bringing together Jew and Gentile into the same community of faith is in jeopardy, at least in the manner that he had envisioned. His opponents in Galatia agree that Jews and Gentiles may worship together in one community of faith. They, however, demand that Gentiles earn that inclusion by adhering to all of the expectations of the Jewish Law, particularly the ritual components dealing with circumcision and dietary matters. Paul, though, is already on written record in his correspondences to Thessalonica (1 Thess 2:12; 3:3; 4:7; 5:9, 24)[47] and Corinth (1 Cor 2:2) arguing that inclusion into the people of God is based on God's election through the gospel of Christ, specifically the gospel that records Christ's death on the cross. It is God's action, through Christ that determines one's inclusion into the people of God, not one's adherence to and compliance with the Jewish Law.

Focusing particularly on circumcision, Paul presses his point by demonstrating that faith is the measure of one's standing before the Lord (2:1-21). Appealing to Abraham as a model, he argues that one is determined to be righteous in God's sight through faith and not through accomplishing works of the law (3:1-29). In other words, what Paul once declared in his Thessalonian and Corinthian correspondences through the language of election and sanctification, he now proclaims in Galatians through the language of justification by faith.[48] Just as Abraham believed God and was reckoned as righteous well before his compliant act of circumcision, so also the one who is made righteous through faith in God's work through Jesus Christ is the one who will live in harmony and right relationship with God (3:11).

Of course, Paul's challenge to the Law and his championing of justification by faith can be, and very often has been, seen very individualistically as a matter of personal redemption, as though God's field of concern were limited to the justification of sinful individuals alone. There are, however, other considerations; there is yet more potential to be explored. A look at Galatians through a liberation lens suggests that a social and political boundary-breaking edge courses through Paul's theological discussion. "However, whereas the more traditional Reformation approach tends to view justification in terms of the sinful individual, the new perspective on Paul emphasizes the communal and social dimensions of justification: how one group of people is to relate to another."[49] Paul recognizes that "one group of Christians (Jewish Christians) attempted to impose its cultural and national identity upon another (Gentile Christians)."[50] The apostle handled this social and ethical crisis theologically. But it is theology with a potent socio-ethical edge. Indeed, if Gal 3:28 is to be taken seriously, a new kind of community must develop.

A community whose theology of justification by faith led to a social reality where slave and free, male and female, Jew and Gentile lived on an equal plane would have been a radically countercultural one indeed. The key though is that Paul's ethics for living here derive directly from his understanding of justification by faith. This theological understanding that results in the removal of the Law as the standard bearer for right relationship with God also opens up the possibility that Gentiles and Jews may *together* populate the people of God.

Paul makes this clear at the close of Romans 3 when he argues that the Jew no longer has room for boasting because the Law in which the Jew delighted does not possess the divisive ability it was once thought to have. Because it could not save the one people who held to it, it also could not keep them set apart as the one and only people acceptable before God. Surely, this is what he means when he writes:

> Then what becomes of boasting? It is excluded. By what law? By that of works? No, but by the law of faith. For we hold that a person is justified by faith apart from works prescribed by the law. Or is God the God of Jews only? Is he not the God of Gentiles also? Yes, of Gentiles also, since God is one; and he will justify the circumcised

on the ground of faith and the uncircumcised through that same
faith. (Rom 3:27-30)

The matter of circumcision and all the other ritual components
of the law, like dietary rules and Sabbath observance, that separated Jew from Gentile become symbolically important as Paul
moves on into his Romans 4 exegesis of Gen 15:6. There, once
again using Abraham as his prime witness, he takes the matter of
the law's ability to separate and divide head-on. Abraham was
considered righteous through his faith, well before his legal act of
circumcision represented his new status in the flesh. Circumcision,
then, a key ritual component of the law, which was also a preeminent physical marker of distinction between the ethnicities, no
longer had the kind of salvific power it was once thought to have.[51]
That distinction now belonged to a divinely enabled faith. Though
circumcision remained a physical marking in the flesh of some
note (Rom 3:1-2), it no longer counted as a work, indeed a critical
work, in one's progression toward a legally obtained justification.
Gentiles who did not become circumcised were thus no longer
automatically considered incapable of being part of the people of
God. The implications were huge; Gentiles were no longer considered ritually unclean by legal default. As Paul's argument in
Galatians 2 makes clear, they could, therefore, participate with
those who were circumcised and followed the other ritual requirements of the law in a free and unencumbered way. A more universal understanding about the human place before God and the
possibilities for humans living among each other was developing
instead. "For Christ is the end of the law so that there may be righteousness for *everyone* who believes" (Rom 10:4, italics added). In
other words, as Tamez interprets, justification by faith is, in its final
essence, a radical, boundary-breaking theological reality. "Paul
affirmed all peoples as equals, on the same plane in their relationship with God. With this theological principle the division of the
world's people into Jews and Gentiles was overcome, and the
Christian faith made universal, so that all people might have the
possibility of access to the promises made to Abraham."[52] In this
theological way a new anthropological reality was socially and
ethically enabled. This is why Paul can argue at Gal 6:15: "For neither circumcision nor uncircumcision is anything; but a new cre-

ation is everything!" and quite conclusively at 5:6: "For in Christ Jesus neither circumcision nor uncircumcision counts for anything; the only thing that counts is faith working through love."

Liberating Ethics

It is important that we hear what Paul is saying here. Faith works. It does not work to earn salvation. Neither does it work as a result of salvation. It works because justification is in its essential nature a kinetic, not a static reality. Or, as Furnish puts it, "Obedience is *constitutive* of the new life."[53] Paul's theology of grace is about enablement, not celebration. Believers are justified into a new reality where a new law holds sway. Paul calls it the law of faith (Rom 3:27). This "law of faith," is important because it lives itself out ethically as the "law of Christ." One's faith in God's Christ act of justification enables an ethical living that is driven by love. This love is enabled by faith, not requisitioned by the law. It is therefore more a fruit for Paul than it is a work. "In short, in Pharisaic ethics people must *change their ways* in order to accomplish works. In the Christian Paul's ethic people must *let themselves be changed*, so they can bear fruit."[54] This love that bears fruit is the "law of Christ" that Paul exhorts (Rom 13:9; Gal 5:14).

But, if Gal 3:28 is any guide, it is a love that realizes a radically unique ethical reality. "There is no longer Jew or Greek, there is no longer slave or free, there is no longer male and female; for all of you are one in Christ Jesus." Faith works itself out through love in an incredibly liberating, boundary-breaking, countercultural way. "In the one body of Christ, all secular categories are transcended, even distinctions inherent in the created order."[55] This is a crucial point. Paul's understanding of God's actions in Christ lead him to the almost insane conclusion that even the categories that God established in the act of creation have now been superseded. "The statement has been widely heralded as the 'Magna Carta of the New Humanity,' for it sets forth a relationship 'in Christ Jesus' in which believers through baptism not only have been 'united with Christ' and 'clothed with Christ' (v. 27) but also have entered into a new relationship of openness with one another."[56] The boundaries standardized for all time at the very beginning of time have been eschatologically smashed down in the act of Jesus' coming, death, and resurrection. Here is a place where Paul's Christ theology crashes hard up against his creation theology, shattering the territorial lines it imposed, redrawing the orders of separation it enacted, and, along the way, inaugurating the genesis of a very different kind of human social and ethical landscape.

How important was this new perspective for Christian understanding in the first century? The formulaic recording of such broken boundaries occurs in other Pauline (1 Cor 12:13) and post-Pauline (Col 3:11) materials alike. Longenecker concludes that the formula figured prominently in the baptismal liturgy of the early church. Given the celebrated role of baptism in clarifying the Christian's new reality, this is no small point. At the moment of theologically identifying themselves with the death and rebirth of Christ, Christians simultaneously declared a new social and ethical relationship of oneness in the human community.

> Regardless of how the specific details concerning the provenance of the confessions are to be settled, the point to note here is that when first-century Christians spoke of being "sons of God," "baptized into Christ," and "clothed with Christ" (3:26-27), they also spoke of their faith in terms of a new relationship socially in which there is "neither Jew nor Greek, slave nor free, male nor female" (3:28)— three pairings which cover in embryonic fashion all the essential relationships of humanity.[57]

The implications are staggering, for if indeed indicative and imperative are commingled in Paul's thought, then God's doing becomes the mandate for human living. The shattering of creation's boundaries that occurs with Jesus' death and resurrection is the gracious provocation of a new eschatological reality that enables human transgressions of the same kind. All people, regardless of gender, ethnicity, race, status, or stature are equally acceptable in God's sight and therefore must be equally treated in human living. *It is precisely here, through its boundary-breaking intent that Pauline theology enables liberating human ethics.*

> Rather, the cultural mandate of the gospel lays on Christians the obligation to measure every attitude and action toward others in terms of the impartiality and love which God expressed in Jesus Christ, and to express in life such attitudes and actions as would

break down barriers of prejudices and walls of inequity, without setting aside the distinctive characteristics of people.[58]

Nowhere is this Pauline concern to "break down barriers of prejudices and walls of inequity," on grander display than in his written material about food sacrificed to idols and the love feast that was connected early on with the Lord's Supper. In 1 Corinthians 11, the apostle demanded that the kinds of status separations that may have had significant meaning between non-Christians should not impact the manner in which Christian believers came together in the meal. Provisions must be made so that differences in social circumstance do not translate into differences in the way believers share with one another, particularly at a moment as critical as the meal. "Therefore to celebrate the Lord's Supper while disregarding social obligations perverts the celebration of the sacrament. Here, too, the sacrament has an ethical dimension encompassing everyday reality."[59] Since the most barbed comments are reserved for those in the more favorable status positions, Elliott is right, I think, to argue that Paul is ultimately bringing a challenge to the ideology of privilege. The ones who were socially privileged enough to arrive early and therefore imbibe all of the food are chastised for their callous disregard of their less fortunate brothers and sisters.

Just so, when he writes to both the Corinthian and Roman congregations about food sacrificed to idols, another issue that threatens to divide rather than unite communities of faith, Paul focuses his exhortations on the privileged. In this case, though, he targets those who consider themselves privileged with a stronger faith. They must alter their behavior. They must surrender their privilege to eat meat sacrificed to idols in order to protect the more fragile faith of those to whom such behavior was a sin. They must do so in order to enable unity. As Tamez points out, the entire meat-eating discussion shows that Paul's interest is in communal solidarity,[60] something that cannot occur where the ideology of social or spiritual privilege erects divisive boundaries.

It is important to view Paul's statement at Gal 3:28 in this way, as a part of his overall boundary-breaking theological perspective, so as to demonstrate that it is not an aberration in his thought, but is wholly representative of it. Indeed, the more one understands the theological foundations of Paul's ethics, the more one appreciates just how socially and politically liberative his ethics can be. Consider, for example, the foundational presence of the cross in Paul's thought. In fact, the cross is so instrumental that Elliott and Matera describe his as a cross ethics; "the cross becomes the ruling metaphor for Christian obedience."[61] Through baptism, in imitating Christ, believers are called to let their living experience a "death like his." It is the kind of living, as 1 Thess 1:6 proclaims, whose countercultural orientation of believing and acting against the socially expected behaviors connected to the worship of pagan deities that provokes and then endures the kind of persecution that Paul himself once inflicted.

In fact, the mere alignment of his theology with the language of the cross gave Paul's ethics a politically liberative bent right from the start. Few historians of reason would disagree that the Romans utilized crucifixion as a form of political and military terror. Targeted specifically against those who threatened imperial interests with sedition, insurrection, and even outright rebellion, this ancient form of capital punishment was as awash in politics as it was in blood. And there is more! Like contemporary capital punishment in the twenty-first-century United States, Roman crucifixion was a weapon wielded primarily against those of lower social, economic, political, and ethnic standing. "Crucifixion was the 'supreme Roman penalty,' yet 'almost always inflicted only on the lower class . . . the upper class could reckon with more 'humane' punishment (such as decapitation)."[62]

Not only, then, does the form of Jesus' execution place him in a social category with those whose lives or movements represented some sort of political threat; it also placed him in solidarity with the wretched who eked our their existences at the bottom of Greco-Roman society. Taken in this light, Paul's calls for unity and community as the one body of Christ (e.g., 1 Cor 12:3-16) formed through the image of a Christ *crucified* have a striking social and political emphasis that goes beyond merely holding a struggling church together. We are talking about a body that is to a large extent composed of what Greco-Roman society considered to be broken, or at the very least, damaged limbs. Indeed, the very fact that Paul considered it possible to combine not only Greeks and Jews, but slaves and free, women and men, those of lower and menial with those of upper and aristocratic status in one fellow-

ship of believers was damaging and threatening to the social cohe-
sion of a Greco-Roman life of patronage built upon and orchestrated by its various status differentiations.

> To be more precise, his vision of the world, which was a product of
> an environment that was oppressive and difficult for the poor, was
> markedly utopian: Paul longed for a society of equals where soli-
> darity would reign. If he had problems with his society, it was pre-
> cisely because his gospel required a practice that did not agree with
> the pattern of life of Greco-Roman society, where equality was
> almost inconceivable.[63]

How, then, could a first-century hearer of Paul's message of a
crucified Christ possibly miss the social implications? How could
his demand that they baptize themselves into a *death like his* not
have been heard as an ethics laced with transformative challenges
to the manner in which Greco-Roman life was lived? Surely, this is
what the apostle is exhorting in places like 1 Thessalonians and the
Corinthian and Roman correspondences when he reminds his followers to maintain their distance from idols and even all the social
and political perks that idol worship entailed. The same thing is
happening when he assures his readers that they will be saved
from the coming wrath of God "while destruction will come to
those who trust in the Roman imperial *peace and security.*"[64] The
cost for such countercultural intransigence and the threat it raised
to the cult-oriented symbolism of Roman rule was packaged in
Paul's language of expected persecution. Like Jesus, those who
would live in resistance to the social and religious norms of Greco-
Roman life, those who would act as if the social markings of male
and female, Jew and Gentile, slave and free were obsolete, would
face grievous forms of social and political retaliation. This, Paul
warned, was to be expected, and yet believers must continue to
live the kind of lives that provoked it, and, indeed, live it hopefully. Why? Because human power like Rome and the demonic
forces like sin and death that backed it up did not prove victorious
in their battle against Jesus. Jesus was raised by God into new life.
That resurrection is the eschatological assurance that Jesus, and
not the cross upon which he was impaled, would prevail.
Believers, then, were called to take sides with Jesus. They were
called to do so even knowing that once they did, in this life, in this

reality, such an ethical choice would almost guarantee social and political peril. In this life the cross prevailed, even as God's triumph was proclaimed.

> Paul heard in the proclamation of the crucified messiah an apocalyptic announcement and *thus a direct challenge to Rome*. If one crucified by Rome had been vindicated by God—vindicated *by being raised from the dead already*—then the "time given Rome" was at an end, the time of "the kingdom of the saints of the Most High" was at hand. The proclamation of the crucified was a declaration that the changing of the age was at hand."[65]

It is a proclamation of resistance that would be as much at home in the fiery prophecy of Revelation as it obviously is in the theologically enabled ethics of Paul.

Nowhere is this language of resistance more provocative, and controversial, than in the matter of slavery. If my reading is right, Gal 3:27-28 mandates that in and through baptism a person's status as a slave comes to an end. Though Paul's language here has been spiritualized, apparently almost from the moment he penned it, it is clear that the potential for a liberative social ethics is as real here as is the more universally recognized realization of "spiritual" equality. Elliott makes two appeals. First, he follows Allen Callahan's remarks about 1 Cor 7:22, where Callahan observes that in speaking of a baptized slave as becoming a "freedperson" of the Lord, Paul chooses a term that refers to manumission. Second, he points out that the early church father Ignatius was very much like the observant slave owners of the latter-day United States; he realized the liberative and therefore dangerous potential in Paul's language. Elliott, therefore, concludes that "a master's 'duty' to slaves, even to the extent of manumitting them, was among the expectations that Paul would have communicated to householders during their formation as Christians."[66]

Is such a read of Paul's language possible? This seems especially unlikely given the fact that in 1 Cor 7:17-24, where Paul speaks to the issue of slavery directly, he appears to counsel slaves to be happy maintaining their social status as they have it in anticipation of the imminently arriving eon of God's triumph. Only then would the world that Gal 3:28 represents be literally as well as "spiritually" realized. Paul's return of the slave Onesimus to his slave master Philemon makes matters even worse. The liberative potential, at least in this eon, seems radically limited.

But before we arrive at such a depressing conclusion, we ought to remember that what Paul says even in these particular moments ought to be considered in the larger light of a boundary-breaking theology that enables a transformative ethics. This realization alone guarantees a wider potential than is usually allowed. But, as Elliott and others point out, there are also contextual issues closer to home that allow for a more liberative potential in Paul's language regarding slavery and slaves. First, 1 Cor 7:17-24 ought to be seen in the light of its larger narrative context before ultimate conclusions are drawn about what it can possibly or possibly not mean. Once again building from work pioneered by Amos Jones, Jr.,[67] Elliott reminds us to consider Paul's use of language carefully. He is particularly concerned about the language of *klēsis*, or calling. In English, he points out, calling can refer to one's occupation or "station in life." But this connection does not hold in the Greek usage of early Christianity. "In fact throughout early Christian literature, and particularly Paul's letters, *klēsis* means one thing: the 'calling' to belong to Christ."[68] If he is right, then Paul's statement that a person should remain in his or her calling would not necessarily refer to his or her slave station in life. Instead, it would refer to one's calling "to belong to Christ, or (at Rom 11:29) the analogous "calling" of Israel."[69] In such a scenario, when Paul says at 7:20 that each person should remain in the "calling" to which they were called, he has their original place of orientation toward God in mind instead. Such would make sense, of course, in the light of Paul's attempt to bring Jew and Gentile *together* into the body of Christ. Never does he attempt to make the believing Jew a believing Gentile or the believing Gentile a believing Jew. Each should abide in the "calling" in which they were called. The message here is a positive, boundary-breaking one, not a limiting one. He's not trying to make everyone the same; he's trying to get different peoples to worship the same Christ, *together.* That's the liberating point. Because to accomplish his goal he must break down the institutionalized boundaries that culture, politics, and religion have erected between them.

A broader look at 1 Corinthians 7 seems to support such a reading. As Elliott, Jones, and Schüssler Fiorenza point out, nowhere in the entire chapter does Paul argue that believers be limited to their current "stations in life." "In fact, *the whole chapter is structured by a series of concessions, in each of which Paul allows, in the light of circumstance, an alteration to his personal preference for conduct or lifestyle.*"[70] Unmarried widows are allowed to marry, though Paul would rather they not; wives are allowed to remain separated from their husbands, though Paul counsels against it; believers are allowed divorce from their pagan partners, though the apostle abhors divorce; and marriage itself is allowed, though Paul himself would opt against it. In each case, Paul allows for a transformation in "stations of life." Incredibly, some of those stations, like marriage (and divorce), are ones in which the Lord himself would have resisted change. Schüssler Fiorenza goes even further. She points out correctly that "Paul clearly does not advise the former Jew or the former gentile to remain in their Jewish or pagan state."[71] It seems highly unlikely that Paul would hold a view for slaves, that they faithfully maintain their present "station in life" as a matter of faith, that he does not hold for anyone else.

The possibilities for interpreting 7:21-22 are now opened up immeasurably. We have not come to the conclusion that they *must* be interpreted in a liberating manner, but we have rejected the conceit that they cannot be so interpreted. As volumes of scholarship have shown, the interpretative problem rests with the manner in which an interpreter translates the phrase *mallon chrēsai* in 7:21. Loosely translated, the contested phrase means something like "take advantage of." The question is, advantage of what? There are two probable options; each one dramatically alters the way in which the verse is ultimately translated. If the object of the phrase is "slavery," then the verse would read something like, "even if you can become free, make use of your slavery instead." But if the object of the phrase is "freedom," then the verse would have an exactly opposite, liberative meaning: "if you can become free, then do [take advantage, make use of] it." Traditional interpretations have favored the former translation. Now that we know that there is a broader meaning for "calling" than traditional interpreters have always believed, as well as a broader, boundary-breaking theology into which that "calling" fits, the probability for the more liberative interpretation increases. What seems to be less probable is a Pauline world where a boundary-breaking life dedicated to Christ and a life lived in slavery could co-exist.

> In effect, slaves live in two worlds: on the one hand, they are a member of the *ekklesia*; on the other hand, they continue as slaves in the world. The slaves return to their master, in keeping with their obligations, to become totally subject to him as the *dominus*, lord and master. They must participate in the family worship of images and celestial beings and hold the emperor to be divine. Then, when the church meeting is held, the slaves return to the congregation to worship Jesus the Savior of their souls, who only has fit them for heaven.[72]

Imagine the unacceptable lifestyle and the resulting kinds of problematic behaviors that slaves attached to pagan masters would be obliged to perform. Imagine even the difficulty of deferring to the lordship of a Christian master when one's only enslavement was supposed to be to Christ. Could the apostle who did not even want people eating meat sacrificed to idols because of the problems such actions could cause tolerate slaves beholden to earthly masters?

Paul's letter to Philemon offers a similarly complicated perspective on the apostle's position regarding slavery. The traditional view has been that Paul simply returned Onesimus to his owner, Philemon, thereby acknowledging the efficacy of the laws that enslaved him, even if he did try to ameliorate matters in this particular situation by asking the master to treat his slave as a brother in Christ. "Rather than engaging in a head-on confrontation with slavery, Paul sought to elevate the quality of personal relationships within the existing structures of society."[73]

Even here, though, there is dramatic liberative potential that enables Paul's thought to be consistent with the boundary-breaking theology that characterizes him overall. First, most interpreters argued, Onesimus is a runaway. That identification in itself would have put him in a very precarious situation. Runaways were treated harshly as criminals in the Roman world.[74] Added to this is the thought that this runaway who had most certainly "stolen himself" from his master's employ may have stolen money or material as well (Philemon 18). Paul's call for a pardon subverts the socio-political expectations and ethics of the time. Or, as Schrage puts it, "Paul's asking pardon for the runaway (Philem.

12, 17) shows that love does not leave sociological and legal customs untouched; it penetrates and shapes the structures of society."[75] But there is more. The manner of Paul's appeal initiates a faith transformation that implies a substantial shift in a key societal structure. As Jones observed earlier, when Paul asks Philemon to treat Onesimus as a "brother" he is asking for a dramatic change in how the two men must now relate to one another in the faith community to which they belong (Philemon 2). This is something more than Paul's request that Onesimus be released to God's service with the apostle; it is also an indication that the "station in life" which Onesimus formerly occupied was no longer consistent with who and what he now was in Christ, and that the entire community of faith, not just Philemon alone, must recognize it.

Allen Callahan wants to push that liberative potential even further.[76] He challenges the very notion that Onesimus is a runaway or even a slave at all. In fact, he notes that it is not until the late fourth century that John Chrysostom initiates the novel, unsubstantiated view of Onesimus's identity as a slave. Attempting to thwart Christian libertarians who maintained that faith in Christ was incommensurate with the lived reality as a slave, Chrysostom, according to Callahan, appealed to Paul's letter as a way of supporting the status quo of slavery and thereby defusing the possibility that Christianity could be seen as championing the subversion of the present order. Obviously, proslavery forces in the American antebellum South picked up on such a perspective and mined it for all it was worth. But this does not change the fact, Callahan argues, that nothing in the language of the letter confirms that Onesimus was a slave. In fact, he points out that Paul calls Onesimus Philemon's brother in the flesh as well as in the Lord. The critical reference, he notes, is in verse 16, where Paul uses the language "as a slave." Callahan argues that "as" here is more important than "slave," for Paul is making a rhetorical, not a literal argument. His point? Onesimus should no longer be treated as someone subordinate, but as someone equal to Philemon because of his status in Christ. Such an argument, of course, would be quite commensurate with Paul's boundary-breaking message throughout.

And this is the point I wish to make with regard to Paul's standing on slavery. The potential for a liberative interpretation exists.

Why is this helpful? Because the act of interpretation is one of gauging which potential understanding is more probable within a given set of interpretative parameters. I have been pressing throughout this chapter that Pauline ethics must be understood in the light of the theological context in which it is situated. In that context, with its absorbing boundary-breaking tendencies, I would argue that the liberative options for interpretation in the matter of slavery are just as probable, and indeed more so, than the traditional interpretations that would oppose them. In other words, I have been trying to demonstrate that not only does such a liberative potential exist, but that, given the overall character of Paul's theologically enabled ethics, it would have been accessed as the most meaningfully interpretative option by Paul's earliest readers, and thus can certainly be so accessed by us.

Sometimes

Obviously, the African American slaves were not impressed. Paul clearly was no abolitionist, and though his writings, at least when accessed through a liberative, African American lens, do suggest a liberative critique and challenge, Paul apparently did not possess the full ethical courage of his Gal 3:28 convictions. If Callahan is wrong and traditional interpreters are right, Onesimus would be a good case in point. The African American slaves utilized running away as a primary form of resistance against the institution of chattel slavery. An entire underground network railroaded fugitives who by their very act of flight risked their lives trying to reach safe houses and later free destinations in the northern United States and Canada. The "ethical" act of sending a slave back, for whatever religious or spiritual reason, would have been absolutely unthinkable. Even in the most charitable liberative light, then, if Onesimus was a slave, Paul's move to return him to his owner would have been, at least to the slaves, ethically incomprehensible. The fact that assembled slaves walked out on a South Carolina Philemon sermon testifies to the validity of such a conclusion. Indeed, it was precisely at the point where the preacher began to use the letter to Philemon as the grounds against running away that many of the slaves gathered themselves, got up, and ran away from his service and the Paul on whom he had prepared it.

Paul, then (and this is certainly no revelation!), is not a monolith; though a strong boundary-breaking tendency runs through his theology and so enables a liberating ethics, he is by no means himself always a voice of social and political liberation. There are times when he is as forceful as can be about breaking down the barriers that isolate humans from God and from each other, and other times when he allows those barriers to stand. As Longenecker notes, Paul's "perception was not anywhere as clear or his actions anywhere as decisive in this area [of slavery] as it was with respect to the principle 'neither Jew nor Greek'" (cf. Rom 1:29-31; 13:13; 1 Cor 5:10-11; 6:9-10; 2 Cor 6:6; 12:20-21; Gal 5:19-23). The man who penned Gal 3:28 is the same man who did not speak out against slavery and who may have even returned a runaway slave to his master and left the adjudication of the slave's status in that master's hands.

Why this kind of complexity? I think, as I have already noted, that the answer lies in the fact that his ethics are enabled by his theology, and his theology is also not monolithic. The creation theology, for example, that was so instrumental in checking the negative Greek dualism that degraded the body in favor of a pure and interior soul, was also instrumental in setting up the very categories of theological order that enabled particular divisions of social status. When the apostle made his theological moves here, rather than from his focus on what God had done and was doing through Christ Jesus, the liberative potential in his ethics suffered dramatically.[77] As his appeal to standard virtue and vice lists demonstrate,[78] when operating from this perspective Paul was much more likely to entertain and accept the ethical standards of the surrounding society. This tendency is quite evident in particular ethical categories where creation theology was the apostle's primary working program. "Paul's attitude toward work, marriage, and the state also shows that we must not be too hasty in ignoring the structures and circumstances of the life we have received from the Creator."[70]

The status of women is illustrative. Because I agree with the bulk of scholarship that understands the very hostile statements in 1 Cor 14:34-35 to be a later interpolation to Paul's work, I shall not consider it here. But even without that remark, from a liberative standpoint, Paul offers us a rather checkered portrait. On the one hand, it seems clear that he has taken his own manifesto at Gal 3:28 to heart. Women, it seems are considered fellow workers with Paul himself (Rom 16:3; Phil 4:2-3). Many appear in leadership positions in the various church communities (Rom 16:1, deacon; 16:7, apostle). The female leaders appear to be co-equals with their male counterparts. They prophesy and speak as authoritative voices in worship (1 Cor 11:5). Truly, in matters of practice, it seems, in Christ there is no male or female; a key creation status of distinction has been destroyed.

And yet, in crucial moments of discussion and decision making, Paul seems to end up arguing with himself about just how far this break down of boundaries can be taken. As he waffles in 1 Cor 11:2-16, it becomes clear that the hold his creation theology has on his ethics can be, at least from a liberative standpoint, as disabling as his Christology is in other places enabling. "More important, however, is the nature of the justification Paul gives for his ruling. He clearly injures his own case, not arguing on his usual high level."[80] Scholars can protest all they want about Paul here being concerned more about men and women disgracing themselves in worship through improper attire than about establishing orders of relationship between men and women. But the fact remains that Paul clearly argues from a perspective of created orders that has God first, men second, and women deriving from them both (v. 7). Verse 3 ("But I want you to understand that Christ is the head of every man, and the husband is the head of his wife, and God is the head of Christ") and verses 8-9 ("Indeed, man was not made from woman, but woman from man. Neither was man created for the sake of woman, but woman for the sake of man") frame the discussion about the head coverings and thus orient it, and those verses are concerned with the ordered relationship between men and women, an ordering that places men literally and figuratively at the head. Verse 10 ("For this reason a woman ought to have a symbol of authority on her head, because of the angels") establishes a preliminary conclusion to the matter based on the issue of authority that is itself earlier derived from the distinct orders established at creation.

No sooner, though, than one has Paul pegged as a creation theologian whose theology disables any pretense of liberative thought, in verse 11, he turns to a christological formulation ("Nevertheless, in the Lord") that once again shatters status boundaries and brings men and women into equal partnership with one other and therefore gives them equal responsibility toward one another. It even appears, if verse 12 ("For just as woman came from man, so man comes through woman; but all things come from God.") is to be a guide, that even the created orders themselves are reevaluated. All things come from God. No longer does one repeat the creation myth that woman came through man and not the other way around (Gen 2:21-25); men and women come mutually through each other. "These words in fact contradict v. 8 and in effect retract what has already been said, even though Paul does not surrender his position (cf. vv. 13-16)."[81] Apparently, at least in this matter, Paul cannot accept the ethical consequences of emancipation that his own radical christology has enabled.

The same confliction haunts Paul in his discussions on church and state. I have noted earlier that much of what Paul expected from his followers was contrary to the expectations the Greco-Roman world had for its citizens and subjects. Indeed, in some cases Paul's apocalyptic faith claims would have enabled such a radical resistance to the ethos of the surrounding culture that I dared compare him to the witness of resistance that we find in Revelation. But that does not sound at all like the Paul who penned Rom 13:1-7, where Christians are to subject themselves unconditionally to the authority of the state. Here, as Schrage and others point out, the apostle seems more inclined to operate from principles of creation and then the ethics of the surrounding culture than from the provocative Christology that enables a more liberative ethics.

> There can be no doubt as to Paul's interest: the subordination of Christians must agree with the ordered disposition ordained by God. This subordination includes the hierarchy of office holders, authorities, officials, magistrates, and the like. . . . The proper attitude of Christians, like others, to the civil authorities is subservience. . . . What subservience means is "participation in an order established by God."[82]

The traditional interpretation has been that because Paul believed God's triumph was imminent a believer could and should endure the state as a temporary fixture at best. One need not, therefore, strive against it since its time was in any case quite limited. This "interim ethic" position is, however, no longer the only theory that seeks to explain Rom 13:1-7. There have, of late, been attempts to see Paul's counsel here in a more charitable light. Certainly, it is the case that Paul is speaking occasionally here as in all of his letters, and is thus not making a universal proclamation about church state matters for all time. But this does not dismiss the fact that for his particular place and time he here champions a conservative stance toward the state that seems to contradict his own more challenging perspectives to it elsewhere. This is why some exegetes have argued that perhaps the apostle meant in this very particular situation to prevent a tragedy in the life of the Roman congregation and therefore, out of social necessity, counseled an ethics of unconditional subservience. Elliott, for example, envisions a circumstance seen against the contextual backdrop of Claudius's expulsion of Jews from the city because of their conflict over a certain "Chrestus."[83] In an attempt to head off any such future exile, Paul in effect asks the Roman Christians to lay low. This would mean that because the Jewish and Gentile combatants put an end to their internal bickering over matters of faith, the united community would give the Roman government no other cause to consider it a contentious and threatening entity. It would have been for this very practical reason that Paul encouraged the believers in Rome to obey the government and show themselves responsive to it.

I doubt the slaves who walked out on the Philemon sermon would have been impressed with the latter-day scholarly attempts to rehabilitate Paul's counsel to unconditional subservience. In fact, it is just this kind of Pauline (creation) theologically enabled ethics that made the slaves and the freedmen and women who looked back upon their lives as slaves hesitant about reading and studying Paul as a biblical and apostolic authority. Still, if they had engaged him, with the kind of illiterate clarity and sophistication that they brought to their song, sermon, and written study of other biblical materials, I think they might have wondered where their point of departure with Paul actually took place. For, like the apostle, they found themselves occupied and oppressed by an imperial authority. Furthermore, like Paul, they believed that such human authorities were orchestrated by satanic principalities and powers that were not sympathetic to the designs God had for creation. It was for this reason that they resisted, and, they might have reasoned, Paul would have counseled resistance as well. Certainly, such resistance risked the possibility of persecution and even death. But the slaves willingly faced this risk time and time again. So did Paul. And so did anyone who might have adhered to Paul's counsel in Thessalonica and Corinth. So, what happened here? Once again, at least where Romans 13 is concerned, Paul seems not to possess the liberative courage of his christologically enabled convictions.

The apostle is similarly conflicted on matters of marriage and human sexuality. Take, for example, his theologically enabled counsel at 1 Corinthians 7. In responding to a Corinthian view of extreme sexual asceticism, "that a man ought not to touch a woman," Paul, though himself an active proponent of celibacy (v. 7), opens up the possibilities for human living. Here, he's being consistent with the boundary-breaking, christologically enabled ethics that he has counseled elsewhere. Sexual asceticism, like any other "work" of the law, cannot earn justification before God. It should therefore not be used as a divisive weapon separating those who presume themselves saved from those whom the self declared righteous ones consider condemned.

The apostle goes on to press a case for mutual submission (v. 4). In reading these verses one gets the impression of equality between men and women; they have mutual obligations toward one another where matters of marriage and sexuality are concerned. What Paul wrote at Gal 3:28, he obviously here intends the Corinthians to live. "When spelling out those new relationships which are meant by God to exist in the fellowship established by God in Christ Jesus, Paul explicitly says that in the same way that Jews are to have no exclusive privilege over Gentiles and free men to have no exclusive advantage over slaves, so men are to have no exclusive prerogatives over women."[84]

That sounds grand, of course, but we know all too well that what Paul gives he also takes away later on in the letter at places like chapter 11. In fact, many would argue that the less than liberating ethics enabled by a focus on creation theology is evident already even here. One cannot help but notice how Paul links marriage to the checking of flaming passion in such a way that the "holy estate" appears to have more a defensive than a righteous purpose. Why might this be the case? For Paul "marriage is consonant with the created order; it is an effective barrier against the demonic power of unchastity and the triumph of evil."[85]

Schrage goes on to say that this "ordered" foundation for marriage does not exhaust its meaning; we have already seen that this is the case. Still, it is clear that even as Paul senses the liberative and boundary-breaking essence of marriage and sexuality and counsels his Corinthian adherents so, he cannot pull himself fully away from a creation orientation that maintains the kind of orders that perpetuate division rather than eliminate it.

The entire matter of homosexuality, which has been discussed at such great lengths that I see no need to detail it here,[86] follows this train of tortured apostolic thinking. It is clear that Paul condemns homosexual activity in the first century. The non-liberative reasons are once again associated most clearly with his understanding of creation theology. Sexuality, in this view, is an ordered function of reproduction and not relational intimacy; homosexual activity, which breaks down that order, is provoked by idolatry.

It is unclear, however, how the boundary-breaking apostle might deal with more contemporary issues regarding homosexuality as a way of life genetically predisposed, rather than as a compilation of idolatrous acts. Would the man who understood that God's act in Christ Jesus shattered ethnic, gender, social and political boundaries between human beings have allowed genetically prescribed sexual preference boundaries to stand instead? I am not sure of the answer, because, as I have been trying to show, I am simply not sure of Paul.

There is a common sports adage that comments on the future quality of a sports team's performance with the conditional statement, "it depends on which team shows up." I think I would have to give the same conditional response to the aforementioned question. What would Paul do were he hypothetically faced with the question of homosexual orientation and lifestyle as humans understand the reality today? It would depend, I think, on which theologically enabled Paul showed up.

A Concluding Thought

I have spent a great deal of time working in this chapter on Pauline ethics precisely because I do not think that as a whole the

African American community has spent enough time on it. I have tried to outline the reasons why I think this is the case, but, in so doing, I hope I have also suggested why African Americans must ratchet up their study of Paul. The liberative benefits that can be gleaned from his counsel are legion. Too often Paul has been a target of attack and derision, not only in African American slave accounts, but, as Jones pointed out over a decade ago, in the language and literature of African American scholarship as well. African American preachers too often use his words as uncritical supports for the less than liberative way in which the church works with women, gays and lesbians, church and state issues, and other matters of grave, contemporary social consequence. Paul, as Jones and Elliott argue, and as Tamez demonstrates, must be seen through his own writings, not through the canonical lens of the post-Pauline commentaries on him.

It would have been a tremendous historical gift if the African American slaves could have brought themselves to the point of this kind of creative, challenging engagement with Paul's writings. As Howard Thurman makes note in regard to the spirituals, they certainly possessed the necessary gifts of transformative interpretation. For indeed, not just Paul, but the entire corpus of biblical material was presented to them as supportive of their slave status and the slave society that institutionalized it. But they were able to see through the interpretative farce and, even in their imposed state of illiteracy, "read" the Bible in a provocatively liberative manner.

> The existence of these songs is in itself a monument to one of the most striking instances on record in which a people forged a weapon of offense and defense out of a psychological shackle. By some amazing but vastly creative spiritual insight the slave undertook the redemption of a religion that the master had profaned in his midst.[87]

Thurman's claim is endorsed by Vincent Wimbush in his introduction to *African Americans and the Bible*:

> Almost from the beginning of their engagement with it, African Americans interpreted the Bible differently from those who introduced them to it, ironically and audaciously seeing in it—the most

powerful of the ideological weapons used to legitimize their enslavement and disenfranchisement—a mirroring of themselves and their experiences, seeing in it the privileging of all those who like themselves are the humiliated, the outcasts and the powerless.[88]

Why could not the slaves see in and do with Paul what they were able to do successfully with the rest of the biblical tradition? I suspect that it was because they came to believe that the problem lay as much with Paul as it did with the perverted interpretations coming out of slaveholding Christianity. My effort in this chapter has been to demonstrate that while such an understanding is sometimes true, it is not always so, and, indeed, most of the time it is not. Paul's theological understanding of what God did in Christ Jesus enabled a boundary-breaking ethics with a strong liberative potential. Developing that potential is the task of the current African American church. It is a place where the church can build upon the rich and creative legacy its slave forefathers and mothers bequeathed it.

CHAPTER SIX

Revelation: The Witness
of Active Resistance

> My Lord, what a mornin,'
> My Lord, what a mornin,'
> My Lord, what a mornin,'
> When de stars begin to fall.
>
> You'll hear de trumpet sound,
> To wake de nations underground,
> Lookin' to my God's right hand,
> When de stars begin to fall.[1]

Those words represent a vision of hope for a world weary people. Like John who authored the Apocalypse, the Revelation of Jesus Christ that anchors the canonical Christian Bible, the slave singer-songwriters looked to the future because the present was so abhorrent. In fact, much of the slave imagery about the future is Revelation imagery: trumpets sound, stars fall, nations crumble, a Lamb arises, an altar appears, and a beaten, bloodied people sit vindicated upon it. Finally.

> John saw, Oh, John saw,
> John saw the holy number,
> Sitting on the golden altar,
> On the golden altar.
>
> Worthy, worthy is the Lamb,
> Is the Lamb, Is the Lamb,

> Oh, worthy, worthy is the Lamb,
> Sitting on the golden altar.
>
> Mary wept, an' Martha cried,
> Martha cried, Martha cried,
> Oh, weeping Mary weeps no more,
> Sitting on the golden altar.[2]

Perhaps in a world where desperation and death are intimate, though unwelcome, housemates, and hope is a faraway presence who keeps promising to visit but never does, all a people have are dreams and visions. Perhaps those dreams are like an opiate, a narcotic nirvana that strives spiritually even though those addicted to it know it will never reach reality. Perhaps what John saw on Patmos had no clear connection to the actual lives his people were living, except to divert their attention. Perhaps what the spiritual creators and singers envisioned averted the gaze of their listeners for a time without doing anything to change the horrors haunting their historical horizons. Perhaps John spouted painkiller prophecies and the slaves arranged for artistic, antebellum inoculations. Perhaps.

I do not buy it. I do not buy it because the people who lived the symbolic language also lived contrary lives of opposition to the political and religious powers in their respective worlds. John was not on Patmos because he saw visions. Indeed, according to his own recollection, it was only after he arrived that the visions occurred. He was on Patmos because he had himself witnessed to the very cause the visions were now exhorting upon others. So, too, is the case with the slave creators and singers of the spirituals. Harriet Tubman used them as a signal on the outlawed Underground Railroad. She did not use them to salve the wounds of an escapist people. She used them to engage, encourage, and inspire those who had risked their lives to flee their enslavement. Nat Turner did not create and sing spirituals like "Steal Away to Jesus" as an encouragement to hide black faces in the sand. He sang them to arouse black anger until it fought back against white oppression. These were not folk given to escapist tendencies; these were folk used to retorting, running, and rebelling. They employed their visions and dreams as weapons in a war of resistance; they unleashed them so as to unbind a people from their fear. A people who are assured of their standing and existence in the world to come are more likely to risk their standing in the present to secure their future. This, I believe, is what John and the slaves were doing; they were envisioning the future in the hopes that a people emboldened by the portrait they saw in their minds would use their lives as brushes to help draw it in their history. They were using their faith, through vision and song, to inspire their readers and listeners to hope, to endure, and, ultimately, to resist. Indeed, what George Cummings says about the slaves and their spirituals, he might very well just as accurately say about John and his revelation.

> The common black experience of tragic suffering lived in and through the dialectic of hope and resignation is set on a powerful journey in the context of worship, where a qualitative shift in the community's consciousness takes place and serves to liberate momentarily and keep alive the hope of permanent liberation.[3]

In other words, the visions do not just suggest a new future, in the lived experience of the worshiping community, they create the future within the present. It is as though a people occupied by the power and force of Rome can, already, in their moment of worship when they read John's Revelation, sense the liberation that God's triumph will bring. Just as a people devastated by slavery could, even as they worked the fields, tended the master's home and children, or endured the master's sexual and vindictive fury, be free in the North at the very moment they were shackled in the South. A taste of freedom, John knew, the slave singers understood is a powerful inducement for the solicitude of freedom. That is what those visions and these songs were all about.

I do not make these opening connections between the spirituals, just one of the many forms of slave narratives I have talked about in this work, and the Apocalypse because I believe that an uncritical parallel exists between them. Obviously, millennia separate them; they were written to and for people of vastly different circumstances and needs. And yet, there are striking correspondences between what John wrote and the slaves crafted, because there are striking correspondences between their two target audiences. In an earlier book, *Go Preach! Mark's Kingdom Message and the Black Church Today*, I attempted to demonstrate such a correspondence of relationships between the circumstance of contemporary

African Americans and the circumstance of Mark's reading community.[4] My primary interest was to demonstrate that the Roman occupation endured by Mark's readers corresponds to the "psychological occupation" that continues to haunt African Americans. If anything, the correspondences of oppression are even more striking when the historical circumstances of the slaves are included in the mix. John believed that he was writing to a people whose occupied lives were threatened at every turn; the creators of the slave narratives justifiably believed the same.

John's language about the suffering of God's people can be striking. Of that, there is no doubt. Consider the prophecy about the fate of two key witnesses who proclaim the lordship of Christ over against the lordship of Rome.

> When they have finished their testimony, the beast that comes up from the bottomless pit will make war on them and conquer them and kill them, and their dead bodies will lie in the street of the great city that is prophetically called Sodom and Egypt, where also their Lord was crucified. For three and a half days members of the peoples and tribes and languages and nations will gaze at their dead bodies and refuse to let them be placed in a tomb; and the inhabitants of the earth will gloat over them and celebrate and exchange presents, because these two prophets had been a torment to the inhabitants of the earth. (Rev 11:7-10)

Evidently, this was the fate of many who would dare make such a witness: "When he opened the fifth seal, I saw under the altar the souls of those who had been slaughtered for the word of God and for the testimony they had given; they cried out with a loud voice, 'Sovereign Lord, holy and true, how long will it be before you judge and avenge our blood on the inhabitants of the earth?' "(Rev 6:9-10).

There is language just as striking in the historical ledgers of the slave narratives. Consider the recounting of one Solomon Bradley who, when he was interviewed in South Carolina in 1863, was a twenty-seven-year-old slave who had recently joined a Union Army regiment.

> I went up to [Mr. Farrarby's] house one morning from my work for drinking water, and heard a woman screaming awfully in the

door-yard. On going up to the fence and looking over I saw a woman stretched out, face downwards, on the ground her hands and feet being fastened to stakes. Mr. Farrarby was standing over and striking her with a leather trace belonging to his carriage-harness. As he struck her the flesh of her back and legs was raised in welts and ridges by the force of the blows. Sometimes when the poor thing cried too loud from the pain Farrarby would kick her in the mouth. After he had exhausted himself whipping her he sent to his house for sealing wax and lighted a candle and, melting the wax, dropped it upon the woman's lacerated back. He then got a riding whip and, standing over the woman, picked off the hardened wax by switching at it. Mr. Farrarby's grown daughters were looking at all this from a window of the house through the blinds. The punishment was so terrible that I was induced to ask what offence the woman had committed and I was told by her fellow servants that her only crime was in burning the edges of the waffles that she had cooked for breakfast. The sight of this thing made me almost wild that day. I could not work right and I prayed the Lord to help my people out of their bondage. I felt I could not stand it much longer.[5]

There are also very poignant accounts that relay the same devastating conviction between witnessing to the Lord and persecution on account of that witness. The matter of the would-be slave preacher James Smith is a case in point.

He was finally received into the church and baptized. Not long after this, he felt loudly called upon to go out and labor for the salvation of souls among the slave population with whom he was identified. At this conduct his master was much displeased, and strove to prevent him from the exercise of what the slave considered to be his duty to God and his brethren, on the Sabbath day. He was sometimes kept tied all day Sundays while the other slaves were allowed to go just where they pleased on that day. At other times he was flogged until his blood would drip down at his feet, and yet he would not give up laboring whenever he could get an opportunity, on the Sabbath day, for the conversion of souls. God was pleased to bless his labors and many were led to embrace the Saviour under his preaching.

At length his master sold him to a slave trader, who separated him from his family and carried him to the State of Georgia. His parting words to his wife were that if they proved faithful to God, He would bring them together again in a more free land than Virginia.[6]

There is as much correspondence in the responses as in the circumstances; in both situations the authors pray not for spiritualistic escape, but historically engineered vengeance and transformation.

In fact, I would argue that the more one reads Revelation and then turns to the slave narratives, the more one appreciates the kinds of correspondences that led the slaves themselves to pick up on so much of the apocalyptic imagery and thinking that are characteristic of the Apocalypse. It is, for example, clear when reading Revelation, that John envisions two powerful world eons. This eon is controlled by the forces of Satan; the future one will be controlled by God (Revelation 21–22). Indeed, this is how John, like Paul, could explain the suffering of God's people in a reality where God was both all-powerful and interested in and caring about the lives of God's people. In this age Satan had been (and will be) allotted power and rule (12:12; 20:7); it the future, however, that rule will be forever curtailed. Followers of God who lived in the present must take heart in their knowledge of this truth that one day soon Satan and Satan's forces would be overthrown (12:9; 20:1-15). As I will demonstrate momentarily, this knowledge was the basis upon which John called upon them to resist those forces and maintain their allegiance to God.

This kind of dualistic worldview also pervaded the thinking of the slaves. Their writings exhibit the same kind of cognitive dissonance; they know that human beings are meant by God to be free, and that God is in control of history, and yet, unbelievably, they are not free. This is the kind of conundrum whose reasoning lies in an apocalyptic understanding of a present age that looks very different from the imminently approaching future age.

> Children, we shall be free,
> When the Lord [as Messiah] shall appear.
> Give ease to the sick, give sight to blind,
> Enable the cripple to walk;
> He'll raise the dead from under the earth,
> And give them permission to talk.[7]

Just as John expressed his hope for the coming triumph in well known supernatural visions, so, too, do the slave narratives use visions of transformative power that induce hope for real transformative change. As was the case with John, what the slave sees in his or her mind has implications for what God will soon do in his or her historical circumstance. That is, effect freedom. Consider, for example, the legend of Simon Legare Island.

> An extensive slave owner had brought back over a new batch of blacks direct from Africa. According to the custom of the time this group was given two weeks in which to adjust themselves to their new surroundings before they were set to work. But . . . these were not ordinary beings. "When dey left by dey self you could hear a tapping, tapping, tapping all day and all night. And dey would not crack dey teet to dem" (would not speak to anyone).
> Finally, the time came for the slave driver to call them to work with the crack of his whip. "Dey come out and dey stretch out dey han jest like dey gwine to tek de tools to wuk like de rest. But when dey stretch dey han dey rise. At middle day you could see dem far out ober de ocean. At sundown you could hear "o voice, but dey couldn't shum no mo." Dem gone home."[8]

Neither in the Apocalypse, as, for example, when the woman clothed with the moon is given wings and escapes the dragon (Rev 12:13-17), nor in the slave narratives, however, is personal escape from the horror the hoped-for and enacted conclusion. Divine judgment that would transform the human historical landscape was anticipated instead. In the Johannine vocabulary it was the symbolic language of a fallen Babylon (Rev 17-18); in the slave narratives it was the portent and horrific realization of the Civil War. As monstrous an event as it was in the life of the United States of America, the slaves had prayed fervently for it, believing it to be the only form of judgment that could punish the system that had enslaved them and at the same time wipe it out forever. As Dwight Hopkins notes, "Various slave stories, accordingly, attribute the success of the Yankee forces over the Confederates to God's will." He quotes a certain Charles Grandy as a case in point.

> Den a gra' big star over in de east come right down almos' to de earth. I seed it myself. 'Twas sign o' war alright. Niggers got glad. All dem what could pray 'gin to pray more 'n ever. So glad God sendin' de war.[9]

And, as this interchange between Robert Smalls, a twenty-four-year-old slave interviewed in South Carolina in 1863, indicates, the slaves were most eager to participate with God in this historic enterprise.

Q. Have the colored people any general idea of fighting for their liberation?

A. They have a great idea. If they had a chance there would be no difficulty in raising a military force. If our headquarters were in Charleston we would have ten or fifteen regiments. The people there have been constantly praying for this day.[10]

This is not the language or imagery of an escapist people who look to otherworldly visions to drug out their historical realities. Just as John foresaw a new earth as well as a new heaven (21:1), so the slaves believed that God's accomplishments in the heavenly realm could and would lead to liberation on the earthly one. "The coming of the Civil War and Emancipation validated the slave's belief that God acts in human history. 'Shout the glad tidings o'er Egypt's dark sky/ Jehovah has triumphed, his people are free!' they sang."[11]

This is why they could sing in images that talked about other worlds, but in their essence challenged the structure of this world, and, even more important, beckoned their participation in that challenge.

> Singin' wid a sword in ma han,' Lord,
> Singin' wid a sword in ma han,'
> Singin' wid a sword in ma han,'
> Singin' wid a sword in ma han.'
>
> Purtiest singin' ever I heard,
> 'Way ovah on de hill,
> De angels sing an' I sing too,
> Singin' wid a sword in ma han,' Lord.[12]

This is the language of resistance, not escapism. It is the kind of language that I believe characterizes the slave narratives[13] and corresponds with the ethical exhortation that John wanted his visionary imagery to impress upon his first-century readers and hearers.

Apocalyptic Theology: The Truth Is Out There

In John's world of Asia Minor (1:4), where the pagan attraction to the emperor cult was at its foremost level of appeal in the empire,[14] a Christian believer in one of John's churches might rightly ask, "Who is in control? God? Or the Emperor and Rome?" For all practical purposes, and in the understanding of every reasonable man and woman, the truthful answer appeared to be the Emperor and Rome. John even acknowledged this "truth" in his portrayal of Rome as the great and mighty "Babylon," whose unrivalled wealth and power was idolized by the entire world. Satanically empowered, she wielded the force and terror of a great beast (17:18; 18:16, 18).

John's truth, though, is an alternative to this one, a hidden truth that cannot surface above the mighty claims of all powerful Rome. Caesar is lord, and Rome rules. That is the public truth that drowns out all other truths and, with the might of the Roman legions, declares them all to be lies. But John offers his visionary prophecy anyway. In the future that he foresees the lie will be put to this Roman conceit. This is the message his mythology brings.

The truth is out there, and the truth is, despite what you see in this very out of control world, where the powers and forces of chaos and destruction seem to be victorious at every turn, *God is in control.*[15] In John's time this message translated but one way. The truth is: God is Stronger than Rome. To any objective observer the claim is a ludicrous one.

Of course, one would first want to ask, whose God? *Whose God* is stronger than Rome? John will say that Jesus' God is that God. That is where it really becomes ridiculous. Jesus' God? Jesus, the same Jesus who died like a dumb animal on the cross? His God? Precisely. His God! *That is* the truth. *His* God is stronger than Rome.

But even John knows he's fighting an uphill battle. That is why he does not waste any time acknowledging the precarious nature of his argument. And yet his vision seems to turn the apparent truth of Roman authority on its head. John's vision gives Jesus the symbolic characteristic of *exactly* a dumb animal, a lamb, a helpless animal used continuously as an offering of sacrifice, and most particularly as a paschal sacrifice offered for the liberation of the people from their sins and their historical captivity. But, then, that is exactly why the image of a Lamb, meek though it may be, is so fitting. The lamb imagery recalls the great feat of Passover (where the lamb's blood was placed on the doorposts of the Hebrew lodgings as protection from the wrath of God's death angel), the ultimate act of unlikely liberation from an apparently all-powerful human force.

It is not all that odd, then, that this lamb has the character traiting of a lion. Notice how John opens his discussion of Jesus' role in God's plan. At 5:5, he writes, "Then one of the elders said to me, 'Do not weep. See, the Lion of the tribe of Judah, the Root of David, has conquered, so that he can open the scroll and its seven seals.' " The elder points out a Lion, a conquering Lion who wields the power of almighty God. And then John looks. And he sees this lion. And *this* is what he records at 5:6 about *that Lion*: "Then I saw between the throne and the four living creatures and among the elders *a Lamb* standing as if it had been slaughtered, having seven horns and seven eyes, which are the seven spirits of God sent out into all the earth."

A Lamb, standing *as if* slaughtered, is the *Lion* that John sees. The oddly ironic message is clear. *Looks deceive.* The Lamb has all the markings of one who was slaughtered. But apparently the slaughtering did not take. It was a real slaughtering, the markings show that. But it was not consummate. For the Lamb apparently rose beyond the slaughtering, but with the markings in tact so that his followers who believed in him might be consoled, and his enemies who slaughtered him might be afraid. For it is clear, despite how it looks, that this Jesus is a conquering Lion. The fact that he now wields the seven spirits of God are proof of that (cf. Isa 11:2, where the spirits are various attributes of God). This Jesus and the God whose plan he represents is the one in control of human history. The Romans, and those who collaborated with the Romans, to slaughter him are not.

But to claim such a truth is nonsense. It does not compute, any more than does the image of a lamb as a powerful lion compute. This is cognitive dissonance, the tension that develops because what one expects is not what actually occurs. There is a tension between what is and what should be. And this tension creates a feeling of dis-ease, of dissonance in the person afflicted by it.

John's goal was to overcome this unbearable tension; he wanted, at least in the symbolism of his revelation, to show that what his people believed was indeed the truth that governed human reality and history. Despite how it appeared on the surface, God, not Rome, was in charge. And so, to demonstrate this Truth, John imaged two key polar oppositions, God and Satan. On the heavenly, or mythological, level, these two were at war; despite how it seemed at times, God was destined to win. In fact, in the future that John foresaw, that victory had already taken place. This is what his mythological presentation, borrowing liberally from mythologies before his, is trying to say. As Adela Yarbro Collins puts it:

> The beasts rising from the sea called to mind Yahweh's battles with Leviathan and Rahab, those sea monsters whose rebellion against God symbolized the forces of chaos, sterility, and death. Their defeat represents the victory of order, fertility, and life, which is associated with God's creative acts. These symbols were not unique to Israel. . . . The plots of ancient myths of combat vary, but they have certain elements in common. A rebellion, usually led by a dragon or other beast, threatens the reigning gods, or the king of the gods. Sometimes the ruling god [re: Lamb] is defeated, even killed, and then the dragon reigns in chaos for a time. Finally the beast is defeated by the god who ruled before, or some ally of his. Following his victory the reestablished king of the gods (or a new, young king in his stead) builds his house or temple, marries and produces offspring, or hosts a great banquet. . . . This basic plot or pattern is found in every series of visions in Revelation, beginning with the seven seals.[16]

On the ground, here on earth, that mythological battle had direct human, historical referents. God was represented by Christ, the slaughtered Lamb with the conquering power of a Lion. Satan was represented by the graphic, beastly portrayals of Rome and the conquering power of her Caesars. Rome's dominance is only an appearance, an illusion, a mirage. That is the truth Revelation says is out there, the truth the satanic forces who support Rome do not want the believer to find out.

Why is it so important to Rome that the Christian believer not find out the truth? Because then, out of fear, out of a desire to protect this physical life and the things that go with it, the believer would be willing to compromise his or her beliefs and accommodate them to the belief structure offered by Rome. But if John's truth is THE truth, to ally oneself with Rome, even to cooperate with Rome, would be to make an alliance with the devil. And in a world where everything, even history itself, is rushing headlong towards the end where God's rule will be shown to be the only true rule, a believer does not want to find him or herself allied with the wrong power.

All of this also tells us a little bit about the community to which John was writing. Socially, politically, and economically, these were people of some means.[17] And yet, because they are an occupied people, they also felt themselves to be oppressed. Even so, they are still allowed to maintain a semblance of economic success and political self-sufficiency. Even in Palestine where the Jews were often at odds with their Roman occupiers, there was a semblance of self-governance, allowed to the Herodians first, and then later in Judea to the Sanhedrin operating with the Roman prefect or procurator. Politically, then, the people populating John's seven churches are an occupied people in Asia Minor. And yet they have some sense of self-determination as allowed by Rome. If you listen to the text and hear John's arguments against accommodation such as 18:4, it appears that they are also people with at least enough standing and money to want to avoid losing it.

One might also start with the presumption of general religious tolerance. Rome encouraged the demonstration of fidelity that subject peoples wanted to pay their gods and goddesses as long as their worship also included appropriate recognition of Roman deities. Since acknowledgement of Roman religious figures and practices also carried with it an explicit claim of loyalty, or at least obedience, to the Roman political infrastructure, refusal of cultic participation attracted suspicion and hostility. In such a circumstance, religious fidelity and political homage were one in the same.

Christians were bound to have problems. As was the case with their Jewish forebears, they were beholden to the first commandment's prohibition against the worship of other gods. Christians were, by definition, religiously intolerant. While there is some debate as to whether Domitian demanded that the populace acclaim him in worship as Lord and God,[18] there does seem to be a growing consensus that the requirements of the imperial cult in general and the demands of the Christian faith were mutually exclusive social and religious positions. "According to a tradition which probably represents the actual situation, they were required to make the two-word acknowledgement of Roman sovereignty, 'Kurios Kaisaros' ('Caesar is Lord'), an exact counterpart to the basic Christian confession 'Jesus is Lord' (see Rom 10:9; 1 Cor 12:3)."[19]

John realizes that his reader/hearers are coming before a situation where they will have to decide whether to progress societally and politically and economically or declare themselves followers of Christ at the risk of losing everything. They have status to protect and material to conserve and they may well think that those are more important than their commitment to God's future. John is afraid the time may come when they might be willing to sacrifice their commitment and allegiance to that future in a futile attempt to conserve their economic present by buying into the Roman economic way of life, participating in societal gatherings that may require them to compromise their faith, or even denying that faith if declaring it might mean loss of property, privilege, or life. It seems to me that people who have some status in life are precisely the kinds of people who have these kinds of concerns about fitting in. So, while they may be powerless in comparison to Rome, they are, many of them in their own smaller communities, people of some means.

The letter of Pliny, an Asia Minor governor, to the Emperor Trajan explains why believers might be coerced to accommodate themselves to the power and force of Rome. Schüssler Fiorenza quotes the pertinent part:

> In the meanwhile the method I have observed towards those who have been denounced to me as Christians is this: I interrogated them whether they were Christians; if they confessed it I repeated the question twice again adding the threat of capital punishment; if they still persevered, I ordered them to be executed. . . . Those who denied they were, or had ever been Christians, who repeated after me an invocation to the Gods, and offered adoration with wine and frankincense to your image, which I ordered to be brought for that purpose, together with those of the Gods, and who finally cursed Christ——none of which acts it is said, those who are really Christians can be forced into performing,——these I thought it proper

to discharge. Others who were named by that informer, at first confessed themselves Christians and then denied it. . . . They all worshipped your statue and the images of the Gods and cursed Christ.[20]

There is, in this world, a lot of incentive to accommodate oneself to the powers represented by Rome. Indeed, any force that has the power of capital punishment over one's life appears, in truth, to be the power in charge of one's life.

This is why John creates a world from his vision, a world in the symbolism of his narrative, that presents an alternative truth. And this kind of truth works best in the kind of community I am envisioning for John, where people of some means must make a decision about choosing *those* means and the life that goes with it or choosing Christ. In his mind's eye of faith, as ridiculous as it may seem, the truth is that God and God's Christ are in control. Here, John reveals, is not only an alternative truth; here is *the* Truth. It is on the basis of this truth and the historical circumstances of his believers that John fashions an ethics of active resistance.

An Ethics of Active Resistance

In some ways John is more helpful than the authors I have studied thus far; he clarifies his ethics with his language. He describes himself as a witness whose prophecy is given in the hope of seeking witness (those who hear and who keep what is written in it, 1:3) from those who, like him, follow the Lamb and attest to the truth that the Lamb, by the power of God, is in control of human history. It is in this language of stated and requested witness that he develops the ethics of active resistance against the false truth that Rome is Lord and Master of human history. It is to that language of witness, then, that I now turn in order to develop a better understanding of his ethics.

Revelation 1:1-3

This is an action text. The first three verses script out a delivery sequence for the Revelation of Jesus Christ that moves quickly from God's heaven to John's Patmos. "The means whereby this revelation was given can be depicted in the analogy of a chain whose main links are God-Jesus-the angel-John-his readers."[21] The language John uses to build this chain suggests a literary equivalence between the term "revelation" and the formula "word of God and witness of Jesus Christ." What started with God ended up with John. Verse three adds another dimension; it represents that same revelation as John's written prophecy. A kind of literary equation has developed. The Revelation of Jesus Christ is "the Word of God and witness of Jesus Christ," each of which is also the written prophecy that John's hearers and readers are to keep.

But what does all that equivalence mean for our consideration of John's witness language? *What*, actually, are they supposed to be keeping? H. Strathmann pushes us in the right direction: "The Word of God and the witness of Jesus Christ are inseparably interwoven."[22] But what are the parameters of that relationship? What can we determine about either the Word or the witness from the fact that they are so integrally connected? David Aune makes a suggestion. He correctly observes through his translation, "the message from God, that is, the witness borne by Jesus," that Jesus' witness specifies the exact nature of God's word. " 'The word of God' and 'the testimony of Jesus' are not two different things, but rather the second is an aspect of the first."[23] And there lies the crux of the problem. The testimony of Jesus Christ cannot clarify the Word of God unless we know what that testimony is. What exactly is the witness of Jesus Christ?[24]

We can say that it is not a believer's witness about Jesus, but, as Aune translates, a witness "borne" by Jesus himself. The genitive in the clause is subjective. In fact, early use here sets the pattern for use later on. John is consistent; when he talks about the "witness of" he is referring to the "witness borne by."[25] In most cases, it is borne by Jesus Christ.

What does this have to do with John's ethics? The answer lies not in *what* he says but *how* he says it; in verse 3 he uses the language of commendation. The commendation takes the specific form of a macarism, a blessing.[26] John celebrates, or makes it known that he, along with God and Jesus Christ, will celebrate particular people who do particular things. Not surprisingly, those particular things pertain to the witness borne by Jesus Christ. The person who reads this witness aloud so that others may hear it, and the persons who hear this witness and keep it, are those whom

John considers blessed. This is the action he's commending, then, the action he wants his readers to perform. It is so important that before he closes he will pronounce the commendation again at 22:7. Indeed he encourages them throughout to realize the importance of this "keeping" (3:3, 8; 14:12; 16:15; 22:9) and promises eschatological victory to those who do (2:26-29; 3:10). He wants them to proclaim and keep the witness that is borne by Jesus Christ, a witness so powerful and true that it is, for them, in their circumstance, the Word of God. They may not yet know what it is, but right from the start they know what to do with it.

Revelation 1:4-8

John is writing to churches specifically located in an area of the Empire famous for its attraction to the emperor cult. But he is writing in the symbolic language of apocalyptic that is noted for its characterization as resistance literature.[27] And he chooses his words very carefully. He brackets this small section with a provocative characterization of God: "the one who is, who was, and who is coming." Boring points out that in the Greek-speaking world a three-fold formulation like this one was a commonplace way of celebrating a deity's eternity and immutability. "It was said, for example, that 'Zeus was, Zeus is, and Zeus will be' (Pausanias)."[28] John testifies that this notoriety belongs to God, but with a twist. God is not only the eternal one, he is also the coming one. And he is coming for a purpose. John hints at that motive when he follows up on the formulation in verse eight with the term *pantocrator*. God, the eternal and coming one, is also the Almighty one. God is the true and supreme power in the cosmos. In the eastern provinces of John's seven churches, where Rome was also making precisely this claim, God's coming, as the Almighty, was bound to make headlines. And conflict.

John heightens the probability for that conflict by the way he describes the second key figure, Jesus Christ. He does not use proper grammar. Of course, John's problems with Greek are legendary; many have argued that his flawed speech is the work of someone who thinks in Hebrew or Aramaic. But Allan Callahan makes the important observation that John operates this way intentionally. Because "most of the grammatical rules violated are flawlessly observed elsewhere in the work,"[29] he believes that John *chooses* to write in a Greek that is heavily influenced by Semitic principles. He does so because he wants his use of language to be a representation, a working symbol as it were, of the social and political resistance his people must wage.

He therefore intentionally mismanages his characterization of Jesus Christ; "the connection of the three titles with the name 'Jesus Christ' is grammatically incorrect."[30] Since "Jesus Christ" is in the genitive case, operating as the object of the preposition "from," the titles that follow should also be in the genitive. Instead, John puts "the faithful witness," "the first born of the dead," "and the ruler of the kings of the earth," in the nominative case. As Callahan might say, John is not making a mistake; he's making a point. G. K. Beale notices that he is following the same pattern he initiated in verse four, where the threefold formula about God is in the nominative case even though its function as the object of the preposition "from" should have it in the genitive. There, as here, Beale argues, John stays with the nominative because he wants to direct attention to an allusion he is making to Old Testament Ps 89:37 (88:38 LXX) where the controlling moniker "faithful witness" also occurs in a nominative formulation.[31] But it occurs there with a specific orientation, as does "first born" in 89:27 (88:28 LXX). The context of the two references in their Old Testament location is one of kingship, "the unending reign of David's seed on his throne (cf. likewise Ps. 88:30[89:29]). John applies the phrase directly to the Messiah's own faithful witness, which led to establishment of his eternal kingship."[32] Indeed, the reference to "first born" in the Psalm is directly associated with not only kingship, but the highest kingship on the earth. That is exactly the kind of kingship John envisions for Jesus Christ here ("And I will make him firstborn, highest among the kings of the earth," author's trans.; "I will make him the firstborn, the highest of the kings of the earth," NRSV).

The initial access that John wants his hearers/readers to make of Jesus Christ as faithful witness, and even first born, then, is one of kingship. If Callahan and Beale are correct, John has skewed his grammar in order to shepherd his hearers/readers towards this very pointed connection. Now the actual content of the titles can have the force the visionary intended they have.

Witness is key, not only because of its lead position in the chain of three, but also because it follows up on John's opening three verses which convey his entire work as the witness borne by Jesus. We already know Jesus is the central witness figure, so that here John is not really telling us something new. It is also not surprising that Jesus Christ would be described as *faithful* since his witness is the Word of God for their particular cultural circumstance.[33] The strikingly new component is that this faithful witness is the first born of the dead and, using a phrase he highlights by appealing to it only here, the ruler of the kings of the earth. Once again, at a key moment, "and" connects two of John's key descriptive components. Here, as in verse 2, a better translation would be, the first born of the dead, who is the ruler of the kings of the earth. Not only does the entire phrase clarify what it means for Jesus to be a faithful witness, but the image of universal kingship clarifies what it means for Jesus to be first born of the dead.

This fits a context of situation where John has intentionally mishandled the Greek in order to draw attention to a particular psalm reference that has a primary interest in the establishment of secure and abiding kingship. He is using his warped grammar to straighten out his readers; he's telling them how to access the reality of Jesus Christ. Jesus Christ has a witness to make; he is the first born, the ruler of all the kings of the earth. As God is ruler of all, *pantocrator*, Jesus is ruler of the entire human realm. *This* is the revelation of Jesus Christ.

In a cultural context where Rome already lays claim to ultimate kingship, it is also a Revelation bound inevitably for trouble. Indeed, as Beale points out, this awareness is already present in the language John chooses to use. "Kings of the earth" is a reference used "typically elsewhere in Revelation to antagonists to God's kingdom (6:15; 17:2; 18:3,9; 19:19; cf. 16:14). This includes not only the kingdoms and peoples represented by the kingdoms but also the satanic forces behind those kingdoms."[34] Jesus' kingship, by claiming to be the one abiding and universal kingship, necessarily *resists* the already established kingdoms who are making the same claim. In John's context of culture there is only one: Rome.

What does such an interpretative perspective *do*? The answer lies again in the kind of language John uses. The tone of his writing commends his characterization of Jesus as the faithful witness. "The phrase 'the faithful witness' points to Jesus, not only as the revealer from heaven but as the one who also, like the Christians in John's churches, once stood before the Roman authorities. He had borne his witness, even at the cost of his life (cf. John 18:33-19:16; 1 Tim 6:13)."[35] Indeed, this is the one part of the description that Christians can emulate. They cannot be the first born of the dead, nor the ruler of the kings of the earth, but they can, like Antipas (2:13), like John himself (1:2), be faithful witnesses to the witness that Jesus himself bears, that God is the Almighty, and Jesus Christ is his coming king. In their cultural context, to bear such witness is also to broker a very dangerous form of political as well as religious resistance.

Revelation 1:9-11

John's appeal to the formula, "the word of God, that is, the witness borne by Jesus," in 1:9 acts as a bookend to his use of it in verse 2. But what is most interesting here is John's *causal* point. He says that he is on the island of Patmos "because of," "on account of" that witness. Boring points out that the phrase "on account of" is always used in Revelation "for the result of an action, not its purpose. John has been banished to Patmos because he had been preaching the Christian message."[36] That message is Jesus' own witness to his universal and abiding kingship.

John is here commending his own actions, lifting himself up as a model to be imitated. And therein also lies the text's ethics. John calls himself their partner; in doing so he also challenges them to live up to the parameters of the partnership. As he held to the witness borne by Jesus, despite the consequences, so must they. But this suggests a kind of active resistance, does not it? To harbor the view that Jesus Christ is king in a world that actively proclaims the lordship of Rome and its Caesar is to act obstinately. It is to resist, to refuse to fit in. Even more, if you add to that declaration of witness the belief that God is coming soon to inaugurate that kingship and make a kingdom of Christ's followers, it is to invite "tribulation." Endurance in such a context of situation cannot mean passive waiting in spite of what Rome is doing. It suggests instead a continued resolve to keep to that witness even though that witness, by its very nature, provokes an angry Roman response.

Revelation 2:12-17

In a place like Pergamum a hostile response to the witness of Jesus' universal and exclusive Lordship would be expected. The capital city of the entire Asian province, the city was a hotbed of pagan cults and emperor interest. Schüssler Fiorenza calls it a "citadel of Hellenistic civilization in Asia," which, even more important, claimed to be "the official center of the imperial cult."[37] Beale notes that the city referred to itself as the "temple warden" of a temple devoted to Caesar worship.[38] No wonder Richard claims that it was "the center of imperial worship for the entire region."[39]

But not every believer in Pergamum resisted accommodation to the institutions that proclaimed imperial lordship. Not only were there those who accepted the rites and expectations of foreign cults; there were also prophetic leaders like Balaam and prophetic communities like the Nicolaitans who argued that such behavior was consistent with a holding to the witness borne by Jesus Christ.

The particular issue at hand was the eating of meat sacrificed to foreign deities. Participation in feasts where such food was available was one of the key ways in which members of a community integrated themselves into the fellowship of the larger populace. John believed that such "integration" came at too high a price. He believed that followers of Christ needed to make a stand. If they truly believed that Jesus was the Lord of history, then they must live in a way that showed it. He therefore demanded that they refuse to partake of any rite, or eat any food consecrated to another person's or power's lordship. No matter what the consequences.

And so, through his portrayal of Antipas as the key characterization, he commends an opposing action: resistance. John commends him by the way he describes him. He is *like Jesus*. Once again John uses what appears to be a grammatical error to make his theological point. Beale points out that "witness" here should be in the genitive case, as should the adjective "faithful" and the noun "witness" that follow it. John, however, against rule, forces them into the nominative. "Again, the awkward nominative is a device directing attention to the OT allusion in order to make clear the identification of Antipas' witness with that of Jesus."[40] That not only suggests that he witnesses to what Jesus witnesses to, the kingship of Jesus, and then dies because of it; it also makes his tragic character one worthy of emulation. Indeed, John already commends those who have behaved like him in 2:13 and condemns those who have not in 2:14-16.[41] He celebrates those who have held fast *even* though such defiance in such a place can lead to the kind of end that claimed Antipas.

The directive that develops is clear: The community at Pergamum, in spite of the consequences, must be what Antipas has been, a faithful witness to the kingship of Christ. But that will also require them to do what he has done, to resist the temptation to acquiesce to the demands of the Roman cultic/political infrastructure, demands that stem from the foundational belief that Caesar is Lord and Rome is the universal and abiding kingdom. This kind of activity is bound to be seen as contrary and treated as provocative in *this* kind of context. In other words, the language of witness, whether it is related to Jesus Christ, John, or one of John's fellow believers, seems to suggest an active resistance to contemporary cultic and political expectations. In fact, it is so controversial a resistance that it can lead to death. He is not commending them to act passively, then, but to act oppositionally, to resist what *this* context desires, celebration of and devotion to the Lordship of Rome and its many client deities. He is asking them to testify to the Lordship of another, and, in so doing, to put themselves directly in harm's way.

Revelation 6:9-11

The formula "the word of God, which is the testimony borne by Jesus" is back.[42] This time John uses it to make his causal connection perfectly clear; it *is* because of their witness to Jesus' Lordship that believers have suffered. Aune's grammatical investigations confirm the point.[43] Specifically attending to Boring's broad evaluations, he notes that the overwhelming occurrences of "because of" in Revelation deal either with cause or reason, even to the point of conveying the sense of instrumentality. He includes the uses in 6:9 and 20:4, which also speaks of those who have been beheaded "because of" their testimony, as prominent examples. Witnessing to the lordship of Christ *causes* their physical deaths.

This is why the souls are crying out for justice. They want God

to vindicate their testimony that Christ is King. For as long as justice is delayed those who deny that witness will continue to
believe and promote Rome's lordship instead. So now they wait
beneath the heavenly altar for action. But one should not confuse
the issue. Their waiting passively in heaven does not imply that
they also waited passively on earth. They are in heaven, as slaughtered souls (or as beheaded ones in 20:4), precisely *because* they
actively witnessed to the testimony that Jesus is the ultimate Lord
of human history in a world where Rome laid vicious claim to its
own witness of ultimate authority.

Ironically, this oppositional witness that has caused their deaths
also participates in the transformation that it seeks. Even as the
souls cry out for God to act, John's description of their situation
leaves one with the impression that the efforts of their earthly com-
patriots continue the transformative effort they began. He implies
in verse 11 that the souls in heaven have but a little while to wait
for the justice they seek, just until the deaths of witnesses like
themselves have come to a completion. Their deaths, in this way,
contributed, then, to the coming of God's vindication and justice,
God's kingdom. John, though, is not commending death. In none
of the literary situations that revolve around "witness" has this
been the case. He has instead been commending witness, even
though he knows that such witness, given its content and their cultural context, will inevitably lead to tribulation and perhaps death.
A kind of narrative formula lies beneath his descriptive symbolism. Yes, the deaths of the witnesses lead to the coming of God's
kingdom. But it is the active witnessing that *causes* the deaths. The
witnessing, not the dying, is in the first and primary position of
activity. It is the witnessing that believers can control. They cannot
control whether Rome will respond with censure, appropriation of
property, denial of social privilege, exile or death. But they can
control whether they witness to the lordship of Jesus Christ. The
more who witness, the more intolerable will become the word that
is witnessed, and the more belligerently Rome will be forced to act.
The witnessing, the provocative activity John has been commending all along, will set up the circumstances of Rome's response. It
is the witnessing, then, that leads to the coming of God's justice
and vengeance, God's kingdom. Dying is a result; witnessing is the
cause. It is witnessing that he commends. For it is witnessing that

plays a synergistic role with God's own efforts to accomplish the universal and abiding Lordship of Jesus Christ. *This* is the Revelation of Jesus Christ.

Final Discourses: Completing the Case

The study thus far provides the access points we need to *read* the witness material that follows. I select two such sections of material as cases in point. The language that encompasses 11:3 and 7 is a good place to begin. The two witnesses presented here are clearly commended characterizations. John's narration highlights them as positive models, role models, in fact, for those aspiring to be true witnesses. Here the intent of prophecy becomes clear. The witnesses are not given a gift to hold in passive waiting; they are given a mandate to prophesy for a specified period of time. They are, in other words, to be active witnesses, energetically spreading a particular prophecy.

But John also repeats the warning he has issued before. Rome, in the symbolic guise of the beast, will make war upon them and kill them. We now see that it would be perfectly reasonable for a reader or hearer to access the language to mean that John is making a causal point. The beast is not simply killing two witnesses who prophesy the lordship of Christ; it kills two witnesses *because* they prophesy the lordship of Christ. Still, Rome's response, the slaughtering, is not the focus; the activity of the witnesses is the focus. Their deaths are a result of their witnessing, and are thus secondary to that primary activity that John wants to commend. They are commended because of what they do, not because of what is done to them.

What they do will have a transformative effect. The language in 12:1-17 makes this clear; 12:11 is the key: here lies the access point for reading what John wants to say. In this verse the key characterization is neither the divine child, the supernatural woman, or the aggrieved dragon. It is instead the almost anonymous "them" of 12:10 who become the active "they" of 12:11. "They" are the people who do what John has been commending since 1:3; "they" *keep* the word of God which is the testimony borne by Jesus (12:17). There is consistency; the relationship between witnessing and suffering remains causal. Because they keep witnessing they are continually hounded by the power that denies that testimony. But 12:11 says something more, something that on the surface seems startling, but given our earlier discussion is really only a confirmation of what has been claimed before. "They" will conquer the dragon. "They" will break the back of the force that backs Rome. "They" will shatter its claim to Lordship.

Once again John uses the language of instrumentality.[44] The relationship between witnessing and transformative victory is causal. "They" will conquer "because of" the blood of the Lamb. Here, of course, "they" are dependent upon divine action that they themselves cannot emulate. Though their blood too will spill it cannot have the redemptive and victorious effect of the blood of the Lamb. But John does not stop here. Pressing on, he continues with another "because of" statement of instrumentality that places them in partnership with God. Because of their witness they will conquer.

John's language leads to a particular kind of contextual conclusion: by obstinately proclaiming the lordship of Christ they help effect it, *even* in a world that believes in and prosecutes for the Lordship of Rome. "We must not fail to observe the implications of this. If it is right to say that the basis for a new order of society is God's word of judgment pronounced in Christ, then it follows that the witnesses who proclaimed that word to challenge the prevailing political order, were not acting anti-politically at all, but were confronting a false political order with the foundation of a true one. We must claim John for the point of view which sees criticism, when founded in truth, as genuine political engagement."[45] This is witness as not only active resistance, but as triumphant cultic, social, and political transformation. *This* is the Revelation of Jesus Christ.

Some Concluding Thoughts: Reclaiming the Language of Apocalyptic

For the African American church the apocalyptic language of resistance found in the Book of Revelation ought to be an integral part of the personal and corporate language of faith. Not just in a historical way, but also a contemporary one. It is the language of the powerless; the language of future hope presently realized. It is the language of the future because the present often speaks in such destructive ways.

African American churches read and hear the present news of our collective circumstance. It is news preoccupied with contemporary evils like racial profiling, the return of extensive resegregation of our nation's schools, the revival of hate groups that target people based on ethnicity and race, the pervasive preponderance of the impoverished and the destitute, the cries of the hopeless in our inner cities, and the wave of political conservatism in response that nonetheless exhorts accommodation to life as U.S. society presently endures it. Because the bulk of African Americans in this country still count themselves among the most impoverished and oppressed,[46] John's message to resist, to refuse an accommodating "fitting in" and "acquiescing to" the present social, economic and political way of life as it is presently lived is *still* a necessary message. His language of resistance, as the slaves rightly understood in their time, must remain a vital part of the African American language of the present time, if African American Christian language is to remain the language of hope for the future in the midst of an unbearable present.

African American Christians must therefore reclaim the language. Obviously, it is not needed as much in our well-to-do middle- and upper-class Christian circles. There, Revelation often sounds creepy and misguided, violent and deranged, like some first-century disciple who had gotten the wrong kind of spiritual high. And so the language has been surrendered through its lack of use. It has been given over to extremists like David Koresh who see in it a plan for the violent revolution of any and all sources of authority. Or it has been allowed to be misused by fundamentalist groups who see in it a literal plan for the overwhelming of human history toward *their* kind of future. The crazier the people who use the book, the crazier the book itself seems to be. That is because we are looking at the book through the lens of *their* realities and issues. We allow *those* issues to determine how we should understand the book and whether the book should be preached from and taught out of. Like the earlier Christians in their search for a canon, many contemporary African Americans are just not sure it should be a part of our history and heritage, at least not canonically. To be sure, there is *some* good material: chapters 1–3 and the letters to the churches. That sounds perhaps like Paul. Or maybe the closing chapters, the ones that talk about a new heaven and a new earth; there is good prophetic imagery there. But all that other stuff, the sevens and the twelves, the seals and the bowls and the trumpets, the whores and the madonnas, the lamb and the blood, the lakes of fire and the 144,000 saved from it, all of that seems too far out and too inexplicable except to those who have some kind of extremist or fundamentalist agenda.

I am suggesting, though, as the slaves understood, that the kind of apocalyptic imagery we find in Revelation can be the foundation of a potent social and political ethics if we engage its symbolic potential through the proper lens, the kind of lens the authors of the slave narratives quite obviously used. Through such a glass, it clearly promotes an ethics of social, religious, and political resistance.

John's text, then, has a particular ethical agenda in mind. He wants the hearers and readers of this text to do something. To Endure. To Witness. To resist accommodation to the practices and trends of their time and culture, no matter how much it costs them, and to do so in a way that helps precipitate the rushing in of the kingdom. He shows them a future where what ought to be, God in charge and God's people vindicated, has become what is. In anticipation of that future he wants his people to manufacture a present where what ought to be, God's people in faithful and committed relationship to God and resisting the lure of Greco-Roman religious, social, and political expectations, has become what is. The stakes are high, life and death. It is not about losing this physical life and enduring physical death however. It is about losing the resurrected life and having to endure the second death. Those are the outcomes of the battle that is now being waged. And in that battle, no matter how it looks, Rome will not be the ultimate victor. Believe this and stand against Rome, stand with God.

This is why I say Revelation, like the slave narrative lens through which I read it, acts like a historical apocalypse. Though it envisions the future and the heavenly world, it does not encourage its hearers and readers to escape there. Those visions are encouragement for doing the kinds of things that are necessary in this world, in this time, to transform them. That is what all the imagery and symbolism is about.

Ultimately, this is why I started my discussion on Revelation by appealing to the spirituals and the people who sang them. For I think that what Zora Neale Hurston said about the spirituals, that they were really only spirituals when sung in the context of oppression that birthed them, can and should also be said about Revelation. To understand it one must view it from John's perspective, from below. Otherwise it sounds as vengeful, spiteful, and escapist as many of its critics have claimed it to be. Schüssler Fiorenza makes a good comparative argument. She writes: "The outcry for divine justice in Rev. is borne out of the experience that no Christian who was denounced by his or her neighbors could receive justice from a Roman court. Martin Luther King, Jr.'s *Letter from a Birmingham Jail*, for instance, reflects experiences and hopes similar to the theology of Rev. . . . His indictment of racist White America cannot be construed as 'hatred of civilization' or as 'envy' deficient of Christian love for one's enemies, if the dehumanizing power of racism is understood as evil."[47]

Does Revelation have a place in our present world? Schüssler Fiorenza's comments suggest that it does. What we must do is to be particularly careful that we understand the book in light of its context and apply it to those current situations that correspond with that context, situations from below. For in those circumstances the powerful imagery may well have the same provocative effect; to encourage endurance and provoke transformative witness, the kind of witness that can make what should be what is. There is such a power and that power is available to us. That's Revelation's truth. That's the *truth* that's out there.

CHAPTER SEVEN

New Testament Ethics Through an African American Lens: Some Concluding Thoughts

When I first began this project my goals for this final chapter were a bit more grandiose than they are now. After having spent the bulk of the book talking about approaching Ethics in the New Testament from the African American cultural perspective, I had thought to conclude by explaining precisely how that perspective could inform decisions about particular ethical issues. I am talking, of course, about the most pressing ethical issues that presently face us: marriage and divorce, economics and personal possessions, hetero- and homosexuality, church and state relationships, cloning and other biomedical breakthrough concerns, and so forth. How are you going to be a New Testament ethicist in the twenty-first century if you do not have a biblically informed way of telling someone where they should stand on the issues of abortion and women's rights, even if abortion is not talked about in the Bible and women's rights seems very often to be talked against? But that is where exegetical skill and hermeneutical capability come into play. The objective is to find in the ancient texts an ethical directive for the contemporary believer, a moral that is on target for his or her particular twenty-first-century circumstance. Scholastic procedure allegedly enables such universal ethical applicability. And so, the responsible scholar and pastor describes the state of the problem, points to the biblical texts that deal with the problem (or offers excuses if only a few, or even no texts do so), and then suggests the proper ways in which Christians should behave.

That was, before I completed the beginning and middle of this book, also my plan for the end of it. But my work has brought me to an alternative conclusion. The creation of such universally normative ethical directives for living would contradict everything for which the work in this book has come to stand. I am less interested now in arguing for or against the most biblically appropriate way of governing ourselves ethically on any particular issue. I am more and more interested in provoking a discussion of New Testament ethics from the many different cultural perspectives that characterize contemporary Christians. "Imagine the possibilities for conversation and debate were we all across many different traditions to be able to ask of one another—what are we saying about ourselves and about the others, and what are we doing when we scripturalize?"[1]

I am fascinated by the potential for meaning that exists in the New Testament materials and the manners in which people of different communities approach, access, and draw ethical direction from that potential. Ethics, as Paul so clearly understood, is not law. It is not a code which, when written down, codified, and passed out among the faithful, can be legislated and enforced uniformly across all cultural boundaries. It is instead a spiritual relationship that connects human believers to God's ever-present engagement with the world through the Spirit of Christ Jesus. In that gracious encounter we see possibilities; we do not read writ. The New Testament is itself a written record of that Christ—human encounter and thus a model for our own engagement with it. The Gospel writers, Paul, and the seer John all read the circumstances of their communal times and, through their interactive working with the Spirit, targeted their ethics to their people's particular circumstances and needs. I am suggesting only that we follow their lead, that, directed and molded by the written words they left us, we use those words as guides through which we might sense the leadership and guidance of the Holy Spirit for our living today. That means that we not only take the written words seriously, *but that we also take seriously the way in which the Spirit leads us to those words through the lens of our contemporary cultures.*

This is what a look at New Testament Ethics from a cultural perspective is all about. No one single lens onto the texts is favored as the objective, and therefore singularly accurate one. That has been the case with the Euro-American perspective that has reigned supreme in the study of New Testament Ethics. It is this perspective that has set the agenda for interpretative reading of the Bible and the drawing of ethics from that reading. Any other lens onto the text, if it did not agree in approach and conclusion, was considered suspect and was ultimately rejected. Since only one perspective mattered, conversation, by definition, could not and did not occur. To therefore end this book by substituting a different cultural lens as the "objective" focus and then drawing normative ethics from that lens would have perpetuated the "monologue" method of approaching New Testament Ethics. A new cultural lens would have claimed interpretative priority. A new voice would have championed a different, in this case, more liberative resulting ethics. But in the end the outcome would have been the same. Though key players would have changed places, at least in this book, the idea that there is some New Testament Ethics that objectively and universally guides all human behavior in all spheres of life would have been extended. It would have been a liberation ethics, and for that I would have been excited. But it would nonetheless have been ethics from a single lens masquerading as an ethics for all. It may come to the point that liberation ethics does have such universal possibilities. But this is a conclusion that should be reached through conversation across cultural borders, not, as has been historically the case, mandated as "ethical" from one culture to all others.

In the end, this is precisely why I consciously approached the study of New Testament Ethics through the very particular lens of African Americans, and especially African American slaves. I am NOT suggesting that this is the universal lens that gives us the final answer for dealing with ethical issues. That, again, is why I do not here in this last chapter want to deal with specific ethical issues and thereby give the impression that there is now a single perspective through which we should access them, and a single way that we should live in our encounters with them. Instead, I began with this liberative lens because I believe with scholars like Vincent Wimbush that an approach to New Testament studies from the African American perspective can open up possibilities for conversation across cultural lines that have not existed before. In his book, *African Americans and the Bible: Sacred Texts and Social Texture*, he asks the orienting question, "How might putting African Americans at the center of the study of the Bible affect the study of the Bible?"[2] "What if the reading and thinking about the Bible . . . were read through African-American experience?"[3] This, simply put, is the question I have been asking from the perspective of New Testament Ethics. And I certainly, as my own work here will testify, agree with his answer. When one looks at the matter of ethics in the New Testament from an African American experience, one sees it from below. "With African American experience as the starting point for the study of the Bible a greater sensitivity to the Bible as manifesto for the exiled, the un-homely, the marginal, the critics and inveiglers will be sustained."[4]

Wimbush's words about the benefits of using the African American experience as the starting point for biblical studies are as provocative and challenging to contemporary African American communities as they are to Euro-American ones. Certainly, as I have pointed out, those words critique Euro-American interpreters who have wielded their cultural lens, and the biases that go with it, as the only objective portal through which to approach the subject of New Testament ethics. But his challenge also critiques African American believers and interpreters. The boundary-breaking take on the New Testament that I found shaped through the lens of the African slaves has a powerful and transformative meaning for an African American community still in desperate need of liberation and transformation, not only from without (where the problems are more obvious), but from within (where the problems may be even more destructive). The slave perspective brings a challenge; believers, and the communities they make up, ought to have the courage of their convictions. One remembers particularly the challenge the slaves brought to the Pauline understanding of God's activities in the world. Where it appeared to them that Paul was not faithful to his own liberating Gospel, they withdrew from him. Though they often judged him unfairly, we have come to see, they did, from their perspective and place in life, and from their connection with God through that place in life, challenge the words that Paul used to interpret God's Word of grace and love. Indeed, when one looks back critically, and not romantically at the slaves themselves, one can see that they might well have applied that same standard to themselves. While seeking liberation, male slaves also, for example, treated women in a highly patriarchal, nonliberating manner. The African American church, as many writers have noted, continues to fall prey to this problem of sexist gender relations today.

> Both historical and contemporary evidence underscore the fact that black churches could scarcely have survived without the active support of black women, but in spite of their importance in the life of the church, the offices of preacher and pastor of churches in the historic black churches remain a male preserve and are not generally available to women . . . this issue continues to be a controversial one for the Black Church.[5]

This is only one issue, to be sure. I do not mean to suggest that it is the only place where the slave and contemporary African American communities can and should entertain a prophetic word for themselves. I mean to suggest instead, through such an example, that these communities, too, are in need of the very same transformative, liberative challenge that the slaves brought with them to their engagement with biblical language and imagery. The slave community, being a closed historical one, cannot not learn from this prophetic word. The contemporary African American one can. Where, for example, gender relations are concerned, the boundary breaking ethics that develops through a focus on the cultural lens of African slaves offers a possibility as much for transformed living as for transformed reading.

Such a call for transformation obviously challenges the Euro-American world as Wimbush so clearly and rightly perceives. Approaching the matter of biblical ethics through such a lens champions a call for the relinquishing of Euro-American interpretative dominance and issues instead an invitation for biblical engagement that is a conversation across cultural boundaries. But in a complex, ever-changing contemporary African American reality it not only implores boundary crossing between African American and other American communities; it also exhorts a liberating boundary crossing within the African American community itself. I speak here of what is perhaps one of the most destructive trends in the life of contemporary African America: the socio-cultural splitting along economic lines. This is an emergency that is as visible in the church as it is in the larger African American community.

> As we mentioned, some studies have pointed out the increasing bifurcation of the black community into two main class divisions: a coping sector of middle-income working-class and middle-class black communities, and a crisis sector of poor black communities, involving the working poor and the dependent poor.[6]

The ethical priority here is not just one of education, of teaching African Americans and others about this danger; it is one of boundary-crossing. Here is where there is a correspondence of relationships that speaks from the first century world of believing communities to a contemporary faith community. The Jesus whom the Gospel writers described as a boundary crosser seeking to break down the ethnic barriers separating God's people, and the Paul whose message of faith had an ultimate societal realization of Jew and Gentile together in the one body of Christ each model an ethics of liberation for contemporary African American religious leaders. But this time the boundary to be broken down is not one which separates white and black; it is instead one that separates a minority of well-to-do African Americans from the majority of their still struggling ethnic brothers and sisters.

> The gradual emergence of two fairly distinct black Americas along class lines—of two nations within a nation—has raised a serious challenge to the Black Church. . . . But black pastors and churches have a difficult time in attempting to reach the hard-core urban poor, the black underclass, which is continuing to grow. . . . The challenge for the future is whether black clergy and their churches will attempt to transcend class boundaries and reach out to the poor, as these class lines continue to solidify with demographic changes in black communities.[7]

A liberating, boundary-crossing ethics crafted through the lens of the African American slaves can shape the kind of people who can meet such a challenge. My hope is that a book like this one can spark a conversation about bringing this lens and the lenses of other communities together in conversation rather than indoctrination about New Testament ethics. In this dialogue the primary focus would not be on the establishment of universally normative ways of dealing with particular issues. It would instead encourage a cross fertilization of different cultural perspectives which would in turn spark new encounters with the text's meaning potential. Then and only then would the real goal be within reach. Then we would approach an interpretative reality where ethics enables the crossing of those boundaries that separate humans from God and disable productive and transformative human contact with one other.

Notes

1. Liberation as Lens

1. Dwight N. Hopkins, "Slave Theology in the 'Invisible Institution,'" in *Cut Loose Your Stammering Tongue: Black Theology in the Slave Narratives*, ed. Dwight N. Hopkins and George Cummings (Maryknoll, N.Y.: Orbis Books, 1991), 44.

2. Zora Neale Hurston, "High John De Conquer," in *The Book of Negro Folklore*, ed. Langston Hughes and Arna Bontemps (New York: Dodd, Mead, and Co., 1958), 93.

3. E. Hammond Oglesby, "Cutting the Cheese a Different Way: Ethics, Hermeneutics, and the Black Experience," *The Journal of the Interdenominational Theological Center* 19, 1 & 2 (1991–92): 88.

4. Vincent L. Wimbush, ed., *African Americans and the Bible: Sacred Texts and Social Textures* (New York: Continuum, 2000), 8.

5. Ibid., 9.

6. Ibid., 16.

7. Oglesby, "Cutting the Cheese a Different Way," 41.

8. Leander E. Keck, "Rethinking 'New Testament Ethics,'" *Journal of Biblical Literature* 115, 1 (1996): 3.

9. Halvor Moxnes, "New Testament Ethics—Universal or Particular: Reflections on the Use of Social Anthropology in New Testament Studies," *Studia Theologica* 47 (1993): 156.

10. Eduard Lohse, *Theological Ethics of the New Testament*, trans. M. Eugene Boring (Minneapolis: Fortress Press, 1991), 2.

11. Keck, "Rethinking 'New Testament Ethics,'" 7.

12. Schrage makes the same point: "New Testament ethics is neither autonomous nor teleological. Its criterion and basis is God's saving act in Jesus Christ. Ethics follows from this act and reflects it—is indeed implicit in it." See Wolfgang Schrage, *The Ethics of the New Testament*, trans. David E. Green (Philadelphia: Fortress Press, 1988), 8.

13. Dan O. Via, *The Ethics of Mark's Gospel—in the Middle of Time* (Philadelphia: Fortress Press, 1985), 3.

14. Keck, "Rethinking 'New Testament Ethics,'" 4.

15. Frank J. Matera, *New Testament Ethics: The Legacies of Jesus and Paul* (Louisville: Westminster/John Knox, 1996), 7.

16. Via, *The Ethics of Mark's Gospel*, 14.

17. Keck, "Rethinking 'New Testament Ethics,' " 8.

18. Daniel Patte, "New Testament Ethics: Envisioning Its Critical Study in This Day and Age," *Journal of the NABPR* 23 (1996): 193.

19. Enrique Dussel, *Philosophy of Liberation,* trans. Aquilina Martinez and Christine Morkovsky (Maryknoll, N.Y.: Orbis Books, 1985), 2.

20. See Brian K. Blount, *Cultural Interpretation: Reorienting New Testament Criticism* (Minneapolis: Fortress Press, 1995), 16-17.

21. Stephen Charles Mott, "The Use of the New Testament for Social Ethics," *The Journal of Religious Ethics* 15 (1987): 227.

22. Ibid., 236.

23. Walter Wink, "Biblical Theology and Social Ethics," in *Biblical Theology: Problems and Perspectives,* ed. Steven J. Kraftchick, Charles D. Myers, and Ben C. Ollenberger (Nashville: Abingdon Press, 1995), 264.

2. Reconfigured Ethics

1. Albert J. Raboteau, *Slave Religion: The "Invisible Institution" in the Antebellum South* (New York: Oxford University Press, 1978), 241.

2. Delores S. Williams, *Sisters in the Wilderness: The Challenge of Womanist God-Talk* (Maryknoll: Orbis Books, 1993), 188. Dwight Hopkins agrees: "The experiences of enslaved African Americans, in line with our understanding of religious culture, indicate that questions of ultimate concern are embodied, embedded, or incarnated, if you will, in the everyday life represented by manifold sources." Dwight N. Hopkins, "Theological Method and Cultural Studies: Slave Religion as a Heuristic," in *Changing Conversations: Religious Reflection and Cultural Analysis,* ed. Dwight N. Hopkins and Sheila Greeve Davaney (New York: Routledge, 1996), 167.

3. Brian K. Blount, *Go Preach! Mark's Kingdom Message and the Black Church Today* (Maryknoll: Orbis Books, 1998), 216-32.

4. Tom Teepen, editorial, *The New York* Times, November 29, 1999, 19A.

5. Orlando Patterson, *Rituals of Blood: Consequences of Slavery in Two American Centuries* (Washington, D.C.: Civitas Counterpoint, 1998), 4. See especially chapter 1, "Broken Bloodlines: Gender Relations and the Crisis of Marriages and Families Among Afro-Americans," 3-167.

6. Ibid., 25.

7. John W. Blassingame, ed., *Slave Testimony: Two Centuries of Letters, Speeches, Interviews, and Autobiographies* (Baton Rouge: Louisana State University Press, 1977), lxv.

8. Arna Bontemps, *The Book of Negro Folklore,* ed. Langston Hughes and Arna Bontemps (New York: Dodd, Mead, and Co., 1958), 56.

9. Joan M. Martin, "The Slave Narratives and Womanist Ethics," in *Women's Sacred Scriptures,* ed. Elisabeth Schüssler Fiorenza and Kwok Pui-Lan (Maryknoll: Orbis Books, 1998), 66.

10. Ibid.

11. Ibid.

12. Ibid., 66-67.

13. Hopkins, "Theological Method and Cultural Studies," 169.

14. Ibid. See also Bontemps, *The Book of Negro Folklore,* viii-ix.

15. See Dwight N. Hopkins, *Down, Up, and Over: Slave Religion and Black Theology* (Minneapolis: Fortress Press, 1999), 130. See also Brian K. Blount, *Cultural Interpretation: Reorienting New Testament Criticism* (Minneapolis: Fortress Press, 1995).

16. Quoted in Blassingame, *Slave Testimony,* 52.

17. Ibid., 135.

18. Ibid., 153.

19. Hopkins, "Theological Method and Cultural Studies," 167-69.

20. Ibid., 167.

21. Cheryl Towsend Gilkes, " 'Mother to the Motherless, Father to the Fatherless': Power, Gender, and Community in Afrocentric Biblical Tradition," *Semeia* 47 (1989): 58.

22. Williams, *Sisters in the Wilderness,* 192-93.

23. Dwight N. Hopkins, *Introducing Black Theology of Liberation* (Maryknoll, N.Y.: Orbis Books, 1999), 17.

24. Dwight N. Hopkins, "Slave Theology in the 'Invisible Institution,' " in *Cut Loose Your Stammering Tongue: Black Theology in the Slave Narratives,* ed. Dwight N. Hopkins and George Cummings (Maryknoll, N.Y.: Orbis Books, 1991), 7.

25. Hopkins, *Down, Up, and Over,* 11.

26. Hopkins, "Slave Theology in the 'Invisible Institution,' " 25.

27. Ibid., 14.

28. Albert J. Raboteau, *A Fire in the Bones: Reflections on African-American Religious History* (Boston: Beacon Press, 1995), 27.

29. Ibid., 33.

30. Ibid.

31. M. Shawn Copeland, " 'Wading Through Many Sorrows': Toward a Theology of Suffering in Womanist Perspective," in *A Troubling in My Soul: Womanist Perspectives on Evil and Suffering,* ed. Emilie M. Townes (Maryknoll, N.Y.: Orbis Books, 1993), 120. Hopkins agrees: "By stationing Jesus back with Moses, the entire Exodus event becomes a paradigmatic foreshadowing of the liberation consequences of Jesus' death and resurrection." Hopkins, "Slave Theology in the 'Invisible Institution,' " 21.

32. Thomas Hoyt, Jr., "Facing Today's Issues, Why Study the Bible?" *Engage/Social Action* 11/7 (1983): 35.

33. Jacquelyn Grant, *White Women's Christ and Black Women's Jesus: Feminist Christology and Womanist Response* (Atlanta: Scholars Press, 1989), 212.

34. Copeland, " 'Wading Through Many Sorrows,' " 120.

35. Renita Weems, "Reading Her Way Through the Struggle: African American Women and the Bible," in *Stony the Road We Trod: African American Biblical Interpretation,* ed. Cain Hope Felder (Minneapolis: Fortress Press, 1991), 61.

36. Raboteau, *Slave Religion,* 102.

37. Blassingame, *Slave Testimony,* 433.

38. Raboteau, *Slave Religion*, 220.

39. Ibid., 102.

40. Ibid., 122.

41. Ibid., 123.

42. See Vincent Harding, "Religion and Resistance Among Antebellum Slaves, 1800–1860," in *African-American Religion: Interpretative Essays in History and Culture,* ed. Albert J. Raboteau and Timothy E. Fulap (New York: Routledge, 1997), 111-12.

43. Katie Geneva Cannon, "Slave Ideology and Biblical Interpretation," *Semeia* 47 (1989): 10.

44. Howard Thurman, *Deep River: Reflections on the Religious Insight of Certain of the Negro Spirituals* (Port Washington, N.Y.: Kennikat Press, 1945), 36.

45. Patterson, *Rituals of Blood*, 223.

46. Raboteau, *Slave Religion*, 295.

47. Blassingame, *Slave Testimony*, 411.

48. Raboteau, *Slave Religion*, 126-27.

49. Ibid., 214.

50. Ibid., 215.

51. Hopkins, *Down, Up, and Over*, 107.

52. Raboteau, *Slave Religion*, 309-10.

53. Hopkins, *Down, Up, and Over*, 114.

54. Copeland, " 'Wading Through Many Sorrows,' " 119.

55. Raboteau, *Slave Religion*, 299

56. Ibid., 297.

57. Ibid., 296.

58. Ibid., 295.

59. Ibid., 296.

60. Hopkins, "Slave Theology in the 'Invisible Institution,' " 32-33.

61. Ibid., 34.

62. Raboteau, *Slave Religion*, 164.

63. Harding, "Religion and Resistance Among Antebellum Slaves," 116.

64. Ibid., 118.

65. Ibid., 121-22.

66. Ibid., 111.

67. Raboteau, *Slave Religion*, 305.

3. The Synoptic Gospels: Kingdom Ethics

1. For an example of exceptions, see Mark 7:19*b*; 13:14.

2. Richard B. Hays, *The Moral Vision of the New Testament* (San Francisco: Harper San Francisco, 1996), 74.

3. Eduard Lohse, *Theological Ethics of the New Testament* (Minneapolis: Fortress Press, 1991), 1.

4. Willi Marxsen, *New Testament Foundations for Christian Ethics* (Minneapolis: Fortress Press, 1993), 51.

5. Allen Verhey, *The Great Reversal: Ethics and the New Testament* (Grand Rapids:

Eerdmans, 1984), 24: "The ethic is rather an ethic of response to the coming king-dom of God and its present impact in Jesus."

6. See, for example, the discussion in Mark 7 and Matthew 5:21-48.

7. James Cone, "The Meaning of Heaven in the Black Spirituals," in *Heaven*, ed. Bas Van Iersel and Edward Schillebeeckx (New York: Seabury Press, 1979), 58.

8. Brian K. Blount, *Go Preach! Mark's Kingdom Message and the Black Church Today* (Maryknoll: Orbis Books, 1998), 55-76.

9. Christopher Rowland, "Reflections on the Politics of the Gospels," in *The Kingdom of God and Human Society: Essays by Members of the Scripture, Theology and Society Group*, ed. Robin Barbour (Edinburgh: T. & T. Clark, 1993), 232-33.

10. Christopher Rowland and Mark Corner, *Liberating Exegesis: The Challenge of Liberation Theology to Biblical Studies* (Louisville: Westminster/John Knox, 1989), 89.

11. Lohse, *Theological Ethics of the New Testament*, 41.

12. Frank J. Matera, *New Testament Ethics: The Legacies of Jesus and Paul* (Louisville: Westminster/John Knox, 1996), 15.

13. Blount, *Go Preach!* 192-94.

14. Jack T. Sanders, "Ethics in the Synoptic Gospels," *Biblical Research* 14 (1969): 19.

15. Matera, *New Testament Ethics*, 22.

16. Ibid., 35.

17. Donald H. Juel, *A Master of Surprise: Mark Interpreted* (Minneapolis: Fortress Press, 1994), 36.

18. One notes that in each instance where Mark connects the language of "preaching" directly to Jesus' Palestinian activities that transformative acts of healing or exorcism are integrally related (Mark 1:38-39; 3:4 and 6:12, where dis-ciples preach). This, of course, excludes the programmatic statement in 1:14-15 where Jesus preaches the kingdom's coming. But even in this case there is a notable transformative follow up: the instigation of a new life for the first four disciples. The language itself, when connected with Jesus or his disciples, is trans-formative.

19. Verhey, *The Great Reversal*, 79.

20. Ibid., 80: "Moral obligation is no longer determined by external observance of the prescriptions and prohibitions of the law; moral obligation is determined instead by the nature and activity of God and his Christ."

22. Rudolf Schnackenburg, *The Moral Teaching of the New Testament* (New York: Herder and Herder, 1965), 93.

23. Matera, *New Testament Ethics*, 28.

24. Joel Marcus, "The Jewish War and the Sitz Im Leben of Mark," *Journal of Biblical Literature* 111 (1992): 441-62; Brian K. Blount, "The Apocalypse of Worship: A House of Prayer for All the Nations," in *Making Room at the Table: An Invitation to Multicultural Worship*, ed. Brian K. Blount and Leonora Tubbs Tisdale (Louisville: Westminster/John Knox, 2000).

25. Verhey, *The Great Reversal*, 74-75.

26. Consider, for example, the parallels between Jesus' activity and that of the disciples in Mark 1:38 and 6:12; 1:21 and 6:30; 1:27 and 6:7; 1:23 and 6:13.

27. Wolfgang Schrage, *The Ethics of the New Testament* (Philadelphia: Fortress Press, 1988), 139.

28. Ched Myers, *Binding The Strong Man: A Political Reading of Mark's Story of Jesus* (Maryknoll, N.Y.: Orbis Books, 1988), 5: "The naming functions as a literary fiction, connoting Jesus' consolidation of his alternative community."

29. Verhey, *The Great Reversal*, 77.

30. Compare Mark 14:23-24 ("Then he took a cup, and after giving thanks he gave it to them, and all of them drank from it. He said to them, 'This is my blood of the covenant, which is poured out for many' ") with Matt 26:27-28 ("Then he took a cup, and after giving thanks he gave it to them, saying, 'Drink from it, all of you; for this is my blood of the covenant, *which is poured out for many for the forgiveness of sins,*' " italics added).

31. Juel, *A Master of Surprise*, 41.

32. Marxsen, *New Testament Foundations*, 139-40.

33. M. Shawn Copeland, " 'Wading Through Many Sorrows': Toward a Theology of Suffering in Womanist Perspective," in *A Troubling in My Soul: Womanist Perspectives on Evil and Suffering*, ed. Emilie M. Townes (Maryknoll, N.Y.: Orbis Books, 1993), 120.

34. Dwight N. Hopkins, *Down, Up, and Over: Slave Religion and Black Theology* (Minneapolis: Fortress Press, 1999), 66.

35. John W. Blassingame, ed., *Slave Testimony: Two Centuries of Letters, Speeches, Interviews, and Autobiographies* (Baton Rouge: Louisana State University Press, 1977), 198-99.

36. Ibid., 261-2.

37. Hopkins, *Down, Up, and Over*, 67-68.

38. Marxsen, *New Testament Foundations*, 245.

39. Richard A. Horsley, *The Liberation of Christmas: The Infancy Narratives in Social Context* (New York: Crossroad, 1989).

40. Ibid., 47.

41. John P. Meier, *The Vision of Matthew: Christ, Church and Morality in the First Gospel* (New York: Paulist Press, 1979), 55.

42. Daniel J. Harrington, *The Gospel of Matthew* (Collegeville, Minn.: Liturgical Press, 1991), 47.

43. Horsley, *The Liberation of Christmas*, 48.

44. Leander E. Keck, "Ethics in the Gospel According to Matthew," *Iliff Review* 41/1,2 (1984): 47.

45. See Schrage, *The Ethics of the New Testament*, 145. He points to such illustrative passages as Mark 5:14ff.; 6:1ff.; 7:21ff.; 13:41ff.; 22:11ff.; 24:45ff.; 25:14ff., as places where a mention of eschatological reward for proper behavior or eschatological punishment for improper behavior is cited.

46. Matera, *New Testament Ethics*, 37. See pages 37-42 for Matera's full discussion that includes a look at the parable chapter, Matthew 13, and other parables located in chapters 18, 21–22, and 24–25.

47. Matera, *New Testament Ethics*, 42.

48. Verhey, *The Great Reversal*, 86.

49. Brian K. Blount, "Righteousness from the Inside: The Transformative Spirituality of the Sermon on the Mount," in *The Theological Interpretation of Scripture: Classic and Contemporary Readings*, ed. Stephen Fowl (Cambridge, Mass.: Blackwell Publishers, 1997), 270.

50. Frank H. Gorman, Jr., "When Law Becomes Gospel: Matthew's Transformed Torah," *Journal of Religion and Culture* 24/3 (1989): 227; Leander E. Keck, "Rethinking 'New Testament Ethics,' " *Journal of Biblical Literature* 115/1 (1996): 44; Colin Hart, *The Ethics of the Gospels* (Cambridge: Grove Books Limited, 1998), 9; Schrage, *The Ethics of the New Testament*, 144.

51. Hays, *The Moral Vision of the New Testament*, 97.

52. Blount, "Righteousness from the Inside," 265; Lohse, *Theological Ethics of the New Testament*, 62; Richard Mohrlang, *Matthew and Paul: A Comparison of Ethical Perspectives* (Cambridge: Cambridge University Press, 1984), 48-49; Frank J. Matera, "The Ethics of the Kingdom in the Gospel of Matthew," *Listening* 24/3 (1989): 243. Matera points out helpfully that a significant amount of interpretative controversy surrounds the seven uses of the term *righteousness* in Matthew's text (3:15; 5:6, 10, 20; 6:1, 33; 21:32). There are three primary claims about its meaning: (1) that it refers to God's act of salvation; (2) that it refers to the demand for proper human response in the face of that act, which would be conduct in conformity with God's will as the Law displays that will; (3) that it is a combination of both. I agree with Matera that Matthew always has both connotations in mind. It is for this reason that I argue that one cannot begin a discussion about Matthean ethics without understanding how the kingdom (God's salvific gift as demonstrated through Jesus' preaching and life) and ethics are integrally related.

53. Blount, "Righteousness from the Inside," 267-69; J. Andrew Overman, *Matthew's Gospel and Formative Judaism: The Social World of the Matthean Community* (Minneapolis: Fortress Press, 1990), 4. Overman offers a very persuasive contextual reconstruction. He traces five critical aspects of Judaism during the period from 165 BCE to 100 CE. This suggests, of course, that Judaism of the time was quite multifaceted. Its many sectarian components (e.g., Qumran, Pharisees, Sadducees, the communities responsible for literature like 4 Ezra, 2 Baruch, *Psalms of Solomon*) battled with each other regarding the efficacy of their interpretative strategies and conclusions. He offers five aspects that characterize Jewish groups of the time: fragmentation and factionalism, a language of sectarianism, hostility toward Jewish leadership, centrality of the Law, and a concern for the future of God's covenant people. The Matthean text, he argues, has language representative of each. He, therefore, argues that the Matthean community was one of many sectarian Jewish communities vying for interpretative control in the latter half of the first century CE.

54. Harrington, *The Gospel of Matthew*, 12-16.

55. Marxsen, *New Testament Foundations for Christian Ethics*, 80.

56. Overman, *Matthew's Gospel and Formative Judaism*, 4.

57. Ibid., 24.

58. Schnackenburg, *The Moral Teaching of the New Testament*, 57; Matera, *New Testament Ethics*, 36-37; Verhey, *The Great Reversal*, 82-84; Mohrlang, *Matthew and Paul*, 9-13; Gorman, "When Law Becomes Gospel," 227-36. One might point, for

example, to Mark 7:1-23 and its Matthean parallel, Matt 15:1-20. Matthew omits Jesus' remark (Mark 7:19) that all foods are clean. Obviously, such a remark would abolish a large section of the written law. In Matthew, Jesus does not abolish the kosher laws; he subordinates them to weightier matters of the law instead (see Matt 23:23-28).

59. Harrington, *The Gospel of Matthew*, 91.

60. It is helpful to point out here that Matthew's presentation of the narrative of the Pharisees is an intentionally pejorative one. This is due in no small part to the fact that in Matthew's own time the Pharisaic wing that Overman termed "formative Judaism" was his community's primary competition for the religious affections of the people. Matthew, writing to demonstrate the flaw in their program, opposes them against Jesus in the same way that he felt they had opposed themselves to his faith community. The struggles between Jesus and the narrative Pharisees thus represents the sectarian Matthean conflict between his Jewish "Christian" contingent and the populace of "formative Judaism." In order to demonstrate his belief that "formative Judaism" did not accurately reflect the perspectives of true Israel, the evangelist, therefore, overemphasized and, no doubt, caricatured key Pharisaic positions. For example, they were presented as a legally oriented cultic community so preoccupied with ritual that they lost complete hold on contemporary applications of true spirituality. In truth, though, the Pharisees were themselves reform oriented. It was their intention to interpret the Torah by way of the oral law so that it maintained contemporary usefulness despite the continually changing life circumstances of its people. Thus, while it is certainly true that the Pharisees wanted persons to obey the law carefully as a way of being righteous before God, "By no means did [they] intend to make fulfillment of the law more difficult; their interpretation in fact wanted to make fulfillment possible—for the sake of the rule of God!" Helmut Koester, *Introduction to the New Testament* (Berlin: Walter de Gruyter, 1982), 2:242. See also the wider discussion on the meaning potential of *Pharisee* in Brian K. Blount, "Righteousness from the Inside: The Transformative Spirituality of the Sermon on the Mount," in *The Theological Interpretation of Scripture: Classic and Contemporary Readings,* ed. Stephen E. Fowl (Cambridge, Mass.: Blackwell Publishers, 1997), 267-68. Matthew draws the contrast so sharply because he wants his readers to see clear communal demarcations and then position themselves accordingly.

61. Mohrlang, *Matthew and Paul*, 113-14; Keck, "Rethinking," 51; Sanders, "Ethics in the Synoptic Gospels," 27; Verhey, *The Great Reversal*, 22-23.

62. Matera, *New Testament Ethics*, 49.

63. Ibid., 59.

64. Gorman, "When Law Becomes Gospel," 237.

65. Matera, *New Testament Ethics*, 48.

66. Mohrlang, *Matthew and Paul*, 50.

67. Matera, *New Testament Ethics*, 61. See also Mohrlang, *Matthew and Paul*, 17-18, 78-81, who provides a helpful discussion on the concept of grace in Matthew and how God's grace and the expectation for "better" righteousness interact.

68. Theophus Smith, *Conjuring Culture: Biblical Formations of Black America* (New York: Oxford University Press, 1994).

69. Vincent Harding, "Religion and Resistance Among Antebellum Slaves, 1800–1860," in *African-American Religion: Interpretative Essays in History and Culture*, ed. Albert J. Raboteau and Timothy E. Fulap (New York: Routledge, 1997), 115.

70. Smith, *Conjuring Culture*, 3.

71. Ibid., 58.

72. Ibid., 122.

73. Smith, *Conjuring Culture*, 55. Emphasis mine.

74. Hays, *The Moral Vision of the New Testament*, 99-100.

75. Wayne A. Meeks, *The Moral World of the First Christians* (Philadelphia: Westminster Press, 1986), 139.

76. Ibid., 141.

77. Verhey, *The Great Reversal*, 92.

78. Luke T. Johnson, *The Writings of the New Testament: An Introduction* (Philadelphia: Fortress Press, 1986), 69: "The text of Luke-Acts overwhelmingly suggests that Luke's audience was almost entirely gentile."

79. Hays, *The Moral Vision of the New Testament*, 116.

80. Sharon H. Ringe, *Jesus, Liberation, and the Biblical Jubilee: Images For Ethics and Christology* (Philadelphia: Fortress Press, 1985), 51.

81. Joel B. Green, "Good News to Whom? Jesus and the 'Poor' in the Gospel of Luke," in *Jesus of Nazareth: Lord and Christ. Essays on the Historical Jesus and New Testament Christology*, ed. Joel B. Green and Max Turner (Grand Rapids: Eerdmans, 1994), 59.

82. Ibid., 64 Green notes that Luke uses πτωχός for a variety of Hebrew words: אביון, דל, עני, רוש.

83. Ibid.

84. Ibid., 65.

85. Luke also uses the term separately from such lists at 18:22; 21:3 (where the term obviously applies to economic poverty); and 19:8 (where other nuances besides the economic are possible).

6. Green, "Good News to Whom?" 68. In Green's very helpful reading, even someone like the wealthy Zacchaeus falls within the category of the narratively marginalized. Even though rich, as a tax collector and a sinner, he, too, is an outsider. "In a paradoxical way befitting Luke's portrayal of salvation-as-status transposition, Jesus' encounter with Zacchaeus is a proclamation of good news to the poor." Ibid., 71.

87. Matera, *New Testament Ethics*, 65.

88. See also 8:1 and 9:11, material unique to Luke.

89. Note the similarity in construction with the infinitive use of εὐαγγελίζομαι and the accusative objects "poor" and "kingdom." Compare 4:18: ἔχρισεν με εὐαγγελίσασθαι πτωχοῖς (he anointed me to preach good news to the poor) and 4:43: εὐαγγελίσασθαί με δεῖ τὴν βασιλείαν τοῦ θεοῦ (it is necessary for me to preach the good news of the kingdom of God).

90. Matera, *New Testament Ethics*, 66.

91. Verhey, *The Great Reversal*, 94: "The 'great reversal' theme, first enunciated in the *Magnificat*, emphasized in the inaugural address, and stated in the beati-

tudes, is displayed in Luke's whole portrait of Christ and is related to the key testimony text, Psalm 118:22—that the rejected stone has become the cornerstone (Lk. 20:17; Acts 4:11)."

92. Matera, *New Testament Ethics*, 89.

93. Hart, *The Ethics of the Gospels*, 16.

94. Ringe, *Jesus, Liberation, and Jubilee*, 36.

95. Ibid., 44.

96. Matera, *New Testament Ethics*, 78-79.

97. Ibid., 82.

98. Ibid., 67.

99. Hart, *The Ethics of the Gospels*, 17.

100. Matera, *New Testament Ethics*, 71.

101. James Cone, "The Meaning of God in the Black Spirituals," in *God as Father*, ed. Johannes-Baptist Metz (New York: Seabury Press, 1981), 57.

102. Ibid.

103. Blassingame, *Slave Testimony*, 71.

104. Sylvia R. Frey, " 'The Year of Jubilee Is Come': Black Christianity in the Plantation South in Post-Revolutionary America," in *Religion in a Revolutionary Age*, ed. Ronald Hoffman and Peter J. Albert (Charlottesville: University Press of Virginia, 1994), 87.

105. Blassingame, *Slave Testimony*, 72: "Generally, the slave's longing for freedom was hidden behind biblical symbols."

4. John: The Christology of Active Resistance

1. Frank J. Matera, *New Testament Ethics: The Legacies of Jesus and Paul* (Louisville: Westminster/John Knox Press, 1996), 92. See also Richard B. Hays, *The Moral Vision of the New Testament* (San Francisco: Harper San Francisco, 1996), 138; Johannes Nissen, "Community and Ethics in the Gospel of John," in *New Readings in John: Literary and Theological Perspectives. Essays from the Scandanavian Conference on the Fourth Gospel in Arhus 1997*, ed. Johannes Nissen and Sigfred Pedersen (Sheffield: Sheffield Academic Press, 1999), 194; J. L. Houlden, *Ethics and the New Testament* (Middlesex, England: Penguin Books, 1973), 35; Wayne A. Meeks, *The Moral World of the First Christians* (Philadelphia: Westminster Press, 1986), 317-26.

2. Wolfgang Schrage, *The Ethics of the New Testament*, trans. David E. Green (Philadelphia: Fortress Press, 1988), 297.

3. Brian K. Blount, *Go Preach! Mark's Kingdom Message and the Black Church Today* (Maryknoll, N.Y.: Orbis Books, 1998), 51-54. Here I discuss a correspondence of relationships in the way that I intend that it be understood here.

4. Dwight N. Hopkins, *Down, Up, and Over: Slave Religion and Black Theology* (Minneapolis: Fortress Press, 1999), 117-27.

5. Ibid., 116.

6. Ibid., 119-20.

7. Ibid., 120.

8. Hays, *The Moral Vision of the New Testament*, 138: "Jesus is represented in John

not as a teacher but as a relentless revealer of a single metaphysical secret: that Jesus himself is the one who has come from God to bring life."

9. José Porfirio Miranda, *Being and the Messiah: The Message of St. John* (Maryknoll, N.Y.: Orbis Books, 1977), 85. Miranda's exegetical analysis offers statistical confirmation. "Therefore, in the . . . ninety-eight instances in the Fourth Gospel in which the verb 'to believe' occurs, the historical fact that Jesus is the Messiah is the sole object and content of that belief."

10. Matera, *New Testament Ethics*, 94.

11. Ibid., 103.

12. Nissen, "Community and Ethics in the Gospel of John," 204; Raymond F. Collins, "A New Commandment I Give to You, That You Love One Another," in *These Things Have Been Written: Studies on the Fourth Gospel*, ed. Raymond F. Collins (Louvain: Peeters Press, 1991), 255.

13. Thomas Hoyt Jr., "Facing Today's Issues, Why Study the Bible?" *Engage/Social Action* 11, no. 7 (1983): 34.

14. John W. Blassingame, ed., *Slave Testimony: Two Centuries of Letters, Speeches, Interviews, and Autobiographies* (Baton Rouge: Louisana State University Press, 1977), 395.

15. Matera, *New Testament Ethics*, 105.

16. Allen Verhey, *The Great Reversal: Ethics and the New Testament* (Grand Rapids: Eerdmans, 1984), 143.

17. Schrage, *The Ethics of the New Testament*, 306-8. Schrage's discussion includes information on source- and form-critical issues related to the footwashing episode. As I am interested in the literary shape of the text as we have it before us, while finding this discussion quite interesting, I do not include and expound upon it here. See Hays, *The Moral Vision of the New Testament*, 144: "The character of love is specified in the Fourth Gospel not by an extended body of teaching, as in Matthew's Sermon on the Mount, but by a single enacted parable: Jesus' washing of the disciples' feet." See also Nissen, "Community and Ethics in the Gospel of John," 201. Nissen employs exactly the same wording as Hays in defense of his point about the centrality of the footwashing in John's ethical portrayal.

18. Peter's extreme reticence at John 13:6-8 is ample evidence that this was not the kind of behavior deemed acceptable to someone of Jesus' stature and position.

19. Hays, *The Moral Vision of the New Testament*, 144; Matera, *New Testament Ethics*, 105.

20. Hays, *The Moral Vision of the New Testament*, 145; Willi Marxsen, *New Testament Foundations for Christian Ethics*, trans. O. C. Dean, Jr. (Minneapolis: Fortress Press, 1993), 294-95.

21. Verhey, *The Great Reversal*, 143-44 "John's narrative of the cross, unique and arresting in its description of Jesus' crucifixion as his glorification (13:14; 8:28; 12:32, 34), is related to this new commandment (e.g., 15:13; 10:17, 18). Jesus does not go to the cross as a victim, humiliated and powerless; he is "lifted up" on the cross."

22. Collins, "A New Commandment I Give to You," 246.

23. Marxsen, *New Testament Foundations for Christian Ethics*, 294.

24. Hays, *The Moral Vision of the New Testament*, 150.

25. Rudolf Schnackenburg, *The Moral Teaching of the New Testament* (New York: Herder and Herder, 1965), 325.

26. J. Louis Martyn, *History and Theology in the Fourth Gospel* (Nashville: Abingdon Press, 1979); David Rensberger, "Love for One Another and Love for Enemies in the Gospel of John," in *The Love of Enemy and Non-Retaliation in the New Testament*, ed. Willard M. Swartley (Louisville: Westminster/John Knox Press, 1992), 298-301. Rensberger points to the alternative positions posited by Fernando Segovia and Urban C. von Wahlde. Both conclude that the love commandment in John's Gospel more accurately reflects the historical circumstance of 1 John than that of the Fourth Gospel. The love citations, most notably John 13:34-35 and 15:1-17, were interpolated into the Gospel by a redactor who shared the historical circumstance and outlook of 1 John. It should also be noted that many scholars also point to the literary location of the love commandment as a cause of its more restricted focus in John. The command occurs as an integral part of Jesus' farewell discourse to his community. Since he is addressing this particular community alone at this time, it should, therefore, make sense that when we speaks about the love command he would speak about it in its relationship with them alone.

27. Schrage, *The Ethics of the New Testament*, 316. As Schrage points out, although there are several places where the sense of a more universal love does appear (e.g., 3:16) , this is by no means the Johannine norm. "Nowhere does the Gospel make God's universal love a standard for the life of the Christian community."

28. David Rensberger, *Johannine Faith and Liberating Community* (Philadelphia: Westminster Press, 1988), 22-26.

29. Hays, *The Moral Vision of the New Testament*, 146-7.

30. Rensberger, "Love for One Another and Love for Enemies in the Gospel of John," 300.

31. Wayne A. Meeks, "The Man from Heaven in Johannine Sectarianism," *Journal of Biblical Literature* 91 (1972): 69.

32. Houlden, *Ethics and the New Testament*, 36.

33. Nissen, "Community and Ethics in the Gospel of John," 198: "In the sense in which the term is used in contemporary sociology the Johannine community was a 'sect,' a group whose experience of rejection by its parent body (the synagogue) had pushed it into an increasing sense of alienation from the world at large. It must be emphasized that 'sectarian' in this sense is a descriptive term, not a derogatory one."

34. This is not the negative distinction usually associated with more gnostic forms of dualism, where the physical world is evil and the spiritual good. Since John understands that the physical world occurs as the direct result of God's activity operating in concert with the "Logos," who is sent as the Christ, the world and its physical inhabitations cannot be innately evil.   35. Marxsen, *New Testament Foundations for Christian Ethics*, 295.

36. Schrage, *The Ethics of the New Testament*, 309.

37. David Rensberger, "Oppression and Identity in the Gospel of John," in *The Recovery of Black Presence: An Interdisciplinary Exploration*, ed. Randall C. Bailey

and Jacquelyn Grant (Nashville: Abingdon Press, 1995), 146: "It would seem, then, that Christianity must be prepared, on the basis of the Fourth Gospel, to hold a broad and yet highly specific understanding of 'the world' to which it was sent. It is not the world of creation, of 'nature' as such, of earth and sky, sexuality and labor, health and sickness, that is given us with our physical existence. Rather, it is the world as it has been structured by human will and rationality, but also and especially by human self-absorption and selfishness in opposition to God and to the good of other people. In short, it is human society as such, as it is organized and maintained for the good of some but the harm of others and to the detriment of the love of God."

38. Schrage, *The Ethics of the New Testament*, 309.

39. Rensberger, *Johannine Faith and Liberating Community*, 70.

40. Rensberger, "Oppression and Identity in the Gospel of John," 70.

41. Matera, *New Testament Ethics*, 08.

42. Wayne A. Meeks, "The Ethics of the Fourth Evangelist," in *Exploring the Gospel of John: In Honor of D. Moody Smith*, ed. R. Alan Culpepper and C. Clifton Black (Louisville: Westminster/John Knox Press, 1996), 317-26. Meeks offers an alternative view. He argues that there is no ethics in the Fourth Gospel because John precludes any possibility of choice. The characters' placement in the narrative's dualistic universe is predestined and, therefore, fated. Readers who seek ethical direction from those characterizations must therefore come to a similar conclusion about their own lives. Where there is no choice, there can be no ethics. See especially p. 319.

43. Nissen, "Community and Ethics in the Gospel of John," 210.

44. Werner H. Kelber, "Metaphysics and Marginality in John," in *"What Is John?": Readers and Readings of the Fourth Gospel*, ed. Fernando F. Segovia (Atlanta: Scholars Press, 1996), 129-54. Kelber offers an alternative view. After presenting a very helpful summary of the more significant suggestions for understanding John's perspective on "the Jews," he argues that not only the historical schism that Marytn speaks of, but also the internal dynamics of John's Gospel itself occasion the kind of language John uses. He perceives an internal, theological, metaphysical ambition within the narrative itself that requires the victimization of "the Jews" that occurs. "For in this intricately metaphorical and ambitiously metaphysical narrative the Jews are made to play the role of the letter—the letter which must be overcome in the interest of the Spirit" (ibid., 153-54).

45. Matera, *New Testament Ethics*, 96.

46. J. W. Douglass, "The Assassinations of Martin Luther King and John F. Kennedy in Light of the Fourth Gospel," *Sewanee Theological Review* 42/1 (1998): 41. See also Rensberger, "Oppression and Identity in the Gospel of John," 87-89: "Based on this evidence it has long been clear that the hostile use of the term "Jews" in John does not refer to the Jewish people as a whole, but specifically to the Jewish authorities, i.e., essentially the same body as the Pharisees."

47. Douglass, "The Assassinations of Martin Luther King and John F. Kennedy in Light of the Fourth Gospel," 28-29.

48. Nissen, "Community and Ethics in the Gospel of John," 209.

49. Meeks, "The Ethics of the Fourth Evangelist," 322.

50. Nissen, "Community and Ethics in the Gospel of John," 203.

51. Rensberger, *Johannine Faith and Liberating Community*, 122.

5. Paul: Theology Enabling Liberating Ethics—Sometimes

1. Neil Elliott, *Liberating Paul: The Justice of God and the Politics of the Apostle* (Maryknoll: Orbis Books, 1994), 9.

2. Amos Jones, Jr., *Paul's Message of Freedom: What Does It Mean to the Black Church?* (Valley Forge: Judson Press, 1984), 17. See also Amos Jones, Jr., "Paul's Message of Freedom," in *The Bible and Liberation: Political and Social Hermeneutics*, ed. Norman K. Gottwald and Richard A. Horsley (Maryknoll, N.Y.: Orbis Books, 1993), 504-30; Renita Weems, "Reading Her Way Through the Struggle: African American Women and the Bible," in *Stony the Road We Trod: African American Biblical Interpretation*, ed. Cain Hope Felder (Minneapolis: Fortress Press, 1991), 57-77, for a sense of African American hostility toward the Pauline corpus.

3. Jones, *Paul's Message of Freedom*, 17.

4. Howard Thurman, *Jesus and the Disinherited* (Nashville: Abingdon Press, 1949), 30-31.

5. Albert J. Raboteau, *Slave Religion: The "Invisible Institution" in the Antebellum South* (New York: Oxford University Press, 1978), 103.

6. Vincent Harding, "Religion and Resistance Among Antebellum Slaves, 1800-1860," in *African-American Religion: Interpretative Essays in History and Culture*, ed. Albert J. Raboteau and Timothy E. Fulap (New York: Routledge, 1997), 120.

7. Raboteau, *Slave Religion*, 294.

8. Jones, *Paul's Message of Freedom*, 5.

9. Ibid., 36, 507-9.

10. Elliott, *Liberating Paul*, 23.

11. Elsa Tamez, *The Amnesty of Grace: Justification by Faith from a Latin American Perspective*, trans. Sharon H. Ringe (Nashville: Abingdon Press, 1993), 152-53.

12. Richard N. Longenecker, *New Testament Social Ethics for Today* (Grand Rapids: Eerdmans, 1984), 37.

13. Elisabeth Schüssler Fiorenza, "The Praxis of Coequal Discipleship," in *Paul and Empire: Religion and Power in Roman Imperial Society*, ed. Richard A. Horsley (Harrisburg, Pa.: Trinity Press International, 1997), 226.

14. Willi Marxsen, *New Testament Foundations for Christian Ethics*, trans. O. C. Dean, Jr. (Minneapolis: Fortress Press, 1993), 147.

15. Ibid., 148.

16. Ibid., 150-51.

17. Ibid., 154.

18. Tamez, *The Amnesty of Grace*, 97.

19. Richard B. Hays, *The Moral Vision of the New Testament* (San Francisco: Harper San Francisco, 1996), 46.

20. Rudolf Bultmann, "Das Problem der Ethik bei Paulus" *ZNW* 23 (1924): 123-40.

21. Wolfgang Schrage, *The Ethics of the New Testament*, trans. David E. Green (Philadelphia: Fortress Press, 1988), 169.

22. Jack T. Sanders, *Ethics in the New Testament: Change and Development* (Philadelphia: Fortress Press, 1975), 48.
23. Victor Paul Furnish, *Theology and Ethics in Paul* (Nashville: Abingdon Press, 1968), 225.
24. Schrage, *The Ethics of the New Testament*, 169-72.
25. Marxsen, *New Testament Foundations for Christian Ethics*, 187.
26. Hays, *The Moral Vision of the New Testament*, 18; J. L. Houlden, *Ethics and the New Testament* (Middlesex, England: Penguin Books, 1973), 26.
27. Marxsen, *New Testament Foundations for Christian Ethics*, 161.
28. See Roger Mohrlang, *Matthew and Paul: A Comparison of Ethical Perspectives* (Cambridge: Cambridge University Press, 1984), 88: "In general, it is this view of the Christian life as a response to grace that lies at the heart of the commonly observed link between Pauline theology and ethics." See Rom 6:2-14; 7:4-6; 8:1-14; 2 Cor 5:14-21; Gal 2:20-21; Phil 2:1-15.
29. Schrage, *The Ethics of the New Testament*, 172.
30. Eduard Lohse, *Theological Ethics of the New Testament* (Minneapolis: Fortress Press, 1991), 82. See also Schrage, *The Ethics of the New Testament*, 177. He points to 1 Cor 6:11 and Rom 6:19 in making the similar point that "it is wrong to associate justification with the indicative and sanctification with the imperative. Sanctification, too, is God's work in us. God himself sanctifies and effects sanctification. But it is equally true that sanctification is also God's will and is associated with the imperative. Being sanctified obligates us to achieve sanctification (cf. 1 Thess. 4:3)." Cf. R. E. O. White, *Biblical Ethics* (Atlanta: John Knox Press, 1979), 6.
31. Tamez, *The Amnesty of Grace*, 109.
32. Lohse, *Theological Ethics of the New Testament*, 158.
33. Elliott, *Liberating Paul*, 123.
34. Neil Elliott, "The Anti-Imperial Message of the Cross," in *Paul and Empire: Religion and Power in Roman Imperial Society*, ed. Richard A. Horsley (Harrisburgh, Pa.: Trinity Press International, 1997), 176.
35. Hays, *The Moral Vision of the New Testament*, 25. See also Rom 5:5.
36. See Sanders, *Ethics in the New Testament*, 56-57. "The Christian is for him not merely 'between the times' but rather in two times. At one and the same time, the Christ is in the old aeon of sin and death, in which the fulfilling of the law is impossible, and—in faith and hope—in the new aeon of God's righteousness, where the fulfilling of the law, i.e., *agape* is an accomplished fact."
37. See Schrage, *The Ethics of the New Testament*, 175: "For Paul, this reality is established by incorporation into Christ in baptism, which releases those baptized from the bonds of sin once and for all. To abide in sin is not to evoke the Lord's grace but to ignore it, through refusal to take seriously incorporation into the dominion of Christ's saving rule."
38. Marxsen, *New Testament Foundations for Christian Ethics*, 208.
39. White, *Biblical Ethics*, 135-40.
40. Schrage, *The Ethics of the New Testament*, 298.
41. For a more comprehensive review of the individual uses of the terms, see White, *Biblical Ethics*, 135-40. White's conclusion: "flesh stands simply for human

nature or its material side, for everything—impulses, thoughts, desires, and the like—which belong to the outward man . . . vulnerability, creatureliness, and mortality, which being human implies" (137). See also Rudolf Schnackenburg, *The Moral Teaching of the New Testament* (New York: Herder and Herder, 1965), 264: "Certainly the concept of *sarx* refers to the corporeal and sense-endowed character of man but nevertheless signifies the whole man in his frailty, liability to temptation, and slavery to sin. Man as *sarx* confronts God and, trusting to himself, is powerless and prone to evil. It is in the flesh, then, that sin finds its opportunity. Sin uses the flesh, the humanness of each of us, as its point of attack, as Romans 7:5, 25 suggest." See also Schrage, *The Ethics of the New Testament*, 218: "The body is therefore the locus where we experience life and death, sickness and sexuality—in short, our creatureliness and our position in the realm of nature. The body is the living, breathing person." So also Lohse, *Theological Ethics of the New Testament*, 113-16, who appeals to 1 Cor 3:3; 5:3; 6:15; 12:27; and Gal 6:17: "The body is not seen merely as a part of a person, that could be distinguished from one's real self, for it is precisely in the body that people encounter their fellow human beings and develop relationships with them" (114).

42. Furnish, *Theology and Ethics in Paul*, 214.

43. Lohse, *Theological Ethics of the New Testament*, 123.

44. Ibid., 161-62. See also Mohrlang, *Matthew and Paul*, 28: "The result is that the law, in itself holy and good, nonetheless functions as an instrument of death in the hands of sin (Rom. 7.11)."

45. See Marxsen, *New Testament Foundations for Christian Ethics*, 165: "But after faith came (that is, after Christ came), those who believe no longer live under the disciplinarian law; now they live as people on whom God has already passed his favorable judgment." Marxsen goes on to declare that they had become free. Paul could only see this because, as Marxsen understands it, Damascus represented for him a change of gods. There Paul turned away from a God who demanded proper observation of the law as a precondition to God's verdict, and turned towards a God who has already pronounced judgment in Christ without first demanding achievements. See also Elliott, "The Anti-Imperial Message of the Cross," 177: "Similarly, Christians are 'free from the law,' not because the law has ceased to be valid (to the contrary, as Paul insists in Rom. 3:31; 7:12, 22, 25!), but because Christians have 'died with regard to the law' (Rom. 7:1, 4)."

46. See Hays, *The Moral Vision of the New Testament*, 32: "Jesus' death is an act of faithfulness that simultaneously reconciles humanity to God and establishes a new reality in which we are set free from the power of sin, able to be conformed to the pattern of his life." See also Schrage, *The Ethics of the New Testament*, 172: "The death of Christ establishes the new life and the obedience of Christians, not just as an ethical duty but as reality." See also Furnish, *Theology and Ethics in Paul*, 238: "Where the command is heard, the power to obey is also received."

47. Frank J. Matera, *New Testament Ethics: The Legacies of Jesus and Paul* (Louisville: Westminster/John Knox Press, 1996), 123.

48. Ibid., 161.

49. Ibid., 162.

50. Ibid., 161-62.

51. See Rom 4:11-13: "He received the sign of circumcision as a seal of the righteousness that he had by faith while he was still uncircumcised. The purpose was to make him the ancestor of all who believe without being circumcised and who thus have righteousness reckoned to them, and likewise the ancestor of the circumcised who are not only circumcised but who also follow the example of the faith that our ancestor Abraham had before he was circumcised. For the promise that he would inherit the world did not come to Abraham or to his descendants through the law but through the righteousness of faith."

52. Tamez, *The Amnesty of Grace*, 124.

53. Furnish, *Theology and Ethics in Paul*, 226.

54. Marxsen, *New Testament Foundations for Christian Ethics*, 167.

55. Schrage, *The Ethics of the New Testament*, 223.

56. Longenecker, *New Testament Social Ethics*, 30.

57. Ibid., 33-34.

58. Ibid., 34.

59. Schrage, *The Ethics of the New Testament*, 177.

60. Tamez, *The Amnesty of Grace*, 134-35.

61. Matera, *New Testament Ethics*, 31; Elliott, *Liberating Paul*, 93.

62. Elliott, *Liberating Paul*, 94.

63. Tamez, *The Amnesty of Grace*, 49.

64. Richard Horsley, *Paul and Empire: Religion and Power in Roman Imperial Society* (Harrisburg, Pa.: Trinity Press International, 1997), 6.

65. Elliott, *Liberating Paul*, 170. See also Tamez, *The Amnesty of Grace*, 109: "Thus, Jesus' death on the cross in Jerusalem and Jesus' subsequent resurrection exposed the futility of both the Roman and Jewish systems of law, and both Gentile and Jewish ways of living—in short, the entire present age"; Mark Taylor, *The Executed God: The Way of the Cross in Lockdown America* (Minneapolis: Fortress Press, 2001), 110: "Yet, and this is crucial, *we neither understand the apocalyptic Paul nor his cosmic Christ except through the adversarial stance he assumes and sharpens by critically engaging the political claims of the imperial cult*"; Dieter Georgi, "God Turned Upside Down," in *Paul and Empire: Religion and Power in Roman Imperial Society*, ed. Richard A. Horsley (Harrisburg, Pa.: Trinity Press International, 1997), 152: "If the terms chosen by Paul for his Roman readers have associations with the slogans of Caesar religion, then Paul's gospel must be understood as competing with the gospel of the Caesars. Paul's gospel enters into critical dialogue with the good news that universal peace has been achieved by the miracle of Actium. . . . The *soteria* represented by Caesar and his empire is challenged by the *soteria* brought about by Jesus"; Karl P. Donfried, "The Imperial Cults of Thessalonica and Political Conflict in 1 Thessalonians," in *Paul and Empire: Religion and Power in Roman Imperial Society*, ed. Richard A. Horsley (Harrisburg, Pa.: Trinity Press International, 1997), 217: "All of this, coupled with the use of *euaggelion* and its possible association with the Easter ruler cult, suggests that Paul and his associates could easily be understood as violating the 'decrees of Caesar' in the most blatant manner."

66. Elliott, *Liberating Paul*, 51.

67. Jones, *Paul's Message of Freedom*, 41-44.

68. Elliott, *Liberating Paul*, 34.

69. Ibid., 33.

70. Elliott, *Liberating Paul*, 34.

71. Schüssler Fiorenza, "The Praxis of Coequal Discipleship," 230-31.

72. Jones, *Paul's Message of Freedom*, 53.

73. Longenecker, *New Testament Social Ethics*, 59.

74. Schrage, *The Ethics of the New Testament*, 214.

75. Ibid.

76. See Allen D. Callahan, *Embassy of Onesimus: The Letter of Paul to Philemon* (Valley Forge: Trinity Press International, 1997). Callahan makes the same case in a more abridged form in the introduction and interpretative notes to Philemon in the forthcoming Discipleship Bible by Westminster John Knox Press.

77. Longenecker, *New Testament Social Ethics*, 68.

78. See ibid., 83: "At the heart of the problem as it exists in the church is the question of how we correlate the theological categories of creation and redemption. Where the former is stressed, subordination and submission are usually emphasized—sometimes even silence; where the latter is stressed, freedom, mutuality, and equality are usually emphasized."

79. Schrage, *The Ethics of the New Testament*, 203.

80. Ibid., 224.

81. Schrage, *The Ethics of the New Testament*, 224.

82. Ibid., 237-38.

83. Elliott, *Liberating Paul*, 223-26; Marxsen, *New Testament Foundations for Christian Ethics*, 185; Neil Elliott, "Romans 13:1-7 in the Context of Imperial Propaganda," in *Paul and Empire: Religion and Power in Roman Imperial Society*, ed. Richard A. Horsley (Harrisburg, Pa.: Trinity Press International, 1997), 188.

84. Longenecker, *New Testament Social Ethics*, 75.

85. Schrage, *The Ethics of the New Testament*, 204.

86. See Brian K. Blount, "Reading Versus Understanding: Text Interpretation and Homosexuality," in *Homosexuality: Conversations in a Christian Community*, ed. C. Leong Seow (Louisville: Westminster John Knox Press, 1996), 28-38, where my own views of the matter, quite consonant with the themes I have presented in this chapter, can be found.

87. Howard Thurman, *Deep River: Reflections on the Religious Insight of Certain of the Negro Spirituals* (Port Washington, N.Y.: Kennikat Press, 1945), 36.

88. Vincent L. Wimbush, ed., *African Americans and the Bible: Sacred Texts and Social Texture* (New York: Continuum, 2000), 17.

6. Revelation: The Witness of Active Resistance

1. James Weldon Johnson, ed., *The Book of American Negro Spirituals* (New York: Viking Press, 1931), 162-63.

2. James Weldon Johnson, ed., *The Book of American Negro Spirituals* (New York: Viking Press, 1931), 162-63.

3. George C. L. Cummings, "The Slave Narrative as a Source of Black Theological Discourse: The Spirit and Eschatology," in *Cut Loose Your Stammering*

Tongue: Black Theology in the Slave Narratives, ed. Dwight N. Hopkins and George Cummings (Maryknoll: Orbis Books, 1991), 65.

4. Brian K. Blount, *Go Preach! Mark's Kingdom Message and the Black Church Today* (Maryknoll, N.Y.: Orbis Books, 1998), 51-54, 199-232.

5. John W. Blassingame, ed., *Slave Testimony: Two Centuries of Letters, Speeches, Interviews, and Autobiographies* (Baton Rouge: Louisana State University Press, 1977), 372.

6. Ibid., 276-77. The hoped for reunion did happen seventeen years later in Canada.

7. David Rensberger, *Johannine Faith and Liberating Community* (Philadelphia: Westminster Press, 1988), 58.

8. Will Coleman, " 'Coming Through 'Ligion': Metaphor in Non-Christian and Christian Experiences with the Spirit(s) in African American Slave Narratives," in *Cut Loose Your Stammering Tongue: Black Theology in the Slave Narratives*, ed. Dwight N. Hopkins and George Cummings (Maryknoll, N.Y.: Orbis Books, 1991), 70-71.

9. Dwight N. Hopkins, "Slave Theology in the 'Invisible Institution,' " in *Cut Loose Your Stammering Tongue: Black Theology in the Slave Narratives*, ed. Dwight N. Hopkins and George Cummings (Maryknoll, N.Y.: Orbis Books, 1991), 14-15.

10. Blassingame, *Slave Testimony*, 378.

11. Albert J. Raboteau, *A Fire in the Bones: Reflections on African-American Religious History* (Boston: Beacon Press, 1995), 12.

12. Johnson, *The Book of Negro Spirituals*, 86-88.

13. See, for example, my earlier discussion where I make the argument that the imagery and language in the spirituals is resistance language. Brian K. Blount, *Cultural Interpretation: Reorienting New Testament Criticism* (Minneapolis: Fortress Press, 1995), 55-69.

14. See Elisabeth Schüssler Fiorenza, *Revelation: Vision of a Just World* (Minneapolis: Fortress Press, 1991), 54. Under the Flavians, particularly Domitian, "the Asian provinces strongly promoted the imperial cult."

15. Consider Rev 1:8. " 'I am the Alpha and the Omega,' says the Lord God, who is and who was and who is to come, the Almighty." Or 1:5, where Jesus is described as "the ruler of kings on earth." At 2:12, his words are a sharp two-edged sword. At 2:26-27, he has power over all the nations. At 3:21, he is enthroned with God. At 19:15-16, he rules the nations and is given the title King of kings and Lord of lords. And at 11:15, it is proclaimed that his kingdom shall prevail forever.

16. Adela Yarbro Collins, *Crisis and Catharsis: The Power Of The Apocalypse* (Philadelphia: Westminster Press, 1984), 148.

17. Cf. the descriptions of the churches in the first three chapters of Revelation, only two of which are described as poor. Also note the strong language of economic nonparticipation at places like chapter 18 (see esp. 18:4).

18. Schüssler Fiorenza, for example, makes just this claim. Yarbro Collins maintains that the evidence is incomplete and that no firm determination of Domitian's demands in this regard can be made.

19. M. Eugene Boring, *Revelation* (Louisville: John Knox Pres, 1989), 18.

20. Elisabeth Schüssler Fiorenza, *The Book of Revelation: Justice and Judgment* (Minneapolis: Fortress Press, 1998), 198.

21. Zora Neale Hurston, "High John De Conquer," in *The Book of Negro Folklore*, Langston Hughes and Arna Bontemps (New York: Dodd, Mead and Company, 1958), 13.

22. H. Strathmann, μάρτυς. *Theological Dictionary of the New Testament* (Grand Rapids: Eerdmans, 1967) 4:500.

23. Willi Marxsen, *New Testament Foundations for Christian Ethics*, tran. O. C. Dean, Jr. (Minneapolis: Fortress Press, 1993), 6.

24. One could always point, of course, to Rev 19:10c, where John declares that the witness of (borne by) Jesus is the spirit of prophecy. That clarification only *appears* to help. In fact, it tells us no more than what the opening three verses have already revealed; Jesus' revelation is Jesus' witness which John inscribes as a literary prophecy.

25. Marxsen, *New Testament Foundations for Christian Ethics*, 7: "The phrase μαρτυρίἀ Ιησοῦ occurs five times in Revelation (1:2, 9; 12:17; 19:10; 20:4). In most instances in which a gen. is dependent on μαρτυρία in Revelation, the gen. is subjective (1:9; 11:7; 12:17; 19:10 [2x]; 20:4)."

26. Cheryl J. Sanders, "Liberation Ethics in the Ex-Slave Interviews," in *Cut Loose Your Stammering Tongue: Black Theology in the Slave Narratives*, ed. Dwight N. Hopkins and George Cummings (Maryknoll, N.Y.: Orbis Books, 1991), 67: "That John has exactly seven beatitudes (1:3; 14:13; 16:15; 19:9; 20:6; 22:7,14) is an indication that he considers the form itself important."

27. Jewish apocalyptic thinking and writing had already staked out an identity as oppositional literature in works like Daniel and the Maccabees. Indeed, Adela Yarbro Collins observes that the Hellenizing crisis brought on by the aggressive efforts of the Seleucid empire and leaders like Antiochus IV Epiphanes stirred the fires of apocalyptic feeling and directly contributed to the Maccabean revolt. For an apocalyptic thinker facing such foreign occupation and the real or perceived oppression that was its result there were only two options: accommodation, which would ultimately lead to assimilation, or resistance. The apocalyptist chose to resist. See Adela Yarbro Collins, "The Political Perspective of the Revelation to John," *Journal of Biblical Literature* 96 (1977): 241-2. So, apparently, did Jesus. His "preaching, deeply inspired by apocalyptic, stands in radical opposition to the wise and learned who rule over the people." Pablo Richard, *Apocalypse: A People's Commentary on The Book of Revelation* (Maryknoll: Orbis Books, 1995), 18-19. Christian apocalyptic writings followed Jesus' lead. John's choice of apocalyptic language and imagery to convey his prophecy is therefore significant. He knows what kind of language he is using, and so do those who hear and read his words in their shared context at the close of the first century. He is using the language of resistance; it should be accessed accordingly.

28. Sanders, "Liberation Ethics," 75.

29. Cheryl Townsend Gilkes, " 'Mother to the Motherless, Father to the Fatherless:' Power, Gender, and Community in Afrocentric Biblical Tradition," *Semeia* 47 (1989): 457.

30. Leander Keck, "Rethinking 'New Testament Ethics,' " *Journal of Biblical Literature* 115/1 (1996): 41.

31. Arna Bontemps, "Introduction," in *The Book of Negro Folklore*, ed. Langston Hughes and Arna Bontemps (New York: Dodd, Mead, and Company, 1958), 192.
32. Ibid., 247.
33. John will reaffirm this designation as faithful, and also true, witness at 3:14.
34. Bontemps, "Introduction," 191.
35. Sanders, "Liberation Ethics," 76.
36. Ibid., 82.
37. Keck, "Rethinking 'New Testament Ethics,' " 54.
38. Bontemps, "Introduction," 246.
39. Hopkins, "Slave Theology," 57.
40. Bontemps, "Introduction," 247.
41. His choice of language, "to hold," makes it clear that he is opposing the two characterizations. Those who hold to Jesus name (2:13) are commended; those who hold to the teachings of accomodation and acquiescence (2:14-15) are castigated.
42. Frank J. Matera, *New Testament Ethics: The Legacies of Jesus and Paul* (Louisville: Westminster/John Knox Press, 1996), 75. The fact that Jesus Christ is missing is inconsequential. The reference is plainly to the testimony of Christ to God which they had—that is, had received—and for which they were prepared to die."
43. Marxsen, *New Testament Foundations for Christian Ethics*, clxxvii-clxxviii.
44. Ibid.; Bontemps, "Introduction," 663-64.
45. Walter Wink, "Biblical Theology and Social Ethics," in *Biblical Theology: Problems and Perspectives*, ed. Steven J. Kraftchick, Charles D. Myers, Jr., and Ben C. Ollenberger (Nashville: Abindgon Press, 1995), 90.
46. Blount, *Go Preach!* 199-267; Mark Taylor, *The Executed God: The Way of the Cross in Lockdown America* (Minneapolis: Fortress Press, 2001).
47. Schüssler Fiorenza, *Revelation*, 8.

7. New Testament Ethics Through an African American Lens: Some Concluding Thoughts

1. Vincent L. Wimbush, ed., *African Americans and the Bible: Sacred Texts and Social Texture* (New York and London: Continuum, 2000), 20.
2. Ibid., 2.
3. Ibid., 8.
4. Ibid., 16.
5. C. Eric Lincoln and Lawrence H. Mamiya, *The Black Church in the African American Experience* (Durham: Duke University Press, 1990), 275.
6. Ibid., 384.
7. Ibid.

Bibliography

Allison, James. "The Man Born Blind from Birth and the Subversion of Sin: Some Questions About Fundamental Morals." *Theology and Sexuality* 7 (1997): 83-102.

Aune, David. *Revelation 1-5.* Vol. 52A of *Word Biblical Commentary.* Dallas: Word Books, 1997.

———. *Revelation 6–16.* Vol. 52B of *Word Biblical Commentary.* Dallas: Word Books, 1998.

Bahr, Ann Marie B. "God's Family and Flocks: Remarks on Ownership in the Fourth Gospel." In *Covenant for a New Creation: Ethics, Religion, and Public Policy.* Edited by Carol S. Robb and Carl J. Casebolt. Maryknoll, N.Y.: Orbis Books, 1991.

Bauckham, Richard. *The Climax of Prophecy: Studies on the Book of Revelation.* Edinburgh: T. & T. Clark, 1993.

———. *The Theology of the Book of Revelation.* Cambridge: Cambridge University Press, 1993.

Beale, G. K. *The Book of Revelation: A Commentary on the Greek Text.* Grand Rapids: Eerdmans, 1999.

———. *The Book of Revelation: A Commentary on the Greek Text.* Grand Rapids: Eerdmans, 1999.

Blassingame, John W., ed. *Slave Testimony: Two Centuries of Letters, Speeches, Interviews, and Autobiographies.* Baton Rouge: Louisana State University Press, 1977.

Blount, Brian K. *Cultural Interpretation: Reorienting New Testament Criticism.* Minneapolis: Augsburg/Fortress Press, 1995.

———. "Reading Versus Understanding: Text Interpretation and Homosexuality." In *Homosexuality: Conversations in a Christian Community.* Edited by C. Leong Seow. Louisville: Westminster John Knox Press, 1996.

———. "Righteousness From the Inside: The Transformative Spirituality of the Sermon on the Mount." In *The Theological Interpretation of Scripture: Classic and Contemporary Readings.* Edited by Stephen E. Fowl. Cambridge, Mass: Blackwell Publishers, 1997.

———. *Go Preach! Mark"s Kingdom Message and the Black Church Today.* Maryknoll: Orbis Books, 1998.

———. "The Apocalypse of Worship: A House of Prayer For All The Nations." In *Making Room at the Table: An Invitation to Multicultural Worship.* Edited by Brian

K. Blount and Leonora Tubbs Tisdale. Louisville: Westminster/John Knox, 2001.

Blount, Brian K., and Leonora Tubbs Tisdale. *Making Room at the Table: An Invitation to Multicultural Worship*. Louisville: Westminster John Knox, 2001.

Boesak, Allan A. *Comfort and Protest: The Apocalypse from a South African Perspective*. Philadelphia: Westminster Press, 1987.

Bontemps, Arna. "Introduction." In *The Book of Negro Folklore*. Edited by Langston Hughes and Arna Bontemps. New York: Dodd, Mead, and Company, 1958.

Boring, M. Eugene. *Revelation*. Louisville: John Knox Pres, 1989.

Briggs, Sheila. "Can An Enslaved God Liberate? Hermeneutical Reflections on Philippians 2:6-11." *Semeia* 47 (1989): 137-53.

Caird, G. B. *The Revelation of St. John The Divine*. San Francisco: Harper and Row, 1966.

Callahan, Allen D. "The Language of the Apocalypse." *Harvard Theological Review* 88/4 (1995): 453-70.

———. *Embassy of Onesimus: The Letter of Paul to Philemon*. Valley Forge: Trinity Press International, 1997.

Cannon, Katie Geneva. "Slave Ideology and Biblical Interpretation." *Semeia* 47 (1989): 9-23.

Carson, D. A. "The Purpose of the Fourth Gospel: John 20:31 Reconsidered." *Journal of Biblical Literature* 106/4 (1987): 639-51.

Castelli, Elizabeth, Stephen D. Moore, Gary A. Phillips, and Regina Schwartz, eds. *The Post-Modern Bible*. New Haven: Yale University Press, 1995.

Coleman, Will. "'Coming Through 'Ligion': Metaphor in Non-Christian and Christian Experiences with the Spirit(s) in African American Slave Narratives." In *Cut Loose Your Stammering Tongue: Black Theology in the Slave Narratives*. Edited by Dwight N. Hopkins and George Cummings, 67-102. Maryknoll, N.Y.: Orbis, 1991.

Collins, Adela Yarbro. "The Political Perspective of the Revelation to John." *Journal of Biblical Literature* 96 (1977): 241-56.

———. *The Apocalypse*. Wilmington, Del.: Michael Glazier, 1979.

———. *Crisis and Catharsis: The Power of the Apocalypse*. Philadelphia: Westmister Press, 1984.

———. "The Book of Revelation." In *The Origins of Apocalypticism in Judaism and Christianity*. Edited by John J. Collins. New York: Continuum, 1998.

Collins, John J., ed. *The Origins of Apocalypticism in Judaism and Christianity*. Vol. I of *The Encyclopedia of Apocalypticism*. New York: Continuum, 1998.

———. "From Prophecy to Apocalypticism: The Expectation of the End." In *The Origins of Apocalypticism in Judaism and Christianity*. Edited by John J. Collins. New York: Continuum, 1998.

Collins, Raymond F. "A New Commandment I Give to You, That You Love One Another." In *These Things Have Been Written: Studies on the Fourth Gospel*. Edited by Raymond F. Collins. Louvain, Belgium: Peeters Press, 1991.

Cone, James. "The Meaning of Heaven in the Black Spirituals." In *Heaven*. Edited by Bas Van Iersel and Edward Schilleebeckx. New York: Seabury Press, 1979.

————. "The Meaning of God in the Black Spirituals." In *God as Father*. Edited by Johannes-Baptist Metz. New York: Seabury Press, 1981.

Copeland, M. Shawn. " 'Wading Through Many Sorrows': Toward a Theology of Suffering in Womanist Perspective." In *A Troubling in My Soul: Womanist Perspectives on Evil and Suffering*. Edited by Emilie M. Townes. Maryknoll: Orbis, 1993.

Cormie, Lee. "Revolutions in Reading the Bible." In *The Bible and the Politics of Exegesis*, 173-94. Cleveland, Ohio: Pilgrim Press, 1991.

Cummings, George C. L. "The Slave Narrative as a Source of Black Theological Discourse: The Spirit and Eschatology." In *Cut Loose Your Stammering Tongue: Black Theology in the Slave Narratives*. Edited by Dwight N. Hopkins and George Cummings. Maryknoll, N.Y.: Orbis Books, 1991.

————. "Slave Narratives, Black Theology of Liberation (USA) and the Future." In *Cut Loose Your Stammering Tongue: Black Theology in the Slave Narratives*. Edited by Dwight N. Hopkins and George Cummings. Maryknoll, N.Y.: Orbis Books, 1991.

Donfried, Karl P. "The Imperial Cults of Thessalonica and Political Conflict in 1 Thessalonians." In *Paul and Empire: Religion and Power in Roman Imperial Society*. Edited by Richard A. Horsley. Harrisburg, Pa.: Trinity Press International, 1997.

Douglass, J. W. "The Assasinations of Martin Luther King and John F. Kennedy in Light of the Fourth Gospel." *Sewanee Theological Review* 42/1 (1998): 26-46.

Dube, Musa. "Reading for Decolonization (John 4:1-42)." *Semeia* 75 (1996): 37-59.

Dussel, Enrique. *Philosophy of Liberation*. Translated by Aquilina Martinez and Christine Morkovsky. Maryknoll, N.Y.: Orbis Books, 1985.

Elliott, Neil. *Liberating Paul: The Justice of God and the Politics of the Apostle*. Maryknoll, N.Y.: Orbis Books, 1994.

————. "The Anti-Imperial Message of the Cross." In *Paul and Empire: Religion and Power in Roman Imperial Society*. Edited by Richard A. Horsley. Harrisburg, Pa.: Trinity Press International, 1997.

————. "Romans 13:1-7 in the Context of Imperial Propaganda." In *Paul and Empire: Religion and Power in Roman Imperial Society*. Edited by Richard A. Horsley. Harrisburg, Pa.: Trinity Press International, 1997.

Fenn, Richard K. "Diversity and Power: Cracking the Code." In *Making Room at the Table: An Invitation to Multicultural Worship*. Edited by Brian K. Blount and Leonora Tubbs Tubbs. Louisville: Westminster John Knox, 2001.

Fitzmeyer, Joseph A. *Paul and His Theology*. Englewood Cliffs, N.J.: Prentice Hall, 1989.

Frey, Sylvia R. " 'The Year of Jubilee Is Come': Black Christianity in the Plantation South in Post-Revolutionary America." In *Religion in a Revolutionary Age*. Edited by Ronald Hoffman and Peter J. Albert. Charlottesville: University Press of Virginia, 1994.

Furnish, Victor Paul. *Theology and Ethics in Paul*. Nashville: Abingdon Press, 1968.

————. *The Moral Teaching of Paul*. Nashville: Abingdon Press, 1979.

Georgi, Dieter. "God Turned Upside Down." In *Paul and Empire: Religion and Power in Roman Imperial Society*. Edited by Richard A. Horsley. Harrisburg, Pa.: Trinity Press International, 1997.

Gilkes, Cheryl Townsend. " 'Mother to the Motherless, Father to the Fatherless': Power, Gender, and Community in Afrocentric Biblical Tradition." *Semeia* 47 (1989): 57-85.

Gonzalez, Catherine, and Justo L. Gonzalez. *The Book of Revelation*. Louisville: Westminster John Knox, 1997.

Gorman, Frank H., Jr. "When Law Becomes Gospel: Matthew's Transformed Torah." *Listening: Journal of Religion and Culture* 24/3 (1989).

Grant, Jacquelyn. *White Women's Christ and Black Women's Jesus*. Atlanta: Scholars Press, 1989.

Green, Joel B. "Good News to Whom? Jesus and the 'Poor' in the Gospel of Luke." In *Jesus of Nazareth: Lord and Christ. Essays on the Historical Jesus and New Testament Christology*. Edited by Joel B. Green and Max Turner. Grand Rapids: Eerdmans, 1994.

Halliday, M. A. K., and Ruqaiya Hasan. *Language, Context, and Text: Aspects of Language in a Social Semiotic Perspective*. Oxford: Oxford University Press, 1990.

Harding, Vincent. "Religion and Resistance Among Antebellum Slaves, 1800–1860." In *African-American Religion: Interpretative Essays in History and Culture*. Edited by Albert J. Raboteau and Timothy E. Fulap. New York: Routledge, 1997.

Harrington, Daniel J. *The Gospel of Matthew*. Collegeville, Minn.: Liturgical Press, 1991.

———. *Revelation: The Book of the Risen Christ*. Hyde Park, N.Y.: New City Press, 1999.

Hart, Colin. *The Ethics of the Gospels*. Cambridge, Mass.: Grove Books Limited, 1998.

Hays, Richard B. *First Corinthians*. Louisville: Westminster John Knox, 1997.

———. *The Moral Vision of the New Testament*. San Francisco: Harper San Francisco, 1996.

Herzog, Frederick. *Liberation Theology: Liberation in the Light of the Fourth Gospel*. New York: Seabury Press, 1972.

Hoffman, Joseph R. "The Moral Rhetoric of the Gospels." In *Biblical v. Secular Ethics: The Conflict*. Edited by R. Joseph Hoffmann and Gerald A. Larue. Buffalo, N.Y.: Prometheus Books, 1988.

Hopkins, Dwight N. "Slave Theology in the 'Invisible Institution.' " In *Cut Loose Your Stammering Tongue: Black Theology in the Slave Narratives*. Edited by Dwight N. Hopkins and George Cummings. Maryknoll, N.Y.: Orbis Books, 1991.

———. "Theological Method and Cultural Studies: Slave Religion as a Heuristic." In *Changing Conversations: Religious Reflection and Cultural Analysis*. Edited by Dwight N. Hopkins and Sheila Greeve Davaney. New York: Routledge, 1996.

———. *Down, Up, and Over: Slave Religion and Black Theology*. Minneapolis: Fortress Press, 1999.

———. *Introducing Black Theology of Liberation*. Maryknoll, N.Y.: Orbis Books, 1999.

Hopkins, Dwight N., and George Hopkins, eds. *Cut Loose Your Stammering Tongue: Black Theology in the Slave Narratives.* Maryknoll, N.Y.: Orbis Books, 1991.

Horsley, Richard A. *Paul and Empire: Religion and Power in Roman Imperial Society.* Harrisburg, Pa.: Trinity Press International, 1997.

———. *The Liberation of Christmas: The Infancy Narratives in Social Contest.* New York: Crossroad, 1989.

Houlden, J. L. *Ethics and the New Testament.* Middlesex, England: Penguin Books, 1973.

Hoyt, Thomas, Jr. "Facing Today's Issues, Why Study the Bible?" *Engage/Social Action* 11/7 (1983): 30-36.

Hughes, Langston, and Arna Bontemps, eds. *The Book of Negro Folklore.* New York: Dodd, Mead, and Company, 1958.

Hurston, Zora Neale. "High John De Conquer." In *The Book of Negro Folklore.* Edited by Langston Hughes and Arna Bontemps. New York: Dodd, Mead and Company, 1958.

Johnson, James Weldon, ed. *The Book of American Negro Spirituals.* New York: Viking Press, 1931.

Johnson, Luke T. *The Writings of the New Testament: An Interpretation.* Philadelphia: Fortress Press, 1986.

Jones, Amos, Jr. *Paul's Message of Freedom: What Does It Mean to the Black Church?* Valley Forge: Judson Press, 1984.

———. "Paul's Message of Freedom." In *The Bible and Liberation: Political and Social Hermeneutics.* Edited by Norman K. Gottwald and Richard A. Horsley. Maryknoll, N.Y.: Orbis Books, 1993.

Juel, Donald H. *A Master of Surprise: Mark Interpreted.* Minneapolis: Fortress Press, 1994.

Keck, Leander E. "Rethinking "New Testament Ethics." *Journal of Biblical Literature* 115/1 (1996): 3-16.

———. "Ethics in the Gospel According to Matthew." *Iliff Review* 41/1 and 2 (1984): 39-56.

Kelber, Werner H. "Metaphysics and Marginality in John." In *"What Is John?": Readers and Readings of the Fourth Gospel.* Edited by Fernando F. Segovia. Atlanta: Scholars Press, 1996.

Keller, Catherine. *Apocalypse Now and Then.* Boston: Beacon Press, 1996.

King, Martin Luther, Jr. "Letter from a Birmingham Jail." In *A Testament of Hope: The Essential Writings of Martin Luther King, Jr.* Edited by James M. Washington. San Francisco: Harper & Row, 1986.

Koester, Helmut. *Introduction to the New Testament.* 2 vols. Berlin: Walter de Gruyter, 1982.

Kwok Pui Lan. "Discovering the Bible in the Non-Biblical World." *Semeia* 47 (1989): 25-42.

Lincoln, C. Eric, and Lawrence H. Mamiya. *The Black Church in the African American Experience.* Durham: Duke University Press, 1990.

Lohse, Eduard. *Theological Ethics of the New Testament.* Minneapolis: Fortress Press, 1991.

———. "Changes of Thought in Pauline Theology? Some Reflections on Paul's

Ethical Teaching in the Context of His Theology." In *Theology and Ethics: Essays in Honor of Victor Paul Furnish*. Edited by Eugene H. Lovering. Nashville: Abingdon Press, 1996.

Longenecker, Richard N. *New Testament Social Ethics For Today*. Grand Rapids: Eerdmans, 1984.

MacRae, George W., Jr. "The Fourth Gospel and Religionsgeschichte." *Catholic Biblical Quarterly* 32/1 (January 1970): 13-24.

Marable, Manning. *How Capitalism Underdeveloped Black America: Problems in Race, Political Economy and Society*. Boston: South End Press, 1983.

Marcus, Joel. "Mark 14:61: 'Are You The Messiah-Son-of-God?' " *Novum Testamentum* 31/2 (1989): 125-41.

———. "The Jewish War and the Sitz Im Leben of Mark." *Journal of Biblical Literature* 111 (1992): 441-62.

Martin, Joan M. "The Slave Narratives and Womanist Ethics." In *Women's Sacred Scriptures*. Edited by Elisabeth Schüssler Fiorenza and Kwok Pui-Lan. Maryknoll, N.Y.: Orbis Books, 1998.

Martyn, J. Louis. *History and Theology in the Fourth Gospel*. Nashville: Abingdon Press, 1979.

———. "The Crucial Event in the History of the Law (Gal 5:14)." In *Theology and Ethics: Essays in Honor of Victor Paul Furnish*. Edited by Eugene H. Lovering. Nashville: Abingdon Press, 1996.

Marxsen, Willi. *New Testament Foundations For Christian Ethics*. Minneapolis: Fortress Press, 1993.

Matera, Frank J. "The Ethics of the Kingdom in the Gospel of Matthew." *Listening: Journal of Religion and Culture* 24/ 3 (1989): 241-51.

———. *New Testament Ethics: The Legacies of Jesus and Paul*. Louisville: Westminster/John Knox, 1996.

Mazzaferri, Fred. "*MARTYRIA IESOU* Revisited." *The Bible Translator* 39/1 (1988): 114-22.

Meeks, Wayne A. "The Man from Heaven in Johannine Sectarianism." *Journal of Biblical Literature* 91 (1972): 44-72.

———. *The Moral World of the First Christians*. Philadelphia: Westminster Press, 1986.

———. "The Ethics of the Fourth Evangelist." In *Exploring the Gospel of John: In Honor of D. Moody Smith*. Edited by R. Alan Culpepper and C. Clifton Black. Louisville: Westminster/John Knox Press, 1996.

Meier, John P. *The Vision of Matthew: Christ, Church and Morality in the First Gospel*. New York: Paulist Press, 1979.

Metzger, Bruce. *Breaking the Code: Understanding the Book of Revelation*. Nashville: Abingdon Press, 1993.

Miranda, José Porfirio. *Being and the Messiah: The Message of St. John*. Maryknoll, N.Y.: Orbis Books, 1977.

Mohrlang, Richard. *Matthew and Paul: A Comparison of Ethical Perspectives*. Cambridge: Cambridge University Press, 1984.

Mott, Stephen Charles. *Biblical Ethics and Social Change*. New York: Oxford University Press, 1982.

———. "The Use of the New Testament For Social Ethics." *The Journal of Religious Ethics* 15 (1987): 225-60.

Motyer, Stephen. "Jesus and the Marginalized in the Fourth Gospel." In *Mission and Meaning: Essays Presented to Peter Cotterwell*. Edited by A. Billington. Carlise: Paternoster Press, 1995.

Mounce, Robert H. *The Book of Revelation*. 2nd ed. Grand Rapids: Eerdmans, 1998.

Moxnes, Halvor. "New Testament Ethics—Universal or Particular: Reflections on the Use of Social Anthropology in New Testament Studies." *Studia Theologica* 47 (1993): 153-68.

Myers, Ched. *Binding The Strong Man: A Political Reading of Mark's Story of Jesus*. Maryknoll, N.Y.: Orbis Books, 1988.

Neyrey, J. H. *An Ideology of Revolt: John's Christology in Social-Science Perspective*. Philadelphia: Fortress Press, 1988.

Nissen, Johannes. "Community and Ethics in the Gospel of John." In *New Readings in John: Literary and Theological Perspectives. Essays from the Scandanavian Conference on the Fourth Gospel in Arhus 1997*. Edited by Johannes Nissen and Sigfred Pedersen. Sheffield: Sheffield Academic Press, 1999.

Noel, James A. "The Post-Modern Location of Black Religion: Texts and Temporalities in Tension." In *Changing Conversations: Religious Reflections and Cultural Analysis*. Edited by Dwight N. Hopkins and Sheila Greevey Davaney. New York: Routledge, 1996.

Ogden, Schubert M. "Paul in Contemporary Theology and Ethics: Presuppositions of Critically Appropriating Paul"s Letters Today." In *Theology and Ethics: Essays in Honor of Victor Paul Furnish*, Eugene H. Lovering. Nashville: Abingdon Press, 1996.

Oglesby, E. Hammond. "Cutting the Cheese a Different Way: Ethics, Hermeneutics, and the Black Experience." *The Journal of the Interdenominational Theological Center* 19/1 and 2 (1991-92): 88-101.

Overman, J. Andrew. *Matthew's Gospel and Formative Judaism: The Social World of the Matthean Community*. Minneapolis: Fortress Press, 1990.

O'Donovan, Oliver. "The Political Thought of the Book of Revelation." *Tyndale Bulletin* 37 (1986): 61-94.

O'Toole, Robert F. *Who Is a Christian? A Study in Pauline Ethics*. Collegeville, Minn.: Liturgical Press, 1990.

Patte, Daniel. "New Testament Ethics: Envisioning Its Critical Study in This Day and Age." *Journal of the NABPR* 23 (1996): 175-98.

Patterson, Orlando. *Rituals of Blood: Consequences of Slavery in Two American Centuries*. Washington, D.C.: Civitas Counterpoint, 1998.

Petersen, Norman R. *The Gospel of John and the Sociology of Light: Language and Characterization in the Fourth Gospel*. Valley Forge, Pa.: Trinity Press International, 1993.

Pilch, John J. *What Are They Saying About Revelation?* New York: Paulist Press, 1978.

Pui Lan, Kwok. "Discovering the Bible in the Non-Biblical World." *Semeia* 47 (1989): 25-42.

Raboteau, Albert J. *Slave Religion: The "Invisible Institution" in the Antebellum South.* New York: Oxford University Press, 1978.

———. *A Fire in the Bones: Reflections on African-American Religious History.* Boston: Beacon Press, 1995.

Reid, Stephen Breck. "The Theology of the Book of Daniel and the Political Theory of W. E. B. DuBois." In *The Recovery of Black Presence: An Interdisciplinary Exploration.* Edited by Randall C. Bailey and Jacquelyn Grant. Nashville: Abingdon Press, 1995.

Rensberger, David. *Johannine Faith and Liberating Community.* Philadelphia: Westminster Press, 1988.

———. "Love for One Another and Love for Enemies in the Gospel of John." In *The Love of Enemy and Non-Retaliation in the New Testament.* Edited by Willard M. Swartley. Louisville: Westminster/John Knox Press, 1992.

———. "Oppression and Identity in the Gospel of John." In *The Recovery of Black Presence: An Interdisciplinary Exploration.* Edited by Randall C. Bailey and Jacquelyn Grant. Nashville: Abingdon Press, 1995.

Richard, Pablo. *Apocalypse: A People's Commentary on the Book of Revelation.* Maryknoll, N.Y.: Orbis Books, 1995.

Ringe, Sharon H. *Jesus, Liberation, and the Biblical Jubilee: Images for Ethics and Christology.* Philadelphia: Fortress Press, 1985.

Roetzel, Calvin J. *The Letters of Paul: Conversations in Context.* Louisville: Westminster John Knox Press, 1998.

Rogers, Cornish R., and Joseph R. Jeter, Jr., eds. *Preaching Through the Apocalypse: Sermons From Revelation.* St. Louis: Chalice Press, 1992.

Rowland, Christopher. "Reflections on the Politics of the Gospels." In *The Kingdom of God and Human Society: Essays by Members of the Scripture, Theology and Society Group.* Edited by Robin Barbour. Edinburgh: T. & T. Clark, 1993.

Rowland, Christopher, and Mark Corner. *Liberating Exegesis: The Challenge of Liberation Theology to Biblical Studies.* Louisville: Westmnister/John Knox, 1989.

Ruiz, Jean Pierre. "Holy God/Holy City." In *Humanizing the City: Politics, Religion, the Arts in Critical Conversation.* Edited by Patrick Primeau. San Francisco: Catholic Scholars Press, 1997.

———. "The Politics of Praise: A Reading of Revelation 19:1-10." In *Society of Biblical Literature Seminar Papers.* Edited by Eugene Lovering. Atlanta: Scholars Press, 1997.

Sanders, Cheryl J. "Liberation Ethics in the Ex-Slave Interviews." In *Cut Loose Your Stammering Tongue: Black Theology in the Slave Narratives.* Edited by Dwight N. Hopkins and George Cummings. Maryknoll, N.Y.: Orbis Books, 1991.

Sanders, Jack T. "Ethics in the Synoptic Gospels." *Biblical Research* 14 (1969): 19-32.

———. *Ethics in the New Testament: Change and Development.* Philadelphia: Fortress Press, 1975.

Schnackenburg, Rudolf. *The Moral Teaching of the New Testament.* New York: Herder and Herder, 1965.

Schottroff, Luise. *Let the Oppressed Go Free: Feminist Perspectives on the New Testament*. Translated by Annemarie S. Kidder. Louisville: Westminster/John Knox, 1993.

Schrage, Wolfgang. *The Ethics of the New New Testament*. Philadelphia: Fortress Press, 1988.

Fiorenza, Elisabeth Schüssler. *Invitation to the Book of Revelation: A Commentary on the Apocalypse with Complete Text from the Jerusalem Bible*. Garden City, N.Y.: Image Books, 1981.

———. "The Ethics of Biblical Interpretation: Decentering Biblical Scholarship." *Journal of Biblical Literature* 107/1 (1988): 3-17.

———. "The Praxis of Coequal Discipleship." In *Paul and Empire: Religion and Power in Roman Imperial Society*. Edited by Richard A. Horsley. Harrisburg, Pa.: Trinity Press International, 1997.

———. "Revelation." In *The New Testament and Its Modern Interpreters*. Edited by Eldon Jay Epp and George W. MacRae. Philadelphia: Fortress Press, 1989.

———. *Revelation: Vision of a Just World*. Minneapolis: Fortress Press, 1991.

———. *The Book of Revelation: Justice and Judgment*. Minneapolis: Fortress Press, 1998.

Smith, D. Moody. "Johannine Christianity: Some Reflections on Its Character and Delineation." *New Testament Studies* 21 (1975): 222-48.

Smith, Theophus. *Conjuring Culture: Biblical Formations of Black America*. New York: Oxford University Press, 1994.

Spohn, William C. *What Are They Saying About Scripture and Ethics?* New York: Paulist Press, 1984.

Stein, Stephen J. *Apocalypticism in the Modern Period and the Contemporary Age*. Vol. III of *The Encyclopedia of Apocalypticism*. New York: Continuum, 1998.

Tamez, Elsa. *The Amnesty of Grace: Justification by Faith from a Latin American Perspective*. Translated by Sharon H. Ringe. Nashville: Abingdon Press, 1993.

Taylor, Mark. *The Executed God: The Way of the Cross in Lockdown America*. Minneapolis: Fortress Press, 2001.

Theissen, Gerd. *Social Reality and the Early Christians: Theology, Ethics and the World of the New Testament*. Minneapolis: Fortress Press, 1992.

Thurman, Howard. *Deep River: Reflections on the Religious Insight of Certain of the Negro Spirituals*. Port Washington, N.Y.: Kennikat Press, 1945.

———. *Jesus and the Disinherited*. Nashville: Abingdon Press, 1949.

Trites, Allison A. "Martus and Martyrdom in the Apocalypse: A Semantic Study." *Novum Testamentum* 15 (1973): 72-80.

Vassiliadis, Petros. "The Translation of *MARTYRIA IESOU* in Revelation." *The Bible Translator* 36/1 (1985): 129-35.

Venable-Ridley, C. Michelle. "Paul and the African American Community." In *Embracing the Spirit: Womanist Perspectives on Hope, Salvation, and Transformation*. Edited by Emilie M. Townes. Maryknoll, N.Y.: Orbis Books, 1997.

Verhey, Allen. *The Great Reversal: Ethics and the New Testament*. Grand Rapids: Eerdmans, 1984.

Via, Dan O. *The Ethics of Mark's Gospel—in the Middle of Time*. Philadelphia: Fortress Press, 1985.

Wainwright, Arthur. *Mysterious Apocalypse: A History of the Interpretation of the Book of Revelation*. Nashville: Abingdon Press, 1993.

Ward, Ewing. *The Power of the Lamb: Revelation's Theology of Liberation for You*. Cambridge, Mass.: Cowley, 1990.

Weems, Renita. "Reading Her Way Through the Struggle: African American Women and the Bible." In *Stony the Road We Trod: African American Biblical Interpretation*. Edited by Cain Hope Felder. Minneapolis: Fortress Press, 1991.

Wengst, Klaus. "Babylon the Great and the New Jerusalem." In *Politics and Theopolitics in the Bible and Postbiblical Literature*. Edited by Henning Graf Reventlow and Yair Hoffman. Sheffield: JSOT Press, 1994.

White, R. E. O. *Biblical Ethics*. Atlanta: John Knox Press, 1979.

Williams, Delores. *Sisters in the Wilderness: The Challenge of Womanist God-Talk*. Maryknoll, N.Y.: Orbis Books, 1993.

Wimbush, Vincent L., ed. *African Americans and the Bible: Sacred Texts and Social Texture*. New York: Continuum, 2000.

Wink, Walter. "Biblical Theology and Social Ethics." In *Biblical Theology: Problems and Perspectives*. Edited by Steven J. Kraftchick, Charles D. Myers, Jr., and Ben C. Ollenberger. Nashville: Abingdon Press, 1995.

Index

force/power of, 45, 51
imminent coming of, 48-49, 51, 67-68, 88
Jesus' proclamation of, 47
as object of faith, 97-98
present, 50-51, 56, 82
salvation, 49-50
seeking, 72
klēsis, 145
Koresh, David, 182

labor, 29, 41
Last Supper, 60
Latin America, 122
law, 134-37
    food, 53-54, 55
    forbidding assembled worship, 36, 38
    as gift from God, 70, 124
    Jesus' challenge of, 53-55
    Jewish, 124-25
    of liberty, 32
    purity, 54
    spirit of, 70
    spiritualized, 71
laziness, 35
leaders
    Jewish and Roman, 105, 110, 115, 128-29
    women, 151
legalism, 73
lens, interpretative, 185-91
    African American, 16
    event, 19
    liberation, 13-22, 26-31, 43, 50, 93
    personal, 19
    slavery's legacy as, 24-26
lepers, 53, 84, 85
Letter from a Birmingham Jail (King), 184
Lewis, Isham, 62
Lewis, Lilburn, 62
liberation
    from boundaries, 77
    ethics, 10, 15, 67
    image of, 31

in infancy narratives, 66
inspired by future kingdom, 49-50
as interpretative lens, 13-22, 26-31, 43, 50, 93
Jesus' work for, 80
Jubilee and, 84-85
message of Bible, 31-38
from sin, 33, 97
liberty, law of, 32. See also freedom; liberation
lies, 29, 110. See also lying
life
    eternal, 89, 98-99
    experience, 15, 23-24, 34
    Jesus as, 109-10
    new, 100, 139
    quality of, 24
light, 109-10, 112
Likers, Thomas, 100
location
    spatial and political, 19, 81, 93-94
Logos, 109-10
Lohse, Eduard, 17, 46, 49, 127, 128
Longenecker, Richard, 123, 140, 150
Lord's Prayer, 72
Lord's Supper, 141
love
    commandment, 54-55, 93-94, 100-108
    divine, 101-3
    and faith bond, 99-100, 139-41
    forgiveness of, 88
    for God, 13
    from God, 88
    for Jesus, 101
    as method of resistance, 112
    for one another, 93-94, 99-108, 112, 116-18
    of one's enemies, 86
    works of, 102-4
Luke, Gospel of, 46-47, 50, 79-91
lying, 40, 44.   See also lies

macarisms, 68, 172
Magi, 65, 87
magic, 74-75, 77, 78

Printed in the United States
23575LVS00005B/130-156

9 780687 085897